Part 6

Possessive, Demonstrative, and Interrogative Pronouns

Part 7

Relative Pronouns

Part 8

Prepositions and Conjunctions

French Grammar Drills

SECOND EDITION

Eliane Kurbegov

McGraw Hill

New York   Chicago   San Francisco   Lisbon   London   Madrid   Mexico City
Milan   New Delhi   San Juan   Seoul   Singapore   Sydney   Toronto

Copyright © 2012 by The McGraw-Hill Companies, Inc. All rights reserved. Printed in the United States of America. Except as permitted under the United States Copyright Act of 1976, no part of this publication may be reproduced or distributed in any form or by any means, or stored in a database or retrieval system, without the prior written permission of the publisher.

1 2 3 4 5 6 7 8 9 10   QDB/QDB   1 9 8 7 6 5 4 3 2

ISBN   978-0-07-178949-3
MHID   0-07-178949-9

e-ISBN   978-0-07-178950-9
e-MHID   0-07-178950-2

Library of Congress Control Number 2012931501

McGraw-Hill products are available at special quantity discounts to use as premiums and sales promotions or for use in corporate training programs. To contact a representative, please e-mail us at bulksales@mcgraw-hill.com.

This book is printed on acid-free paper.

Contents

Preface

If you've picked up this book, you know that to learn a language well—to read and write and to understand others and be understood yourself—at some point you just have to buckle down and deal with the grammar. *French Grammar Drills* will enable you to take charge of the grammar that you need to know French well by providing you with plenty of writing drills to reinforce your knowledge and enhance your ability to speak, read, and write with finesse. You will be able to work at your own pace while focusing on those aspects of grammar that require the most attention.

Since so many grammatical elements in French vary as a function of the gender and number nouns, the book starts with a chapter on articles and tips showing you how to distinguish between masculine and feminine genders, as well as singular and plural forms, before moving on to chapters examining adjectives, adverbs, pronouns, prepositions, and conjunctions. The remaining chapters are devoted to verbal forms and tenses. The emphasis in the verb chapters is on those tenses of the indicative and subjunctive modes that are most frequently used in contemporary and conversational French.

A variety of exercises will reinforce your ability to manipulate the French language. There are exercises after each set of explanations so you can immediately apply what you have learned. In addition, ten sets of review exercises follow each group of related chapters. They are found following the study of articles and adjectives (Part 1); after plurals, quantity, and partitive articles (Part 2); after the study of adjectives, including comparatives and superlatives (Part 3); after the study of adverbs (Part 4); after the study of subject, stressed, and object pronouns (Part 5); after possessive, demonstrative, and interrogative pronouns (Part 6); after relative pronouns (Part 7); after prepositions and conjunctions (Part 8); after the study of verbs in the future, conditional, **imparfait,** and **passé composé**, including present and past participles (Part 9); and after the study of the subjunctive, reflexive verbs, the passive voice, negations, interrogatives, irregular verb forms and verbal expressions (Part 10). These review exercises are given specific contexts with the aid of various "vignettes" that give you the opportunity to challenge yourself in communicative, real-life situations. You will find answers to all the exercises in the answer key at the back of the book.

This new edition includes a "Final Review" chapter of exercises that pull together everything you've tested yourself with in the previous drills.

Once you've worked your way through *French Grammar Drills,* not only will you find yourself confidently on your way to fluency, this book will remain a unique resource anytime you need to clarify or review essential grammatical concepts.

Part 1

Articles and Adjectives

1

Definite Articles

Definite articles accompany nouns representing specific things and people. They are usually translated into English as *the*, although they are sometimes omitted in English.

Gender and number of nouns

The definite article (*the* in English) varies according to the gender (masculine or feminine) and number (singular or plural) of the noun it accompanies. Several abbreviations related to articles and nouns, as well as the distinction between familiar and formal speech, are used throughout the book. They are:

m	*masculine*
f	*feminine*
s	*singular*
pl	*plural*
fam.	*familiar*
form.	*formal*

Use **le** before a masculine singular noun starting with a consonant.

le livre	*the book*
le père	*the father*

Use **la** before a feminine singular noun starting with a consonant.

la porte	*the door*
la dame	*the lady*

Use **l'** before a singular noun (masculine or feminine) starting with a vowel or a mute **h**; the definite articles **le** and **la** change to the form **l'**:

| l'homme (m) | the man |
| l'affiche (f) | the poster |

Use **les** before any plural noun (masculine or feminine):

| les garçons | the boys |
| les filles | the girls |

Since the use of **le** or **la** before a singular noun depends on the gender of that noun, there are a few rules of thumb to help you remember the gender of nouns.

Here are some nouns representing male and female subjects and several animals. Male individuals are masculine, while females are feminine. Note that the general term for an animal can be masculine or feminine when one is referring to individuals of both genders: **la grenouille, le crapaud.**

le chéri	the darling (m)	la chérie	the darling (f)
le père	the father	la mère	the mother
l'oncle (m)	the uncle	la tante	the aunt
le frère	the brother	la sœur	the sister
le neveu	the nephew	la nièce	the niece
le charcutier	the deli man	la charcutière	the deli lady
le boulanger	the baker (m)	la boulangère	the baker (f)
le mécanicien	the mechanic (m)	la mécanicienne	the mechanic (f)
l'acteur (m)	the actor	l'actrice (f)	the actress
le lion	the lion	la lionne	the lioness
le coq	the rooster	la poule	the chicken
le crapaud	the toad (m or f)	la grenouille	the frog (m or f)

The ending of a noun can often help determine its gender. Here are some nouns ending in **-e** or in **-on.** These are usually *feminine.*

la réponse	the answer
la danse	the dance
la chanson	the song
la soupe	the soup
la chaussure	the shoe
la maison	the house
la raison	the reason
la solution	the solution

Here are some nouns ending in *consonants* or in the *vowels* -i *and* -u. These are usually *masculine*.

le lac	*the lake*
le ciel	*the sky*
le parti	*the (political) party*
le menu	*the menu*
le reçu	*the receipt*
le château	*the castle*
le tableau	*the painting*
le bureau	*the desk/office*

Exercise 1

Identify the gender of the noun by looking at its ending. Then write the appropriate article (**le**, **la**, or **l'**) before it. When you use **l'**, specify the gender of the noun by indicating (m) or (f).

1. _____ maison

2. _____ chéri

3. _____ bureau

4. _____ raison

5. _____ menu

6. _____ chérie

7. _____ réponse

8. _____ tableau

9. _____ ciel

10. _____ danse

11. _____ coq

12. _____ grenouille

13. _____ boulanger

14. _____ lionne

15. _____ tante

In some cases, all or a majority of the members of a group have the same gender. For example, many names of trees and vegetables are masculine, while many names of fruits are feminine. Here are some common names of trees, vegetables, and fruits:

Arbres	Trees
le chêne	*the oak tree*
le bouleau	*the birch tree*
le saule	*the willow tree*
le palmier	*the palm tree*
le bananier	*the banana tree*
le manguier	*the mango tree*
l'olivier (m)	*the olive tree*
le pommier	*the apple tree*
l'amandier (m)	*the almond tree*

Légumes	Vegetables	*Fruits*	Fruits
le céleri	*celery*	la tomate	*tomato*
le chou	*cabbage*	la banane	*banana*
le poireau	*leek*	la pêche	*peach*
le radis	*radish*	l'orange (f)	*orange*
le brocoli	*broccoli*	la mangue	*mango*
le haricot	*green bean*	la pomme	*apple*
le petit pois	*green pea*	la prune	*plum*
le poivron vert	*green pepper*	la pastèque	*watermelon*
l'oignon (m)	*onion*	la cerise	*cherry*
l'ail (m)	*garlic*	l'amande (f)	*almond*

Exercise 2

Identify the gender of each noun by placing it in the correct category (**Arbre, Légume, Fruit**). Then insert the correct article (**le, la,** or **l'**) before it. If the article is **l'**, indicate its gender by indicating (m) or (f) next to it.

Example: Arbre le chêne

1. _____ poivron

2. _____ radis

3. _____ mangue

4. _____ pommier

5. _____ orange

6. _____ poireau

7. _____ cerise

8. _____ chou

9. _____ saule

10. _____ palmier

11. _____ ail

12. _____ banane

13. _____ olivier

14. _____ petit pois

Units of measurement are masculine (except for **la livre,** *pound*); most words of English origin and the names of languages are also masculine. Here are some examples:

Unités de mesure	**Units of measurement**
le watt	*watt*
le volt	*volt*
le litre	*liter*
le gramme	*gram*
le kilogramme	*kilogram*
le mètre	*meter*
le kilomètre	*kilometer*

Mots d'origine anglaise	**Words of English origin**
le parking	*parking*
le stress	*stress*
le week-end	*weekend*
le bowling	*bowling*
le rock	*rock (music)*
le jazz	*jazz (music)*
le tennis	*tennis*

Langues	**Languages**
l'anglais (m)	*English*
le français	*French*
l'allemand (m)	*German*
l'espagnol (m)	*Spanish*
l'italien (m)	*Italian*
le portugais	*Portuguese*

le chinois	*Chinese*
le russe	*Russian*
l'arabe (m)	*Arabic*
le suédois	*Swedish*
le norvégien	*Norwegian*
le danois	*Danish*
le finlandais	*Finnish*

The names of days, seasons, and months are masculine.

Les jours	**Days**
(le) lundi	*Monday(s)*
(le) mardi	*Tuesday(s)*
(le) mercredi	*Wednesday(s)*
(le) jeudi	*Thursday(s)*
(le) vendredi	*Friday(s)*
(le) samedi	*Saturday(s)*
(le) dimanche	*Sunday(s)*

Les mois	**Months**
janvier	*January*
février	*February*
mars	*March*
avril	*April*
mai	*May*
juin	*June*
juillet	*July*
août	*August*
septembre	*September*
octobre	*October*
novembre	*November*
décembre	*December*

Les saisons	**Seasons**
l'hiver (m)	*winter*
le printemps	*spring*
l'été (m)	*summer*
l'automne (m)	*fall*

Exercise 3

Justify the masculine gender of each of the following words by placing them into the proper category: units of measurement (U), words of English origin (E), days (D), months (M), seasons (S), or languages (L).

1. _____ volt
2. _____ tennis
3. _____ samedi
4. _____ été
5. _____ février
6. _____ mercredi
7. _____ chinois
8. _____ arabe
9. _____ kilomètre
10. _____ basket
11. _____ janvier
12. _____ hiver
13. _____ week-end
14. _____ automne
15. _____ rock

A few nouns can be masculine or feminine; many of these change meaning if they change their gender. Examples:

l'élève (m)	*male student*	l'élève (f)	*female student*
le livre	*book*	la livre	*pound (weight)*
le tour	*tour (visit)/trick*	la tour	*tower*
le mort	*dead man*	la mort	*death*
le physique	*physical appearance*	la physique	*physics*
le voile	*veil*	la voile	*sail*
le poste	*job/post/position*	la poste	*post office*

Exercise 4

Identify the meaning (in English) of each of the following phrases and write the correct article before each noun.

1. _____ voile du bateau
2. _____ mort du poète
3. _____ physique de l'athlète
4. _____ livre de pain
5. _____ poste de professeur
6. _____ voile de la femme
7. _____ poste du village
8. _____ tour guidé du musée
9. _____ mort dans le cercueil
10. _____ physique et la chimie

Exercise 5

Write the correct definite article (**le, la,** or **l'**) before each noun. When the article is **l'**, specify the gender of the noun by indicating (m) or (f) for masculine or feminine.

1. _____ anglais
2. _____ école
3. _____ bateau
4. _____ chanson
5. _____ tableau
6. _____ ami
7. _____ histoire
8. _____ crayon
9. _____ allemand
10. _____ ballon
11. _____ gâteau
12. _____ raison
13. _____ radis
14. _____ menu

15. _____ carte

16. _____ stress

17. _____ palmier

18. _____ tomate

19. _____ pêche

20. _____ boulanger

21. _____ mécanicienne

22. _____ tante

23. _____ grand-père

24. _____ sœur

25. _____ jeudi

26. _____ hockey

27. _____ manguier

28. _____ mangue

29. _____ saule

30. _____ haricot

Use of the definite article

The French definite article is generally used to translate the English article *the*. It is often required in French even though it may be absent in English. The definite article (**le, la, l', or les**) is necessary in the following cases:

- General categories and abstractions

Les fraises mûres sont rouges.	*Ripe strawberries are red.*
La patience est une vertu.	*Patience is a virtue.*

- Name and adjective clusters

Le vieux Paris est fascinant.	*Old Paris is fascinating.*
Surveille **la** petite Émilie.	*Watch little Émilie.*

- Titles and family names

Voici **le** professeur Muller.	*Here is professor Muller.*
Voici **les** Chabrol.	*Here are the Chabrols.*

- Languages

J'étudie **le** français.	*I am studying French.*
Je comprends **l'**allemand.	*I understand German.*

- School subjects

J'adore **la** psychologie.	*I love psychology.*
La physique est intéressante.	*Physics is interesting.*

- Countries

L'Italie est belle.	*Italy is beautiful.*
Je veux visiter **la** France.	*I want to visit France.*

- Seasons

Le printemps est ma saison favorite.	*Spring is my favorite season.*
L'hiver est long au Canada.	*Wintertime is long in Canada.*

- Days. The *singular* definite article (**le**) before the name of a day expresses *on* or *every* (on Monday(s), every Tuesday, etc.).

Je me repose **le** dimanche.	*I rest on Sundays.*
Je sors **le** vendredi soir.	*I go out every Friday night.*

- Parts of the day

Je fais une sieste **l'**après-midi.	*I take a nap in the afternoon.*
L'aube est mystérieuse.	*Dawn is mysterious.*

Omission of the definite article

Compare these sets of sentences, and note that the definite article is omitted in the following cases:

- When the titles **monsieur, madame,** and **mademoiselle** appear before a person's name

Voici **monsieur** Dupuis.	*Here is Mr. Dupuis.*
But: C'est **le** monsieur qui parle français.	*This is the gentleman who speaks French.*

- When the definite article refers to a *specific day*

Viens me chercher **dimanche**.	*Pick me up **on Sunday**.*
But: Je vais à l'église **le** dimanche.	*I go to church **on Sundays**.*

- After the preposition **en**

Je suis forte **en** anglais.	*I am good in English.*
But: L'anglais est ma langue favorite.	*English is my favorite subject.*
Je vais skier **en** hiver.	*I go skiing in the winter.*
But: L'hiver est doux en Provence.	*Winter is mild in Provence.*
Regarde la jolie porte **en** bois!	*Look at the pretty wooden door!*
But: Le bois est joli.	*Wood is pretty.*

Contracted articles

When the preposition **à** (*in, at, to*) or **de** (*of, from*) precedes the definite article **le** or **les**, the contracted form (**au, aux, du, des**) must be used. Note that the preposition contracts with the definite article.

Va **au** bureau.	*Go **to the** office.*
Va **aux** toilettes.	*Go **to the** restroom.*
Sors **du** bureau.	*Come out **of the** office.*
Sors **des** toilettes.	*Come out **of the** restroom.*

Remember to use the preposition **de/d'** to express possession in French:

C'est **la salle des professeurs**.	*This is the **teachers' room**.*
Regarde **la robe de la dame**.	*Look at **the lady's dress**.*

C'est **la femme du monsieur**!   *This is **the gentleman's wife**!*
Voici **la voiture d'Annie**.   *Here is **Annie's car**.*

Exercise 6

Choose the best answer from the two choices:

1. Cette dame s'appelle _____ Roland. (madame, la)

2. _____ amis sont essentiels dans la vie. (L', Les)

3. Je vais sortir avec mes copains _____ prochain. (samedi, le samedi)

4. Tu vas _____ France? Quelle chance! (en, la)

5. J'aime aller _____ concerts de musique rock. (les, aux)

6. C'est la faute _____ parents. (des, du)

7. Va vite _____ maison! (au, à la)

8. Les feuilles _____ arbres rougissent en automne. (d', des)

9. _____ Piriou vous attend. (Docteur, Le docteur)

10. _____ Luc est de plus en plus mignon. (Petit, Le petit)

11. Bonjour, _____ Dufort. (le monsieur, monsieur)

12. _____ santé importe plus que _____ richesse. (—, la)

13. Tu parles _____ anglais? (—, l')

14. C'est la bicyclette _____ Mireille. (de, du)

15. Je suis très bon _____ mathématiques. (en, aux)

16. J'adore _____ melon. (le, —)

17. _____ été est particulièrement chaud cette année. (L', —)

18. _____ samedi soir, je vais toujours au cinéma. (Le, —)

19. Elle est née _____ avril. (en, à)

20. Voilà le livre _____ professeur. (de, du)

21. _____ aube est un moment magique de la journée. (—, L')

22. _____ physique est difficile. (—, La)

23. Viens étudier chez moi _____ samedi après-midi. (—, le)

24. Grand-mère ne sort pas souvent _____ hiver. (en, —)

25. _____ génies sont rares. (Les, —)

2

Indefinite Articles

Indefinite articles accompany nouns unknown to the listener or reader. They are usually translated into English as *a*.

Gender and use of the indefinite article

The French indefinite article varies with the gender (masculine or feminine) and number (singular or plural) of the noun it accompanies:

The article **un** is used before a masculine singular noun:

un livre	*a book*
un ami	*a male friend*

The article **une** is used before a feminine singular noun:

une porte	*a door*
une dame	*a lady*

The article **des** is used before any plural noun (masculine or feminine):

des amis	*some male friends*
des amies	*some female friends*

The French indefinite articles **un** and **une** are generally used to translate the English article *a/an* or *one*. The plural indefinite article **des** is usually translated as *some*.

Donne-moi **une** glace.	*Give me an ice cream.*
Achète-moi **des** pommes.	*Buy me some apples.*

The indefinite article is necessary in French even when it is omitted (but implied) in English:

J'ai acheté **des** chaussures chères.   *I bought (some) expensive shoes.*

Omission of the indefinite article

The indefinite article is omitted after a form of **quel.**

Quel beau garçon!   *What a handsome boy!*
Quelle belle journée!   *What a beautiful day!*

The indefinite article is omitted after **il/elle/on est** or after **ils/elles sont** when one is referring to *unmodified* professions, nationalities, or religions. Compare the following sets of sentences and note the omission of the indefinite article in French before the name of a profession or a nationality when the profession or nationality is not accompanied by an adjective.

Ma sœur, elle est médecin.   *My sister? She is a doctor.*
C'est **un** médecin formidable.   *She is a great doctor.*
Ils sont américains.   *They are American.*
Ce sont **des** Américains célèbres.   *They are famous Americans.*

Exercise 7

Write the correct indefinite article (**un, une, des**) before each noun. Insert — if the article is to be omitted.

1. J'ai _____ nouvelle voiture.

2. J'aimerais _____ petit verre de vin.

3. Apportez-moi _____ menu.

4. C'est vraiment _____ très belle journée!

5. Achète-moi _____ bonbons, s'il te plaît!

6. J'ai _____ nouvelles de Pierre.

7. Tu as _____ gros chien.

8. Prenons _____ billet de métro!

9. Il faut ouvrir au moins _____ fenêtre.

10. Il y a _____ cafés partout.

11. Mon père est _____ ingénieur.

12. M. Boulet? C'est _____ musicien remarquable.

13. Quel _____ beau garçon!

14. J'ai besoin de/d'_____ bon dictionnaire.

15. Je voudrais _____ chambre au premier étage.

3

Demonstrative Adjectives

The French demonstrative adjective varies with the gender (masculine or feminine) and number (singular or plural) of the noun it accompanies.

Ce is used before a masculine singular noun starting with a consonant.

ce bateau	*this/that boat*

Cet (rather than ce) is used before a masculine singular noun that starts with a vowel or mute **h**.

cet arbre	*this/that tree*

Cette is used before any feminine singular noun.

cette porte	*this/that door*
cette idée	*this/that idea*

Ces is used before any plural noun (masculine or feminine).

ces amies (fpl)	*these/those friends*
ces livres (mpl)	*these/those books*

To distinguish between *this* and *that*, or between *these* and *those*, you may add **-ci** or **-là** to the noun.

Cette bicyclette-**ci** est rouge.	*This bike is red.*
Ces bicyclettes-**là** sont bleues.	*Those bikes are blue.*

Exercise 8

Write the correct demonstrative adjective (**ce/cet, cette,** or **ces**) before each noun.

1. Regarde _____ arbre; il est beau, n'est-ce pas?

2. J'aime bien _____ couleur sur toi; elle te va bien.

3. Apporte-moi _____ stylos-là!

4. Je vais ranger _____ chambre tout de suite.

5. _____ pain est délicieux.

6. _____ immeubles sont si hauts!

7. _____ film est très long. Je m'ennuie.

8. _____ homme ressemble à son frère.

9. Je te pardonne _____ faute-ci.

10. _____ tableaux-là sont les plus beaux.

11. _____ amour est éternel.

12. _____ inspiration est rare.

13. _____ maison est adorable.

14. _____ devoirs sont très faciles.

15. _____ menu-ci est cher; _____ menu-là est bon marché.

4

Possessive Adjectives

The French possessive adjectives that express *my*, *your* (fam.), and *his/her* vary with the gender (masculine or feminine) and number (singular or plural) of the noun they precede.

The adjective **mon** is used before a masculine singular noun:

mon vélo	*my bike*

The adjective **mon** is also used before a feminine singular noun starting with a vowel or mute **h**.

mon amie (f)	*my girlfriend*
mon histoire (f)	*my story*

The adjective **ma** is used before a feminine singular noun starting with a consonant.

ma mère	*my mother*

The adjective **mes** is used before any plural noun (masculine or feminine):

mes parents	*my parents*
mes sœurs	*my sisters*

Your (**ton, ta, tes**) and *his/her* (**son, sa, ses**) are used in the same manner as *my* (**mon, ma, mes**). However, note that both possessive adjectives, *his* and *her*, are translated as **son, sa,** or **ses** depending on the gender of the *noun that follows* (not the possessor).

son père (m)	*his father*	**son** père (m)	*her father*
sa mère (f)	*his mother*	**sa** mère (f)	*her mother*
ses parents (mpl)	*his parents*	**ses** parents (mpl)	*her parents*

The French possessive adjectives that express *our*, *your* (plural or formal), and *their* vary only from singular to plural. Gender is not indicated.

		your				your	
notre ami (m)		*our friend*		nos professeurs (mpl)		*our teachers*	
votre affiche (f)		*your poster*		vos affiches (fpl)		*your posters*	
leur père (ms)		*their father*		leurs parents (mpl)		*their parents*	

The table below is a summary of all possessive adjectives by gender and number.

	my	your (fam.)	his/her	our	your (form., pl)	their
ms	mon	ton	son	notre	votre	leur
fs	ma	ta	sa	notre	votre	leur
pl	mes	tes	ses	nos	vos	leurs

Exercise 9

Write the correct possessive adjective on the line provided.

1. _____ père (*my father*)

2. _____ père (*your father*/fam.)

3. _____ père (*his/her father*)

4. _____ mère (*my mother*)

5. _____ mère (*your mother*/fam.)

6. _____ mère (*his/her mother*)

7. _____ parents (*my parents*)

8. _____ parents (*your parents*/fam.)

9. _____ parents (*his/her parents*)

10. _____ sœur (*our sister*)

11. _____ sœurs (*our sisters*)

12. _____ oncle (*your uncle*/form.)

13. _____ oncles (*your uncles*/form.)

14. _____ tante (*their aunt*)

15. _____ tantes (*their aunts*)

Use the definite article, *not* the possessive adjective, before parts of the body, especially in sentences with a reflexive verb (see Reflexive Verbs, Chapter 36).

Lève **la** main!	*Raise your hand!*
Lave-toi **les** cheveux.	*Wash your hair.*
Rase-toi **la** barbe!	*Shave your beard!*

Exercise 10

Ma toilette. *Mireille is getting ready for a party.* Fill in the blank in each French sentence with the correct article to reconstruct all the steps she takes in her preparations.

1. *I tweeze my eyebrows.*

   Je m'épile ＿＿＿＿＿ sourcils.

2. *I shave my legs.*

   Je me rase ＿＿＿＿＿ jambes.

3. *I wash my face and my hair.*

   Je me lave ＿＿＿＿＿ figure et ＿＿＿＿＿ cheveux.

4. *I dry my hair.*

   Je me sèche ＿＿＿＿＿ cheveux.

5. *I put rouge on my cheeks.*

   Je me mets du rouge sur ＿＿＿＿＿ joues.

6. *I powder my nose.*

   Je me poudre ＿＿＿＿＿ nez.

7. *I brush my hair.*

   Je me brosse ＿＿＿＿＿ cheveux.

8. *I curl my bangs.*

   Je me boucle ＿＿＿＿＿ mèches de devant.

9. *I put mascara on my eyelashes.*

   Je me mets du rimmel sur ＿＿＿＿＿ cils.

10. *I spray perfume onto my neck.*

    Je me mets du parfum dans ＿＿＿＿＿ cou.

5

Interrogative Adjectives

Interrogative adjectives vary with the gender (masculine or feminine) and number (singular or plural) of the noun they precede. They are translated as *what* or *which*, and used in questions as well as in exclamations.

Quelle couleur aimes-tu?	*Which color do you like?*
Quel mauvais temps!	*What bad weather!*
Quel courage! (m)	*What courage!*
Quels amis! (mpl)	*What friends!*
Quelle histoire! (f)	*What a story!*
Quelles copines! (fpl)	*What girlfriends!*

Exercise 11

Write the correct form of **quel** before each noun.

1. _____ heure est-il? —Il est une heure.

2. _____ chemise est-ce que je vais porter aujourd'hui? —La blanche!

3. _____ histoires amusantes!

4. _____ réponse intelligente!

5. _____ enfants affectueux!

6. _____ temps fait-il? —Le temps est mauvais. (Il fait mauvais.)

7. _____ question bizarre!

8. _____ copains sympathiques!

9. _____ professeurs stricts!

10. _____ exercice facile!

11. _____ tragédie!

12. _____ pièce intéressante!

13. _____ voyage improvisé!

14. _____ dîner délicieux!

15. _____ vêtements élégants!

Review 1

Exercise 12

Sandrine parle à différentes personnes lors d'une réunion de famille. *Sandrine talks to various people at a family gathering.* Write the definite or indefinite article or the demonstrative or possessive adjective, if necessary, in the space provided to reconstitute what she says.

1. J'adore _____ punch. Et vous? (le, —)

2. Je veux voir _____ photos que Jack a prises. (les, —)

3. _____ Américains n'ont pas souvent de longues vacances d'été. (Les, —)

4. J'ai _____ amis formidables aux États-Unis. (des, —)

5. _____ amis sont importants dans ma vie! (—, les)

6. Jack est _____ américain. (un, —)

7. Vous êtes _____ professeur? (un, —)

8. C'est _____ belle profession. (une,—)

9. Vos élèves lèvent _____ main pour répondre? (la, ta)

10. J'ai deux tantes qui sont _____ professeurs.   (des, —)

11. Voilà. Je vous présente _____ tante! (mon, ma)

12. Tante Jeanne, j'aime _____ chaussures! (cette, ces)

13. Tu les as achetées juste pour _____ soir? (ce, —)

14. J'adore aussi _____ nouveau pull. (ton, ta)

15. Quelle _____ jolie fleur brodée sur ton béret! (—, cette)

Exercise 13

Sandrine va au marché avec sa mère. *Sandrine goes to the market with her mother.* Translate each sentence into English.

1. Je viens de l'école.

_____

2. Je vais au marché avec maman.

_____

3. Les fruits sont chers en hiver.

_____

4. Ces fruits sont encore verts!

_____

5. Les légumes sont toujours frais ici.

_____

6. J'aime la soupe aux légumes.

_____

7. Achète ce céleri. Il a l'air bon.

_____

8. Et ces carottes aussi.

_____

9. Bientôt c'est l'anniversaire de papa.

_____

10. Il adore les animaux.

_____

11. Les chiens spécialement.

_____

12. Qu'est-ce que tu penses de ce petit bulldog?

_____

13. Tu détestes les bulldogs? Zut!

_____

14. Où est-ce qu'on va acheter son gâteau d'anniversaire?

_____

15. À la boulangerie de la rue Rémy?

_____

16. Cette boulangerie-là est très chère, non?

_____

17. C'est lundi, son anniversaire, n'est-ce pas?

_____

18. C'est bien. Le lundi je reste toujours à la maison.

_____

19. On invite toujours tous ses amis.

_____

20. Quelle famille formidable!

_____

Exercise 14

Les projets de vacances de Sandrine. *Sandrine's vacation plans.* Translate the element indicated into French to complete the sentence.

1. D'habitude Sandrine passe _____ avec ses copines. (*Sundays*)

2. Mais _____ elle déjeune au restaurant avec sa famille. (*this Sunday*)

3. Ils discutent de _____ projets de vacances. (*their*)

4. _____ hiver ils pensent aller au Canada. (*This*)

5. L'hiver est _____ saison favorite parce qu'ils aiment tous skier. (*their*)

6. _____ oncle Benoît habite au Québec. (*Her*)

7. Il a une maison en bois à _____ montagne. (*the*)

8. _____ maison magnifique! (*What a*)

9. L'été prochain, Sandrine va voir _____ famille française. (*her*)

10. _____ cousins habitent à Nice. (*her*)

11. Sandrine adore passer _____ été là-bas. (*the*)

12. Elle parle et comprend _____. (*French*)

13. Elle veut être _____ de français un jour. (*teacher*)

14. Elle aime acheter _____ habits et _____ chaussures en France. (*some*)

15. Un de ses passe-temps préférés, c'est _____. (*shopping*)

16. Elle a _____ cousine qui l'accompagne. (*a*)

17. _____ cousine connaît les meilleurs magasins. (*Her*)

18. Avec elle, Sandrine achète toujours _____ vêtements à la mode. (*some*)

19. Elle revient toujours aux États-Unis avec _____ cadeaux pour tous. (*some*)

20. _____ été va être formidable! (*This*)

Part 2

Plurals, Quantity, and Partitive Articles

6

Plural of Nouns

The article in a plural noun phrase must be plural. Review the plural articles and the demonstrative, possessive, and interrogative adjectives:

les	*the*
des	*some*
ces	*these/those*
mes	*my*
tes	*your (fam.)*
ses	*his/her*
nos	*our*
vos	*your (form./pl)*
leurs	*their*
quels/quelles	*which/what*

Generally, to make a noun plural, add the letter -s to the noun.

le stylo	*the pen*	les stylos	*the pens*
la réponse	*the answer*	les réponses	*the answers*

If the singular noun ends in -s, -x, or -z, it remains unchanged in the plural.

le nez	*the nose*	les nez	*the noses*
le fils	*the son*	les fils	*the sons*

If the singular noun ends in -al, change -al to -aux to make it plural.

l'hôpital	*the hospital*	les hôpitaux	*the hospitals*
le journal	*the newspaper*	les journaux	*the newspapers*

If the singular noun ends in -eau, add the letter -x to make it plural.

le tableau	*the painting*	les tableaux	*the paintings*
le morceau	*the piece, morsel*	les morceaux	*the pieces, morsels*

In some cases, the plural form of a noun cannot be obtained by adding **-s** or **-x** to its singular form. Such nouns have *irregular* plural forms which must be memorized.

l'œil *(m)*	*the eye*	**les yeux** *(mpl)*	*the eyes*
le ciel	*the sky*	**les cieux** *(mpl)*	*the skies*
monsieur	*sir (Mr.)*	**messieurs**	*gentlemen*
madame	*Mrs.*	**mesdames**	*ladies*
mademoiselle	*Miss*	**mesdemoiselles**	*young ladies* (form of address)

Exercise 15

Write the plural of each noun phrase.

1. le crayon _____

2. la chaise _____

3. notre bureau _____

4. cette dame _____

5. monsieur _____

6. madame _____

7. leur garçon _____

8. sa fille _____

9. quel fils _____

10. l'hôpital _____

11. l'œil _____

12. un morceau _____

13. le général _____

14. votre bateau _____

15. mon choix _____

16. l'autobus _____

17. le tableau _____

18. le musée _____

19. la porte _____

20. ce bijou _____

7

Quantity

The following adverbs of quantity include the preposition **de**. Do not use an article or a contraction after **de/d'**. The noun that follows may be masculine or feminine, singular or plural.

assez **de**	*enough*
beaucoup **de**	*many, much*
pas mal **de**	*many, much*
peu **de**	*little*
tant **de**	*so many, so much*
tellement **de**	*so many, so much*
trop **de**	*too many, too much*
un peu **de**	*a little*
combien **de**	*how many, how much*

Du lait? Oui, il y a **assez de** lait!	*Milk? Yes, there is **enough** milk.*
De la patience? J'ai **peu de** patience.	*Patience? I have **little** patience.*
Des pêches? J'ai **assez de** pêches.	*Peaches? I have **enough** peaches.*
Combien d'amis as-tu?	***How many** friends do you have?*

The following nouns describe specific measurements. They also include the preposition **de**. Do not use an article or a contraction after **de/d'**. The noun that follows may be masculine or feminine, singular or plural.

une cuillerée **de**	*a spoonful of*
un gramme **de**	*a gram of*
une livre **de**	*a pound of*
un kilo **de**	*a kilo of*
un litre **de**	*a liter of*
un verre **de**	*a glass of*
une tasse **de**	*a cup of*
une bouteille **de**	*a bottle of*
un morceau **de**	*a piece of*

une tranche **de**	*a slice of*
une douzaine **de**	*a dozen*
une centaine **de**	*a hundred*
une boîte **de**	*a box of*

Je voudrais **un kilo de** pêches.	*I would like **a kilo of** peaches.*
Un verre de vin, s'il vous plaît!	***A glass of** wine, please!*

Plusieurs (*several*) and **quelques** (*a few*) do not require **de/d'**.

Voilà **quelques dollars.**	*Here are **a few** dollars.*
Je te l'ai dit **plusieurs fois.**	*I told you **several times.***

Bien des (*many, much*) and **la plupart de** (*most of, the majority of*) can be followed by an article or a contraction.

Bien des fois, j'ai voulu écrire.	*Many times (Often) I wanted to write.*
La plupart du temps, je m'ennuie.	*Most of the time I am bored.*

Quelque chose (*something*) and **rien** (*nothing*) are followed by **de/d'** + a masculine singular adjective.

Apprends-moi **quelque chose** d'intéressant!	*Teach me **something** interesting!*
Je n'ai **rien de** neuf à me mettre.	*I have **nothing** new to wear.*

Exercise 16

Choose the correct completion for each sentence.

1. Je connais plusieurs _____ professeurs de français. (de, —)

2. La plupart _____ gens aiment la paix. (des, —)

3. Il y a trop _____ sucre dans ce café. (de, du)

4. Mets un peu _____ sel dans la soupe. (de, du)

5. Il y a beaucoup _____ lectures pour enfants dans ce livre. (des, de)

6. Tu as tellement _____ amis! (des, d')

7. Voilà quelques _____ sous pour une glace. (de, —)

8. Je voudrais un verre _____ vin. (de, du)

9. Je t'ai répété cela une centaine _____ fois. (des, de)

10. J'ai quelque chose _____ important à te dire. (d', —)

11. J'adore _____ films d'amour. (des, les)

12. Je ne mange pas _____ poisson. (du, de)

13. Je prends _____ fromage après chaque repas. (du, le)

14. Donne-moi _____ salade, mais pas trop! (de, de la)

15. Je prends _____ vin avec les repas. (du, le)

16. Je vais prendre une douzaine _____ œufs. (d', des)

17. Il me faut aussi un kilo _____ jambon. (de, du)

18. Tu as fait bien _____ fautes. (de, des)

19. Combien _____ fautes as-tu? (de, des)

20. Moi, je n'ai rien _____ bon à manger. (de, des)

Partitive Articles

The partitive article, when used in an affirmative sentence, means *some*. The form of the article depends on whether it precedes a feminine singular noun (**de la**), a masculine singular noun (**du**), any singular noun starting with a vowel or mute **h** (**de l'**) or a plural noun (**des**). It is used in French when one is referring to an undefined quantity, even though it may be omitted and implied in English.

Je veux **du** café.	*I want (some) coffee.*
Je veux **de la** crème.	*I want (some) cream.*
Je veux **de l'**eau minérale.	*I want (some) mineral water.*
Je veux **des** petits pains.	*I want (some) rolls.*

The partitive article in a negative sentence is **de/d'**, regardless of whether the noun that follows is masculine, feminine, singular, or plural. It is usually translated into English as *any* or *no*.

Je ne veux **pas de** café.	*I do not want **any** coffee.*
Je ne veux **pas de** petits pains.	*I do not want **any** rolls.*
Pas de sucre pour moi!	*No sugar for me!*

The table below summarizes partitive articles by gender (m/f) and number (s/pl).

	ms	fs	ms or fs (before vowel sound)	pl
some	**du** café	**de la** glace	**de l'**eau	**des** petits pains
not any (no)	**pas de** café	**pas de** glace	**pas d'**eau	**pas de** petits pains

Omission of the partitive article

Note that the partitive article **des**, used in French when one is referring to undefined quantities, is *not* normally used before plural *adjectives*. Compare the following sentences:

| Je raconte **des** blagues. | *I tell (some) jokes.* |
| Je raconte **de bonnes** blagues. | *I tell (some) good jokes.* |

Note that a few French adjective + noun combinations form an entity. **Des** is retained in cases such as: **des jeunes filles, des petits pains, des petits pois.**

The definite article (**le, la, l'**, or **les**) is used instead of the partitive article when one is talking about things in general (such as food items, vegetables, fruit, types of movies, etc.) or when one is dealing with abstractions (review Chapter 1).

| J'aime **les** fruits, mais je déteste **les** légumes. | *I love fruit, but I hate vegetables.* |
| **La** beauté physique est superficielle. | *Physical beauty is superficial.* |

Exercise 17

This is a short exchange between a waiter and a customer. Select the appropriate article from the choices and write it in the space provided.

1. *Serveur:* _____ café, monsieur? (Du, Le)

2. *M. Rémy:* Oui merci. Avec _____ crème! (de la, la)

3. *Serveur:* J'arrive, monsieur. _____ pain avec ça? (Du, Des)

4. *M. Rémy:* Je ne refuse pas. Mais pas _____ croissants! (des, de)

5. *Serveur:* D'accord! _____ eau minérale? (D', De l')

6. *M. Rémy:* Non, non, merci. Pas _____ eau minérale! (d', de l')

7. *M. Rémy:* Mais apportez-moi _____ jus d'orange! (des, du)

8. *Serveur:* Oui, monsieur. _____ jus est très frais aujourd'hui. (Le, Du)

9. *M. Rémy:* Il y a _____ petits pains au chocolat aujourd'hui? (des, de)

10. *Serveur:* Oui. Et _____ délicieuses brioches aussi. (des, de)

Now translate the exchange into English.

11. *Serveur:* _____

12. *M. Rémy:* _____

13. *Serveur:* _____

14. *M. Rémy:* _____

15. *Serveur:* _____

16. *M. Rémy:* _____

17. *M. Rémy:* _____

18. *Serveur:* _____

19. *M. Rémy:* _____

20. *Serveur:* _____

Review 2

Exercise 18

Henri a passé une mauvaise journée. *Henri had a bad day.* Choose the correct completion for each sentence and find out what is wrong.

1. Je me suis arrêté à plusieurs _____ épiceries. (de, —)

2. Mais il n'y avait plus _____ lait frais. (de, —)

3. Il y a trop _____ poivre dans cette salade. (de, du)

4. Mets un peu _____ sel dans la soupe. (de, du)

5. Il y a tellement _____ grammaire dans ce livre. (des, de)

6. Je n'ai pas beaucoup _____ amis! (des, d')

7. Voilà quelques _____ commentaires! (de, —)

8. Je n'aime pas _____ vin. (le, du)

9. Je t'ai répété cela une dizaine _____ fois. (des, de)

10. J'ai quelque chose _____ important à te dire. (d', —)

11. Je déteste _____ films d'amour. (des, les)

12. Je ne mange pas _____ poisson. (du, de)

13. Où est _____ fromage? J'en prends après chaque repas. (du, le)

14. Donne-moi _____ salade! (de, de la)

15. _____ légumes ne sont pas bons. (Les, —)

Exercise 19

Qui sont Henri et Éric? *Who are Henri and Éric?* Translate the following sentences into English and get to know Henri and Éric.

1. J'ai les yeux bleus.

_____

2. J'ai les cheveux blonds.

_____

3. J'achète beaucoup de magazines de sport.

_____

4. Je regarde les matchs de foot à la télé.

_____

5. J'aime les sports.

_____

6. Mon fils Éric me ressemble.

_____

7. Il a les yeux bleus et les cheveux blonds comme moi.

_____

8. Cet enfant connaît tant de jeux.

_____

9. Il est très extroverti. Il parle à tous les gens.

_____

10. Il joue bien des tours à ses copains.

_____

11. Voilà quelques exemples.

_____

12. Il envoie de fausses invitations.

_____

13. Il écrit des notes amusantes à ses camarades de classe.

_____

14. Il raconte des blagues incroyables à tout le monde.

_____

15. Il dessine des caricatures très drôles de ses amis.

_____

Exercise 20

Éric est un petit coquin. *Éric is a little rascal.* Translate the following exchanges between Éric and a waiter at a local café into English and you will find out why Éric is a little rascal.

1. *Éric:* Bonjour, mesdames et messieurs.

   Serveur: Une minute, jeune homme. Je suis en train de servir des clients.

   _____

   _____

2. *Éric:* J'ai un peu d'argent pour un coca.

   Serveur: Les enfants non accompagnés ne peuvent pas entrer.

   _____

   _____

3. *Éric:* Mais je voudrais seulement du pain et du soda.

   Serveur: Écoute, petit. Je vais te servir parce que je n'ai pas beaucoup de clients.

   _____

   _____

3. *Éric:* Merci, monsieur. Il y a du beurre sur ce pain?

   Serveur: Non, je regrette. Mais voilà du coca et de l'eau.

   _____

   _____

4. *Éric:* Je n'ai pas besoin d'eau.

   Serveur: Finis ton coca et rentre à la maison!

   _____

   _____

5. *Éric:* Est-ce que je peux avoir de la glace?

   Serveur: Quoi! Rentre à la maison et reviens avec tes parents!

   _____

   _____

Exercise 21

Éric va à l'épicerie. *Éric goes to the grocery store.* Translate the following exchanges between Éric and the grocery store clerk into English to show your understanding of their conversation.

1. *Éric:* Bonjour, madame Lebon.

   Mme Lebon: Bonjour, mon petit.

   _____

   _____

2. *Éric:* Je voudrais du beurre s'il vous plaît.

   Mme Lebon: Du beurre ou de la margarine?

   _____

   _____

3. *Éric:* C'est jaune, le beurre?

   Mme Lebon: Oui, tu veux du beurre alors.

   _____

   _____

4. *Éric:* Oui, et des petits pains aussi.

   Mme Lebon: Combien de petits pains?

   _____

   _____

5. *Éric:* Deux petits pains et du chocolat noir.

   Mme Lebon: Voilà une tablette de chocolat et des petits pains. C'est pour toi?

   _____

   _____

6. *Éric:* Oui, madame. J'adore les petits pains avec du chocolat dedans.

   Mme Lebon: Tu aimes les bonnes choses, toi.

   _____

   _____

7. *Éric:* J'ai aussi besoin de quelques pommes pour maman.

   Mme Lebon: Tu n'aimes pas les pommes, toi?

   _____

   _____

8. *Éric:* Si, mais maman va faire une tarte aux pommes.

   Mme Lebon: Oh! Désolée! Je n'ai plus de pommes.

   _____

   _____

9. *Éric:* Vous avez des abricots?

   Mme Lebon: Oui, en voilà un demi-kilo.

   _____

   _____

10. *Éric:* Merci madame. C'est cher, les abricots?

    Mme Lebon: Mais non, pas plus cher que les pommes.

    _____

    _____

Part 3

Adjectives

9

Agreement of Adjectives

An adjective helps define the characteristics of a noun. French adjectives have the following forms: masculine singular (ms), masculine plural (mpl), feminine singular (fs), and feminine plural (fpl). They agree with the noun they describe.

Most adjectives are made plural by simply adding -s to the singular form. If the masculine singular form of the adjective ends in a mute -e, its feminine singular form will be the same. Both plural forms will also be the same.

L'homme est **calme.** (m)	*The man is calm.*
La femme est **calme.** (f)	*The woman is calm.*
Les hommes sont **calmes.** (mpl)	*The men are calm.*
Les femmes sont **calmes.** (fpl)	*The women are calm.*

Here are a few examples of adjectives ending in -e:

Masculine/feminine singular	Masculine/feminine plural	English
calme	calmes	*calm*
tranquille	tranquilles	*tranquil*
énergique	énergiques	*energetic*
facile	faciles	*easy*
difficile	difficiles	*difficult*
responsable	responsables	*responsible*
formidable	formidables	*great*
raisonnable	raisonnables	*reasonable*
riche	riches	*rich*
pauvre	pauvres	*poor*
jeune	jeunes	*young*
même	mêmes	*same*
autre	autres	*other*
jaune	jaunes	*yellow*
rouge	rouges	*red*

If the masculine singular form of the adjective *does not end in mute* -e, then -e is usually added to obtain its feminine form.

le petit garçon	*the little boy*
la petite fille	*the little girl*
les petits garçons	*the little boys*
les petites filles	*the little girls*
le monsieur fatigué	*the tired (gentle)man*
la dame fatiguée	*the tired woman*
les messieurs fatigués	*the tired (gentle)men*
les dames fatiguées	*the tired women*

Here are examples of such adjectives:

Masculine	Feminine	Masculine plural	Feminine plural	English
joli	jolie	jolis	jolies	*pretty*
petit	petite	petits	petites	*small*
grand	grande	grands	grandes	*big/tall*
court	courte	courts	courtes	*short*
distrait	distraite	distraits	distraites	*distracted*
méchant	méchante	méchants	méchantes	*naughty/mean*
bleu	bleue	bleus	bleues	*blue*
vert	verte	verts	vertes	*green*
gris	grise	gris	grises	*gray*
mauvais	mauvaise	mauvais	mauvaises	*bad*
français	française	français	françaises	*French*
allemand	allemande	allemands	allemandes	*German*
chinois	chinoise	chinois	chinoises	*Chinese*
démodé	démodée	démodés	démodées	*old-fashioned*
frustré	frustrée	frustrés	frustrées	*frustrated*
désespéré	désespérée	désespérés	désespérées	*in despair*
spontané	spontanée	spontanés	spontanées	*spontaneous*
résigné	résignée	résignés	résignées	*resigned*
fatigué	fatiguée	fatigués	fatiguées	*tired*
épuisé	épuisée	épuisés	épuisées	*exhausted*
énervé	énervée	énervés	énervées	*irritated*

Exercise 22

Complete the corresponding feminine statement for each of the following masculine statements. Follow the example.

Il est frustré.　　　　Elle est <u>frustrée.</u>

1. Il est grand. Elle est _____

2. Mon frère est petit. Ma sœur est _____

3. Il est fatigué. Elle est _____

4. Le petit est énervé. La petite est _____

5. Le chien est méchant. La chienne est _____

6. Il est allemand. Elle est _____

7. Le gazon est vert. L'herbe est _____

8. Le prof est distrait. La prof est _____

9. Le pull est gris. La robe est _____

10. Ce garçon est spontané. Cette fille est _____

11. Ce camion est japonais. Cette voiture est _____

12. Ce roman est mauvais. Cette nouvelle est _____

13. Il est résigné à partir. Elle est _____ à partir.

14. L'homme est désespéré. La femme est _____

15. C'est un film français. C'est une émission _____

16. C'est un joli bouquet. C'est une _____ fleur.

17. Voici un pantalon bleu. Voici une jupe _____

18. Ton short est court. Ta robe est _____

19. Ton costume est démodé. Ta veste est _____

20. Il est épuisé. Elle est _____

Exercise 23

Rewrite in the plural the masculine and feminine statements from Exercise 22 above. The first one has been done for you.

1. <u>Ils sont grands. Elles sont grandes.</u>

2. _____

3. _____

4. _____

5. _____

6. _____

7. _____

8. _____

9. _____

10. _____

11. _____

12. _____

13. _____

14. _____

15. _____

16. _____

17. _____

18. _____

19. _____

20. _____

Other patterns for changing adjectives from masculine to feminine

If the masculine form of an adjective ends in **-l, -n,** or **-s,** the consonant is usually doubled before adding **-e** to make it feminine. Here are a few examples of such adjectives:

bon	bonne	*good*	bas	basse	*low*
gentil	gentille	*nice*	cruel	cruelle	*cruel*
gros	grosse	*thick/fat*	violet	violette	*purple*
muet	muette	*mute*	ancien	ancienne	*ancient/former*

If the masculine form of an adjective ends in **-x**, that **-x** changes to **-se** in the feminine form. Here are a few examples of such adjectives:

affreux	affreuse	*awful*
amoureux	amoureuse	*in love*
chaleureux	chaleureuse	*warm/welcoming*
heureux	heureuse	*happy*
malheureux	malheureuse	*unhappy*
peureux	peureuse	*frightened*

If the masculine form of an adjective ends in **-f**, change this ending to **-ve** to make it feminine. Here are a few examples of such adjectives:

destructif	destructive	*destructive*
facultatif	facultative	*optional*
méditatif	méditative	*meditative*
naïf	naïve	*naïve*
neuf	neuve	*brand-new*
vif	vive	*bright/lively*

If the masculine form of an adjective ends in **-er**, this ending is changed to **-ère** to make it feminine. Here are a few examples of such adjectives:

cher	chère	*expensive/dear*
dernier	dernière	*last*
fier	fière	*proud*
léger	légère	*light*
premier	première	*first*

Irregular adjectives

Some adjectives have unique masculine and feminine forms that do not fit any pattern and must simply be memorized. The following frequently used adjectives have irregular feminine forms.

blanc	**blanche**	*white*
faux	**fausse**	*false*

fou	**folle**	*crazy*
frais	**fraîche**	*fresh*
franc	**franche**	*frank*
long	**longue**	*long*
malin	**maligne**	*sly*
public	**publique**	*public*
roux	**rousse**	*red-haired*
sec	**sèche**	*dry*

The adjectives **beau** (*beautiful*), **nouveau** (*new*), and **vieux** (*old*) have irregular feminine forms; in addition they have *two masculine singular forms* (one form is used before a noun starting with a consonant and the other before a noun starting with a vowel or mute **h**). The following table summarizes the forms of these three adjectives by gender (m/f).

Masculine singular (before consonant)	Masculine singular (before vowel sound)	Feminine (before consonant or vowel sound)	English
beau	bel	belle	*beautiful*
nouveau	nouvel	nouvelle	*new*
vieux	vieil	vieille	*old*

J'ai **un bel arbre** devant ma maison.	*I have a beautiful tree in front of my house.*
J'ai **un beau rosier** dans mon jardin.	*I have a beautiful rosebush in my garden.*
J'ai **une belle terrasse** derrière la maison.	*I have a beautiful terrace behind the house.*

Irregular masculine plural forms

Some masculine forms of adjectives have other ways to indicate the plural form.

For masculine adjectives ending in **-au**, add **-x.**

be**au**	beaux	*handsome/beautiful*
nouve**au**	nouveaux	*new*

For masculine adjectives ending in **-al**, change **-al** to **-aux**.

or**al**	or**aux**	*oral*
amic**al**	amic**aux**	*friendly*

For adjectives ending in **-s**, keep the **-s**.

gri**s**	gri**s**	old

For adjectives ending in **-x**, keep the **-x**.

vieu**x**	vieu**x**	old

Exercise 24

In the three columns write the correct feminine singular, masculine plural, and feminine plural forms of the adjective in italics.

1. Il est *grand.*   Elle est _____.   Ils sont _____.   Elles sont _____.

2. Il est *riche.*   Elle est _____.   Ils sont _____.   Elles sont _____.

3. Il est *séparé.*   Elle est _____.   Ils sont _____.   Elles sont _____.

4. Il est *blanc.*   Elle est _____.   Ils sont _____.   Elles sont _____.

5. Il est *américain.*   Elle est _____.   Ils sont _____.   Elles sont _____.

6. Il est *italien.*   Elle est _____.   Ils sont _____.   Elles sont _____.

7. Il est *fatigué.*   Elle est _____.   Ils sont _____.   Elles sont _____.

8. Il est *gentil.*   Elle est _____.   Ils sont _____.   Elles sont _____.

9. Il est *bas.*   Elle est _____.   Ils sont _____.   Elles sont _____.

10. Il est *bon.*   Elle est _____.   Ils sont _____.   Elles sont _____.

11. Il est *prétentieux.*   Elle est _____.   Ils sont _____.   Elles sont _____.

12. Il est *naïf.*   Elle est _____.   Ils sont _____.   Elles sont _____.

13. Il est *fier.*   Elle est _____.   Ils sont _____.   Elles sont _____.

14. Il est *fou.*   Elle est _____.   Ils sont _____.   Elles sont _____.

15. Il est *sec.*   Elle est _____.   Ils sont _____.   Elles sont _____.

10

Position of Adjectives

Unlike English adjectives, which are placed before the noun, most French adjectives follow the noun.

une histoire **amusante**	*an amusing story*
une pâtisserie **française**	*a French pastry shop*
un roman **passionnant**	*an exciting novel*
un professeur **fatigué**	*a tired teacher*
un pull **gris**	*a gray sweater*
un temple **protestant**	*a Protestant church*

There are, however, a few very common adjectives that precede the noun.

bon	*good*	long	*long*	jeune	*young*	beau	*beautiful*
mauvais	*bad*	court	*short*	vieux	*old*	nouveau	*new*
petit	*small*	joli	*pretty*	même	*same*	premier	*first*
grand	*tall*	seul	*only*	autre	*other*	dernier	*last*

une **bonne** note	*a good grade*
un **petit** garçon	*a little boy*
une **seule** femme	*only one woman*

Remember that the adjectives **beau, nouveau,** and **vieux** have two masculine singular forms depending on whether the noun that follows starts with a vowel sound or a consonant.

un **beau jour** d'été	*a beautiful summer day*
un **bel été**	*a beautiful summer*
un **nouveau gazon**	*a new lawn*
un **nouvel ami**	*a new friend*
un **vieux camion**	*an old truck*
un **vieil arbre**	*an old tree*

Some adjectives can be used before or after the noun. However, their meaning varies according to their position.

un **ancien** élève	*a former student*	une ville **ancienne**	*an ancient city*
un **brave** homme	*a good man*	un homme **brave**	*a brave man*
un **certain** jour	*some day*	un jour **certain**	*a set (certain) day*
un **cher** ami	*a dear friend*	un bijou **cher**	*an expensive jewel*
la **dernière** page	*the last page*	lundi **dernier**	*last Monday*
la **même** idée	*the same idea*	l'idée **même**	*the very idea*
le **pauvre** homme	*the poor man (to be pitied)*	l'homme **pauvre**	*the poor man (no money)*
ma **propre** voiture	*my own car*	ma voiture **propre**	*my clean car*
une **seule** fois	*only one time*	une femme **seule**	*a woman alone*

Exercise 25

Rewrite each sentence, placing the adjective appropriately before or after the noun in italics.

1. J'ai fait un *voyage*. (amusant)

_____

2. Il me faut un *stylo*. (bleu)

_____

3. Les *films* sont pleins d'action. (américains)

_____

4. Ça, c'est un *film*. (passionnant)

_____

5. C'est le/l'*homme* avec toutes ces femmes. (seul)

_____

6. Quelle *journée*! (longue)

_____

7. J'ai ma *voiture*. (propre)

_____

8. C'est la *fois* que je t'écris. (dernière)

_____

9. J'aime mes *amis*. (français)

_____

10. Mireille est une *fille*. (jolie)

_____

11. C'est une *faute*. (petite)

_____

12. C'est une *actrice*. (célèbre)

_____

13. C'est une *femme*. (vieille)

_____

14. Les Alpes sont des *montagnes*. (hautes)

_____

15. Ce sont de *habitations*. (nouvelles)

_____

11

Comparative and Superlative Forms of Adjectives

To compare things and people, use the structures **plus... que, moins... que,** and **aussi... que.**

Marie est **plus grande que** moi.	*Marie is **taller than** I.*
Mme Roux est **moins stricte que** vous.	*Mrs. Roux is **not as strict as** you.*
Marie est **aussi intelligente que** Marc.	*Marie is **as intelligent as** Marc.*

To express superlatives, place **le plus, la plus,** or **les plus** before the adjective. Remember the position (before or after the noun) and the agreement of the adjective (m/f, s/pl). Use the preposition **de** to express *in* in the superlative.

Marie est *la plus grande* fille de la classe.	*Marie is **the tallest** girl in the class.*
M. Botot est **le prof** *le plus strict* de l'école.	*Mr. Botot is **the strictest** teacher in the school.*
Ce sont **les chiens** *les plus mignons* **du** quartier.	*They are **the cutest** dogs in the neighborhood.*

The adjective **bon** has irregular comparative and superlative forms:

Ce gâteau est **bon.**	*This cake is **good.***
Ce gâteau est **meilleur** que le dernier.	*This cake is **better** than the last one.*
Cette école est **meilleure!**	*This school is **better!***
Voici **les meilleurs** amis du monde.	*Here are **the best** friends in the world.*
Voici **les meilleures** notes de la classe.	*Here are **the best** grades in the class.*

Exercise 26

This is what is known about these four young people:

Marc est extrêmement paresseux et très mauvais en français.
Jeanne est souvent paresseuse, mais assez bonne en français.
Lise est un peu paresseuse, mais excellente en français.
Joseph est souvent paresseux, mais assez bon en français.

Now write comparative sentences, translating from English to French as directed below.

1. Marc is lazier than Lise.

_____

2. Jeanne is not as lazy as Marc.

_____

3. Jeanne is as lazy as Joseph.

_____

4. Joseph and Jeanne are lazier than Lise.

_____

5. Marc is the laziest of the four.

_____

6. Marc is the worst one in French.

_____

7. Lise is the best one in French.

_____

8. Joseph is as good in French as Jeanne.

_____

Review 3

Exercise 27

Éric a raison ou tort? *Is Éric right or wrong?* Decide whether little Éric is right or wrong when he makes the following statements. Write **V** for **Vrai** or **F** for **Faux** next to each comparative or superlative sentence.

1. _____ La tour Eiffel est le bâtiment le plus haut du monde.

2. _____ Le basset est le plus grand de tous les chiens.

3. _____ Un avion est plus rapide qu'un train.

4. _____ Un rhume est pire (= plus mauvais) qu'une jambe cassée.

5. _____ Ton père est aussi riche que Bill Gates.

6. _____ Une main est plus grande qu'un doigt de pied.

7. _____ L'été est généralement plus chaud que le printemps.

8. _____ La glace est plus dure que la neige.

9. _____ L'or est moins précieux que l'argent.

10. _____ Depardieu est plus connu que Shakespeare.

11. _____ Brigitte Bardot est l'actrice la plus célèbre du monde.

12. _____ L'élève qui étudie peu est toujours le meilleur de la classe.

13. _____ Le plus vieux des fromages est le meilleur.

14. _____ La pluie est meilleure que la grêle (*hailstones*) pour les plantes.

15. _____ Oprah Winfrey est plus riche que toi.

Exercise 28

Éric parle de ses voisins et de son maître d'école. *Éric talks about his neighbors and his teacher.* Translate the following sentences into French. Use the vocabulary in parentheses. Note that conjugated verbs are supplied; however, you must make adjustments for adjective agreement and position.

1. I have new neighbors. (j'ai/nouveau/voisin)

_____

2. They are friendly people. (ce sont/gens/aimable)

_____

3. But they have a mean dog. (mais/ils ont/méchant/chien)

_____

4. The neighbors' old tree is dry. (arbre/voisin/est/sec)

_____

5. Poor neighbors! (pauvre/voisin)

_____

6. Their daughter Denise is in love with Pierre! (fille/est/amoureux de Pierre)

_____

7. Denise is attentive in class but Pierre is distracted. (est/attentif/distrait)

_____

8. Our teacher is frustrated. (maître/est/irrité)

_____

9. He is not patient. (il n'est pas/patient)

_____

10. But he is very understanding. (mais/il est/indulgent)

_____

11. What a beautiful car! (quel/beau/voiture)

_____

12. I prefer his former car. (je préfère/ancien/voiture)

_____

13. These new cars are expensive. (nouveau/voiture/sont/cher)

_____

14. Dad's car is old. (voiture/papa/est/vieux)

_____

15. It is good only for short trips. (elle est/bon/seulement/ pour/court/voyage)

_____

Part 4

Adverbs

Position of Adverbs

An adverb serves to modify the meaning of a verb and is usually placed right after the verb modified.

Il travaille **vite**.	*He works **fast**.*
Je parle **bien**.	*I speak **well**.*

Sometimes the adverb modifies an adjective, a past participle, or another adverb. In that case the adverb usually precedes the word it modifies.

Elle est **vraiment tenace**.	*She is **really tenacious**. (adjective)*
Le feu est **presque éteint**.	*The fire is **almost extinguished**. (past participle)*
Il marche **extrêmement vite**.	*He walks **extremely fast**. (adverb)*

The position of adverbs that have three or more syllables is flexible. These can be found after the verb or at the beginning or the end of the sentence.

Il a écouté **attentivement** tous les membres du comité.	*He listened **attentively** to all the members of the committee.*
Il a écouté tous les membres du comité **attentivement**.	*He listened to all the members of the committee **attentively**.*

Here is a list of frequently used adverbs or adverbial expressions:

à l'heure	*on time*
ailleurs	*elsewhere*
après	*afterward*
aujourd'hui	*today*
auparavant	*previously*
aussi	*also*
autrefois	*formerly*
beaucoup	*a lot*
bien	*well*

bientôt	*soon*
d'abord	*first*
d'habitude	*usually*
dehors	*outside*
déjà	*already*
demain	*tomorrow*
en avance	*ahead of time, early*
en ce moment	*at this time*
en retard	*late (after the time)*
encore	*still*
enfin	*finally*
ensuite/alors	*then*
hier	*yesterday*
ici	*here*
la veille	*the day (or evening) before*
là/là-bas	*there/over there*
le lendemain	*the next day*
longtemps	*a long time*
mal	*badly*
partout	*everywhere*
peut-être	*maybe*
quelquefois/parfois	*sometimes*
si	*so*
souvent	*often*
tant	*so much*
tôt/de bonne heure	*early*
toujours	*always*
très	*very*
trop	*too much*

Adverbs of time such as **hier, demain, la veille,** or **le lendemain** usually appear at the beginning or at the end of a sentence.

Demain il va partir.	*Tomorrow he will leave.*
Il va partir **demain**.	*He will leave **tomorrow**.*

The adverbs **très** and **si** modify adjectives or other adverbs.

Cet homme est **très fort**.	*This man is **very strong**.*
Il joue **si bien**.	*He plays **so well**.*

Exercise 29

From the list below, choose the adverb that fits best in each sentence. Consider its meaning and position in the sentence.

autrefois	si	dehors	longtemps	partout	encore
beaucoup	déjà	bien	presque	vraiment	d'abord

1. Ici dans la maison il fait bon mais _____ il fait mauvais.

2. Maintenant j'ai une voiture. _____ je prenais le bus.

3. J'attendais quelquefois très _____ que le bus arrive.

4. _____ je vais finir mes exercices et après je vais regarder la télé.

5. J'ai _____ deux exercices à faire.

6. J'ai _____ terminé le premier exercice.

7. Je sais _____. C'est facile.

8. Je ne fais pas _____ de fautes.

9. Je parle le français _____ bien que je peux facilement voyager en France.

10. Je désire _____ voir Paris. C'est mon rêve.

11. Il faut ranger ta chambre! Il y a des livres, des papiers et des vêtements

    _____.

12. Moi, j'ai _____ lu ce livre deux fois.

13

Formation of Adverbs

Many adverbs are formed by taking the feminine form of an adjective whose masculine form ends in a consonant, or the masculine form of an adjective that ends in a vowel, and adding the suffix **-ment** to it.

Consonant ending		**English**	
clair	**clair**ement	*clear*	*clearly*
faux	**fausse**ment	*false*	*falsely*
doux	**douce**ment	*soft*	*softly*
fier	**fière**ment	*proud*	*proudly*
réel	**réelle**ment	*real*	*really*
lent	**lent**ement	*slow*	*slowly*
heureux	**heureuse**ment	*happy*	*happily*
malheureux	**malheureuse**ment	*unhappy*	*unfortunately*

Vowel ending		**English**	
résolu	**résolu**ment	*resolute*	*resolutely*
poli	**poli**ment	*polite*	*politely*
calme	**calme**ment	*calm*	*calmly*
facile	**facile**ment	*easy*	*easily*
vrai	**vrai**ment	*real*	*really*
aisé	**aisé**ment	*at ease*	*comfortably*
Exception: gai	**gaie**ment	*gay*	*gaily*

Adverbs derived from adjectives ending in **-ent** and **-ant** (except for **lent**) are formed by dropping **-nt** from the adjective ending and substituting **-mment**.

élégant	**éléga**mment	*elegant*	*elegantly*
bruy**ant**	bruya**mment**	*noisy*	*noisily*
pati**ent**	patie**mment**	*patient*	*patiently*
évid**ent**	évide**mment**	*evident*	*evidently*

Exercise 30

Write the adverb that corresponds to each adjective.

1. précieux _____

2. tranquille _____

3. réel _____

4. vrai _____

5. doux _____

6. difficile _____

7. impoli _____

8. lent _____

9. heureux _____

10. fier _____

11. élégant _____

12. prudent _____

13. impatient _____

14. aisé _____

15. résolu _____

16. extrême _____

17. total _____

18. rare _____

19. faux _____

20. général _____

Comparative and Superlative Forms of Adverbs

To compare how things are done, use the expressions **aussi... que, plus... que,** and **moins... que.**

Je parle **aussi** bien **que** toi.	*I speak as well as you (do).*
Elle sourit **plus** souvent **que** nous.	*She smiles more often than we (do).*

Superlative constructions require **le plus** or **le moins** before the adverb.

Je travaille **le plus longtemps.**	*I work the longest.*
Elle s'habille **le moins élégamment.**	*She dresses the least elegantly.*

The adverbs **bien** and **mal** have irregular comparative and superlative forms.

Il joue **bien.**	Il joue **mieux.**	Il joue le **mieux.**
He plays well.	*He plays better.*	*He plays the best.*
Il conduit **mal.**	Il conduit **plus mal/pis.**	Il conduit **le plus mal/le pis.**
He drives badly.	*He drives worse.*	*He drives the worst.*

Exercise 31

Translate each sentence into French. Use **doucement** for *softly* and **vite** for *fast*.

1. Denise speaks less softly than Marc.

_____

2. Denise speaks as softly as Jeannine.

_____

3. Denise speaks more softly than me (I do).

_____

4. Marc speaks the most softly.

_____

5. I speak French well.

_____

6. You speak French as well as me (I do).

_____

7. Luc does not speak French as well as us (we do).

_____

8. You and I speak French the best.

_____

9. The teacher speaks French the fastest.

_____

10. Luc speaks French the worst.

_____

Review 4

Exercise 32

Les petites habitudes d'Éric. *Éric's little habits.* Éric tells how he likes to stay up late to read his comics, but has to get up early to go to school. Rewrite each sentence, placing each adverb correctly in the sentence.

1. J'aime les bandes dessinées. (bien)

_____

2. Tu as fermé ton livre? (déjà)

_____

3. Je lis jusqu'à onze heures du soir. (quelquefois)

_____

4. Je fais mes devoirs après le dîner. (toujours)

_____

5. J'écoute de la musique pop. (aussi)

_____

6. Je pars de la maison tôt le matin. (très)

_____

7. Mes copains et moi attendons l'autobus. (patiemment)

_____

8. Ginette a grandi cet été. (vraiment)

_____

9. Elle chante. (gaiement)

_____

10. Le bus s'est arrêté. (enfin)

_____

11. Je parle au chauffeur. (poliment)

_____

12. Je suis fatigué. (aujourd'hui)

_____

13. Je voudrais étudier chez moi. (calmement)

_____

14. Je vais rester à la maison. (demain)

_____

15. Il va au restaurant. (régulièrement)

_____

Exercise 33

Un exercice de vocabulaire dans la classe d'Éric. *A vocabulary exercise in Éric's class.* This is a vocabulary exercise Éric has to do in class today. Help him by crossing out the adverb that *does not* belong in each sentence.

1. Elle fait son entrée *élégamment/bruyamment* en robe longue et satinée.

2. Il va *sûrement/peut-être* à la soirée. Il n'est pas sûr.

3. Elle est ponctuelle. Elle arrive *en retard/à l'heure*.

4. Silence! Ils dorment *encore/partout*.

5. D'abord tu coupes le pain. *Ensuite/Déjà* tu manges.

6. Je suis blonde. *Ailleurs/Autrefois* j'étais brune.

7. Ici il fait chaud. *Dehors/En ce moment* il fait frais.

8. Pars *hier/tôt* pour prendre l'avion.

9. Elle mange *trop/très*, cette petite!

10. *Le lendemain/D'habitude* je passe le week-end chez des amis.

11. Je vais *probablement/rapidement* passer les vacances en France.

12. Mes parents m'accompagnent *la veille/toujours*.

13. Cette musique me plaît *si/beaucoup*.

14. Les gens riches habitent dans des maisons *terriblement/beaucoup* chères.

15. Emballez *bien/tellement* ce paquet. C'est un cadeau.

Exercise 34

Les parents d'Éric préparent une soirée pour leurs amis. *Éric's parents prepare a party for their friends.* Translate the part of the sentence that is in italics from French into English. You will find out how Éric's parents prepare a party for their guests.

1. Ce gâteau-ci est *sans doute* pire que l'autre.

   This cake is _____ worse than the other one.

2. Tu fais *vraiment* une meilleure tarte que moi.

   You _____ make a better tart than I do.

3. *Malheureusement*, les jours de fête, je mange toujours *trop*.

   _____, on holidays, I always eat _____.

4. Regarde! J'ai *presque* fini de préparer mon plat.

   Look! I've _____ finished preparing my dish.

5. *Maintenant* attendons *tranquillement* et *patiemment*!

   _____ let's wait _____ and _____.

6. J'espère que les invités ne vont pas venir *en avance*.

   I hope that the guests do not come _____.

7. Je n'ai *rien de bon* à leur servir *en ce moment*.

   I have _____ to serve them _____.

8. Tu crois que ces hors-d'œuvre seront appréciés *autant que* la dernière fois?

   Do you think these hors d'œuvres will be liked _____ last time?

9. Bon. Préparons *quelque chose de* frais et de délicieux à boire!

   All right! Let's prepare _____ fresh and delicious to drink.

10. *D'habitude* nous servons du champagne.

    _____ we serve champagne.

Exercise 35

Une soirée chez les parents d'Éric. *A party at Éric's house.* Translate the italicized part of each sentence into French to find out how the above preparations have progressed.

1. This casserole is *truly* worse than the first one.

   Cette casserole est _____ pire que la dernière.

2. *Fortunately* you made a coq au vin.

_____ que tu as fait un coq au vin.

3. You cook more *often* than I do.

Tu fais la cuisine plus _____ que moi.

4. Is the tart *almost* finished?

Est-ce que la tarte est _____ finie?

5. It will *surely* be better than my cake.

Elle sera _____ meilleure que mon gâteau.

6. The hors d'œuvres are *probably* ready.

Les hors-d'œuvre sont _____ prêts.

7. Our guests *usually* arrive *on time*.

Nos invités arrivent _____.

8. So let's wait *calmly*!

Alors attendons _____!

9. But *first* let's prepare some drinks.

Mais _____ préparons quelques

rafraîchissements!

10. Otherwise there will be *nothing* refreshing to drink.

Sinon il n'y aura _____ de frais à boire.

Part 5

Subject, Stressed, and Object Pronouns

15

Subject Pronouns

Subject pronouns are used to replace a noun subject; they perform the action of the verb.

je/j'	*I*
tu	*you (fam.)*
il	*he* or *it (m)*
elle	*she* or *it (f)*
on	*one, we, people*
nous	*we*
vous	*you* (to one person formally; to several people)
ils	*they (mpl* or mixed group)
elles	*they (fpl)*

Exercise 36

Insert the correct subject pronoun before each verb.

1. _____ suis Pierre. (*I am Pierre.*)

2. _____ allons au cours d'italien. (*We are going to Italian class.*)

3. Guy et Marc? _____ sont suisses. (*Guy and Marc? They are Swiss.*)

4. _____ aime l'espagnol le mieux. (*She likes Spanish best.*)

5. Toi, Shirley, _____ es ma copine. (*You, Shirley, you are my friend.*)

6. Chloé et Sylvie? _____ sont jumelles. (*Chloé and Sylvie? They are twins.*)

7. _____ êtes prête, mademoiselle? (*Are you ready, Miss?*)

8. _____ viens! (*I am coming!*)

9. _____ adore cette chanson. (*I love that song.*)

10. _____ entend cette musique partout. (*One hears that music everywhere.*)

11. Pierre et moi, _____ va à la plage. (*Pierre and I, we are going to the beach.*)

12. _____ habite à Miami. (*I live in Miami.*)

13. Mes frères? _____ sont si drôles! (*My brothers? They are so funny!*)

14. _____ allons faire des achats. (*We are going shopping.*)

15. Papa, _____ es en retard. (*Daddy, you are late.*)

16

Stressed Pronouns

Stressed pronouns have several uses. They are used after prepositions and before subject pronouns.

Stressed pronouns are used to replace a person after prepositions such as: **à, pour, sur, sous, devant, derrière, à droite de, loin de, près de,** and so on.

près de **toi**	*near **you** (fam.)*
avec **lui**	*with **him***
au-dessus d'**elle**	*above **her***
pour **soi**	*for **oneself***
loin de **nous**	*far from **us***
devant **vous**	*in front of **you** (form. or pl)*
derrière **eux**	*behind **them***
grâce à **elles**	*thanks to **them** (f)*
But: à **ma** droite, à **ma** gauche	*to **my** right, to **my** left*

The structure **chez** + *stressed pronoun* (rather than **à la maison**) is often used to express *at/to someone's home*:

Je suis **chez moi.**	*I am **at home.***
Je vais **chez moi.**	*I am going **home.***
Paul vient **chez moi.**	*Paul is coming **to my house.***
Plus tard j'irai **chez lui.**	*Later I will go **to his house.***
J'arriverai **chez eux** à 8 h.	*I will arrive **at their house** at 8.*
On est le plus à l'aise **chez soi.**	*We feel most comfortable **at home.***

Stressed pronouns are also used to emphasize subject pronouns such as **je, tu, il,** and so on. The list below shows the various stressed pronouns and their corresponding subject pronouns.

moi, je	*I*
toi, tu	*you*
lui, il	*he*
elle, elle	*she*

nous, nous	*we*
vous, vous	*you*
eux, ils	*they (m)*
elles, elles	*they (f)*

| **Toi,** tu restes ici. | **You** *stay here.* (emphatic *you*) |
| Tu restes ici, **toi.** | **You** *stay here.* (even more emphatic) |

Exercise 37

In the following letter from Jessica to Suzie, write the appropriate stressed pronoun in the space provided.

1. _____, je m'appelle Jessica.

2. Je suis heureuse de correspondre avec _____, ma chère Suzie.

3. Mon prof, M. Louis, me dit que _____, tu parles très bien le français.

4. M. Louis a beaucoup d'affection pour _____, les élèves.

5. Mes camarades de classe aiment bien M. Louis aussi. Mais, _____, ils sont un peu

   paresseux.

6. Alors M. Louis s'irrite avec _____. C'est normal!

7. Dans ta réponse à ma lettre, parle-moi de ta famille. Ça va bien chez _____?

8. _____, j'ai deux frères et une sœur.

9. Et _____, combien de frères et de sœurs tu as?

10. Tu te disputes avec _____ quelquefois?

11. J'aime bien étudier chez _____, dans ma chambre.

12. Je rentre d'habitude chez _____ à 4 h de l'après-midi.

13. Ma copine, c'est Marianne. Je vais souvent chez _____ après l'école.

14. Pour _____ deux, Marianne et moi, il n'y a pas de secret.

15. Est-ce que tu as une meilleure amie aussi, _____?

17

Direct and Indirect Object Pronouns

Object pronouns replace nouns that receive the action of the verb. Since there are both direct and indirect object pronouns, it is important to be able to identify and distinguish between direct and indirect object nouns.

Direct objects

Direct object nouns receive the action of the verb directly; they can be things or people; they are *never* preceded by a preposition such as **à, pour, de, sur,** and so on.

    Il appelle **Denise.**   *He calls **Denise.***

The noun **Denise** is the direct object because Denise receives the action of the verb **appelle.** To replace the noun **Denise,** use the pronoun **la.** However, **la** must be changed to **l'** before a following vowel sound.

    Il l'appelle.   *He calls **her.***

In the following sentence, the noun **balle** is the direct object of the verb **jette.** To replace the feminine noun **la balle** in the sentence below, use the pronoun **la.**

    Je jette **la balle.**   *I throw **the ball.***
    Je **la** jette.   *I throw **it.***

The direct object pronouns that replace direct object nouns are: **le, la, l',** and **les.**
Use **le** for *him* or *it* when replacing a masculine person or object receiving the action of the verb.

    Le livre de maths? Tu **le** cherches?   *The math book? You're looking for **it?***

Use **la** for *her* or *it* when replacing a feminine person or object receiving the action of the verb.

La dame? Tu **la** comprends? *The woman? You understand **her**?*

Don't forget to substitute **l'** for **le** or **la** before a vowel sound.

Cette glace? Tu **l'**aimes? *This ice cream? You like **it**?*

Use **les** for *them*, to replace both masculine and feminine objects or people receiving the action of the verb.

Tes amis? Tu **les** écoutes? *Your friends? You listen to **them**?*

Note above that the verb **écouter** takes a direct object in French (**Tu écoutes tes amis.**), even though the English equivalent is *to listen to*.

Indirect objects

Indirect object nouns receive the action of the verb indirectly. Indirect object nouns are normally preceded by the preposition **à**.

The indirect object pronouns that replace indirect object nouns are **lui** and **leur**. These pronouns replace the prepositional phrase **à** + *person(s)*.

Je parle à **Marie**. (à + *person*)   *I speak **to Marie**.*
Je **lui** parle.   *I speak **to her**.*
Je téléphone **aux enfants**. (à + les enfants)   *I give **the children** a call.*
Je **leur** téléphone.   *I call **them**.*

Direct and indirect object pronouns

The pronouns used to express *me/myself, you/yourself,* and so on are direct or indirect depending on the verb that governs them. They are: **me, te, se, nous, vous,** and **se**.

Tu **me** regardes.   *You are watching **me**.*
(Here, **me** is the direct object: **regarder quelqu'un**)

Tu **me** parles.	*You are talking **to me**.*	
	(Here, **me** is the indirect object: **parler** *à* **quelqu'un**)	
Elle **se** regarde.	*She's looking **at herself**.*	
	(Here, **se** is the direct object: **regarder quelqu'un**)	
Ils **se** parlent.	*They are talking **to each other**.*	
	(Here, **se** is the indirect object: **parler** *à* **quelqu'un**)	

The following table summarizes object pronouns with their respective meanings:

Direct/indirect object pronouns (living beings)	Indirect object pronouns (living beings)	Direct object pronouns (living beings or things)
me (m') *(to) me*	**lui** *to him/her*	**le** *him/it*
te (t') *(to) you*	**leur** *to them*	**la** *her/it*
se (s') *(to) him/herself*		**l'** *him/her/it*
nous *(to) us/ourselves*		**les** *them*
vous *(to) you/yourselves*		
se (s') *(to) themselves, each other*		

Exercise 38

What pronoun would replace each underlined noun phrase? Use **le, la, l', les, lui,** or **leur.**

1. J'écris <u>la lettre</u>. Je _____ écris.

2. Nous écrivons <u>à nos amis</u>. Nous _____ écrivons.

3. Je parle <u>à ta sœur</u>! Je _____ parle.

4. Nous écoutons <u>le conférencier</u>. Nous _____ écoutons.

5. Tu respectes <u>tes parents</u>. Tu _____ respectes.

6. Nous parlons <u>à papa</u>. Nous _____ parlons.

7. Tu obéis <u>aux adultes</u>. Tu _____ obéis.

8. Je regarde <u>le film</u>. Je _____ regarde.

9. Tu manges <u>la banane</u>. Tu _____ manges.

10. Elle écoute <u>les informations</u>. Elle _____ écoute.

11. Nous admirons <u>le beau tableau</u>. Nous _____ admirons.

12. Vous préparez <u>les sandwichs</u>. Vous _____ préparez.

13. Ils téléphonent <u>à leurs amis</u>. Ils _____ téléphonent.

14. Je demande <u>à maman</u> de m'aider. Je _____ demande de m'aider.

15. Tu apprécies <u>ce vin rouge</u>. Tu _____ apprécies.

16. Ils aiment <u>la glace</u>. Ils _____ aiment.

17. Je déteste <u>l'hiver</u>. Je _____ déteste.

18. Vous voulez <u>ce bouquet de fleurs</u>? Vous _____ voulez?

19. Elle achète <u>les fruits</u> au marché. Elle _____ achète au marché.

20. Ils descendent <u>l'escalier</u>. Ils _____ descendent.

Exercise 39

Supply the correct pronoun in each French sentence to match the English meaning on the right.

1. Il _____ regarde. (*He watches **us**.*)

2. Maman, nous _____ montrons nos photos. (*Mom, we are showing **you** our pictures.*)

3. Vous _____ payez bien. (*You pay **me** well.*)

4. Je _____ remercie, monsieur. (*I thank **you**, sir.*)

5. Mes amis _____ aiment bien. (*My friends like **me**.*)

6. Annie _____ regarde dans le miroir. (*Annie looks at **herself** in the mirror.*)

7. Je _____ regarde. (*I am watching **her**.*)

8. Luc _____ invite pour demain. (*Luc invites **us** for tomorrow.*)

9. Il _____ invite aussi. (*He invites **them**, too.*)

10. Tu _____ aimes bien? (*Do you like **him**?*)

11. Je veux _____ voir, John. (*I want to see **you**, John.*)

12. Ils _____ admirent de loin, mesdames. (*They admire **you** from afar, ladies.*)

13. Il _____ pose tant de questions. (*He asks **me** so many questions.*)

14. Je _____ ignore. (*I ignore **them**.*)

15. Est-ce qu'il _____ entend parler? (*Does he hear **himself** talk?*)

Position of object pronouns

Direct and indirect object pronouns are placed before the conjugated verb in the present, future, and imperfect (**imparfait**), before the auxiliary verb (**avoir** or **être**) in compound tenses such as the **passé**

composé, and before the infinitive verb in structures that include a conjugated verb followed by an infinitive. The only structure that requires the object pronoun to be placed after the verb is the affirmative command.

Object pronouns

- precede the verb in simple tenses like the present.

    Je **le** vois.   *I see **him/it**.*

- precede the helping verb **avoir** or **être** in compound tenses such as the **passé composé**.

    Je **l'**ai vu.   *I saw **him/it**.*

- precede the infinitive form when the structure consists of a conjugated verb followed by an infinitive.

    Je vais **le** voir.   *I am going to see **him/it**.*

- follow the verb in affirmative commands.

    Regarde-**le**!   *Watch **him/it**!*

The pronouns *moi* and *toi*

Use **moi** and **toi** instead of **me** and **te** in affirmative commands, where the object pronoun follows the verb.

Ne **me** regarde pas!	*Don't look at me!*
Regarde-**moi**!	*Look at me!*
Ne **te** dépêche pas!	*Don't hurry!*
Dépêche-**toi**!	*Hurry!*
Ne **vous** couchez pas!	*Don't go to bed!*
Couchez-**vous**!	*Go to bed!*
Ne **nous en** allons pas!	*Let's not go away!*
Allons-**nous-en**!	*Let's go away!*

Se dépêcher, se fâcher, se lever, se laver, se coucher, se presser, se réveiller, and s'en aller are reflexive verbs. See Chapter 36.

Exercise 40

Answer each question with the appropriate object pronoun: **me (m'), te (t'), se (s'), nous,** or **vous.**

1. Tu t'appelles François?

   —Non, je _____ appelle Olivier.

2. Tu me connais?

   —Non, mais je voudrais _____ connaître.

3. Tu te promènes ici tous les jours?

   —Oui, je _____ promène tous les jours dans ce parc.

4. Qu'est-ce qui te plaît ici?

   —Ce qui _____ plaît, c'est la nature et la tranquillité.

5. Qu'est-ce qui te guide dans la vie?

   —Mes principes _____ guident, et toi?

6. L'entente entre les gens. Tu me trouves idéaliste?

   —Je _____ trouve très sympa.

7. Qui t'aime le plus, toi?

   —Mes parents _____ aiment énormément.

8. Vous vous entendez bien dans ta famille?

   —Heureusement que oui, nous _____ entendons bien.

9. Et tes parents, ils s'aiment beaucoup?

   —Naturellement, ils _____ aiment.

10. Tu me trouves trop curieuse?

    —Oui, je _____ trouve inquisitive.

11. Tu voudrais qu'on se revoie?

    —Oui, j'aimerais bien qu'on _____ revoie.

12. Tu m'appelles demain?

    —D'accord. Je _____ téléphone.

Exercise 41

Answer each question using the appropriate pronoun (**le**, **la**, **l'**, **les**, **lui**, or **leur**) and the correct verb form. Be sure to place the pronoun before the conjugated or infinitive verb.

1. Tu obéis à tes parents?

   —Oui, je _____ d'habitude.

2. Tu lis le journal?

   —Oui, je _____ le matin.

3. Tu téléphones à ta copine?

   —Oui, je _____ tout de suite.

4. Tu finis ta glace?

   —Oui, je _____ avec plaisir.

5. Tes amis aiment la musique pop?

   —Oui, ils _____ beaucoup.

6. Et moi, j'adore la musique classique?

   —Oui, tu _____!

7. J'écoute souvent les opéras?

   —Oui, tu _____.

8. Tu parles aux enfants?

   —Oui, je _____.

9. Tu dis «bonjour» à ton prof?

   —Bien sûr, je _____ «bonjour».

10. Qu'est-ce que tu dis à maman?

    —Je _____ «merci».

11. Tu fais ta rédaction tout de suite?

    —Oui, je _____ tout de suite.

12. Tu sais parler le français?

    —Oui, je _____ assez bien.

13. Ils vendent leur maison?

    —En effet, ils _____.

14. Tu demandes le prix à la vendeuse?

—D'accord. Je _____ le prix.

15. Tu peux dire ça à mes parents?

—Bien sûr, je peux _____ ça.

Exercise 42

Change each negative sentence to an affirmative one. Pay attention to the form of the stressed pronoun.

1. Ne me touche pas! _____
2. Ne te lave pas! _____
3. Ne me demande pas! _____
4. Ne te regarde pas! _____
5. Ne me parle pas! _____
6. Ne nous lavons pas! _____
7. Ne nous dépêchons pas! _____
8. Ne vous pressez pas! _____
9. Ne me cherchez pas! _____
10. Ne te cache pas! _____
11. Ne te réveille pas! _____
12. N'en demande pas! _____
13. Ne nous couchons pas! _____
14. Ne me dites pas ça! _____
15. Ne la couchez pas encore! _____

18

Other Object Pronouns: *y* and *en*

The pronouns **y** and **en** replace specific prepositional phrases.

En

Use this pronoun to replace any phrase introduced by the preposition **de/d'**. Its translation into English will vary depending on what it replaces.

Elle revient **de France**.	Elle **en** revient.
*She comes back **from France**.*	*She comes back **from there**.*
Je voudrais un peu **de sauce**.	J'**en** voudrais un peu.
*I would like a little **sauce**.*	*I would like a little **(of it)**.*
J'ai envie **de sortir**.	J'**en** ai envie.
*I feel like **going out**.*	*I feel like **it**.*

Y

This pronoun has two distinct uses and its translation into English will vary. Use the pronoun **y** to replace any prepositional phrase indicating a location to express *there* (except to say *from/of* a place).

Le livre est **sur le bureau**?	*Is the book **on the desk**?*
—Oui, il **y** est.	*—Yes, it is **(there)**.*
Ta copine est **à la maison**?	*Is your friend **at home**?*
—Oui, elle **y** est.	*—Yes, she is **(there)**.*

The pronoun **y** is also used to replace a prepositional phrase consisting of **à** followed by a thing. Its translation into English will vary.

Tu réponds **à la question?**   —Oui, j'y réponds.
*Are you answering **the question?***   *Yes, I am answering **it.***
Tu penses **à tes vacances?**   —Oui, j'y pense.
*Are you thinking **about your vacation?***   *Yes, I am thinking **about it.***

Changes to the familiar verb ending before *y* and *en*

In familiar affirmative commands, the verb ending for all -er verbs and for the verb **aller** changes (adding an **-s**) before the pronoun **y** or **en**.

Va à Paris.   *Go to Paris!*   **Vas**-y!   *Go there!*
Demande des tickets!   *Ask for tickets!*   **Demandes**-en!   *Ask for some!*

Exercise 43

Select the appropriate pronoun (**y** or **en**) to complete each command in French.

1. De la viande? Prends- _____! (*Meat? Have some!*)

2. Aux cartes? Jouez- _____! (*Cards? Go ahead and play!*)

3. Le Mexique? Vas-_____! (*Mexico? Go there!*)

4. Du vin? Bois-_____! (*Wine? Drink some!*)

5. La plage? Restes-_____! (*The beach? Stay there!*)

6. Des boissons froides? Cherches-_____! (*Cold drinks? Get some!*)

7. Du jus? Mets-_____ dans le frigo! (*Juice? Put some in the fridge!*)

8. Le restaurant? Manges-_____ si tu veux! (*The restaurant? Eat there if you like!*)

9. Du pudding? Gardes- _____ un peu pour moi! (*Pudding? Keep some for me!*)

10. Ce repas va te coûter cher. Penses-_____! (*This meal is going to cost you a lot. Think about it!*)

Exercise 44

Select the appropriate pronoun (**y** or **en**) to complete each answer. The part of the question to be replaced is in italics.

1. Tu comptes toujours aller *en France*?

   —Oui, j'_____ vais cet été.

2. Tu restes *à la maison* ce soir?

   —Oui, j'_____ reste.

3. Tu manges *des chips* en ce moment?

   —Oui, j'_____ mange toujours trop quand je suis nerveux.

4. Tu as besoin *de te reposer.*

   —Oui, j'_____ ai besoin.

5. Tu es *devant ton bureau*?

   —Oui, j'_____ suis.

6. Tu réfléchis *à tes responsabilités*?

   —Oui, j'_____ réfléchis.

7. Tu as envie *de conseils*?

   —Oui, j'_____ ai envie.

8. Viens me voir *au café.*

   —D'accord. j'_____ viens tout de suite.

9. Tu veux que je commande *des sodas*?

   —Oui, commandes-_____!

10. Bon. Je me mets en route.

    —Vas-_____! J'arrive dans deux minutes.

Review 5

Exercise 45

Little Éric has a series of six exercises to complete tonight. Help him. **Le premier exercice d'Éric.** *The first of Éric's exercises.* Add the appropriate stressed pronoun in each sentence so that each person has a chance to go home.

        Example: Je vais chez <u>moi</u>.

1. Marie va chez _____.

2. Nous allons chez _____.

3. On va chez _____.

4. Tu vas chez _____.

5. Jean va chez _____.

6. Luc et toi, vous allez chez _____.

7. Mes amis vont chez _____.

8. Mes copines vont chez _____.

9. Le monsieur va chez _____.

10. La dame va chez _____.

Exercise 46

Deuxième exercice d'Éric. *Éric's second exercise.* Add the appropriate stressed pronoun to emphasize each person's unique characteristics.

1. _____, il est blond.

2. _____, je suis grande.

3. _____, tu es très petite.

4. _____, elle est intelligente.

5. _____, vous êtes les plus gentils.

6. _____, ils sont les plus généreux.

7. _____, nous sommes vraiment honnêtes.

8. _____, elles sont charmantes.

9. Papa et maman? Ils sont formidables, _____!

10. Ta petite sœur? Elle est adorable, _____!

11. Éric, il est coquin, _____!

12. Suzanne, elle est vraiment gentille, _____!

13. Nos amis, ils sont super, _____!

14. Je suis fatiguée, _____!

15. Tu n'es jamais fatigué, _____!

Exercise 47

Troisième exercice d'Éric. *Éric's third exercise.* Underline the direct object in each sentence.

1. Le prof attend Marie?

2. Marie cherche sa sœur Élise?

3. Élise a le sac de Marie?

4. Marie trouve Élise?

5. Marie prend son sac?

6. Elle apporte ses devoirs au prof?

7. Le prof pose les questions?

8. Marie donne les réponses correctes?

9. Le prof donne les notes aux élèves?

10. Marie a la meilleure note aujourd'hui?

11. Luc adore Francine?

12. Il cherche l'amour de sa vie?

13. Ce monsieur paie bien ses employés?

14. Tu prends toujours le métro?

15. Elle comprend le français et l'anglais?

Exercise 48

Quatrième exercice d'Éric. *Éric's fourth exercise.* Complete the answer to each of the above questions with the appropriate direct object pronoun, replacing the underlined noun/noun phrase from the previous exercise. The first one has been done for you.

1. Oui, il l' attend.

2. Oui, elle _____ cherche.

3. Oui, Élise _____ a.

4. Oui, Marie _____ trouve.

5. Oui, elle _____ prend.

6. Oui, elle _____ apporte au prof.

7. Oui, le prof _____ pose.

8. Oui, Marie _____ donne.

9. Oui, le prof _____ donne.

10. Oui, Marie _____ a.

11. Oui, il _____ adore.

12. Oui, il _____ cherche.

13. Oui, il _____ paie bien.

14. Oui, je_____ prends.

15. Oui, elle _____ comprend.

Exercise 49

Cinquième exercice d'Éric. *Éric's fifth exercise.* Answer each question in a complete sentence and use one of the direct object pronouns **le, la, l',** or **les** in each answer.

Example: Il a mon livre? Oui, <u>il l'a</u>.

1. Marc écoute la radio? —Oui, _____.

2. Il entend mal les instructions? —Oui, _____.

3. Il donne les mauvaises réponses? —Oui, _____.

4. Il a la plus mauvaise note? —Oui, _____.

5. Le prof répète la leçon? —Oui, _____.

6. Le prof explique bien cette leçon? —Oui, _____.

7. Marc comprend ses explications? —Oui, _____.

8. Marc fait l'exercice? —Oui, _____.

9. Marc passe le deuxième examen? —Oui, _____.

10. Marc adore le français? —Oui, _____.

Exercise 50

Sixième exercice d'Éric. *Éric's sixth exercise.* Underline the indirect object pronoun in each sentence, then complete the answer to the question with the appropriate pronoun (**lui** or **leur**). The first one has been done for you.

1. Denise obéit <u>à ses parents</u>? —Oui, elle <u>leur</u> obéit.

2. Denise montre sa nouvelle robe à sa copine? —Oui, elle _____ montre sa nouvelle robe.

3. Denise pose des questions à son papa? —Oui, elle _____ pose beaucoup de questions.

4. Son papa parle longtemps à Denise? —Oui, il _____ parle très longtemps.

5. Il téléphone aux grands-parents? —Oui, il _____ téléphone à 6 heures.

Exercise 51

C'est lundi. La grande sœur d'Éric et son copain David rentrent des cours. *It is Monday. Éric's big sister and her friend David are coming back from class.* Complete the following conversation between Sara and David coming back from the university by filling the blank spaces with appropriate personal pronouns.

1. *Sara*: Dis, David, tu aimes cette nouvelle chanson de Chouchou? _____, je ne _____ aime pas trop.

2. *David*: Moi, je _____ trouve vraiment différente, celle-là. Je ne sais pas trop.

3. *Sara*: J'aime beaucoup les autres chansons de l'album. Tu veux _____ entendre?

4. *David*: Je _____ connais toutes, ces chansons. Elles sont bien.

5. *Sara*: Alors, je _____ achète, l'album?

6. *David*: Pourquoi pas? Tu peux _____ apporter à la soirée samedi soir.

7. *Sara*: Tous nos amis vont _____ être.

8. *David*: Je crois que ton album va _____ plaire, à nos amis.

9. *Sara*: Je _____ aime beaucoup, toi, David. Tu es mon meilleur ami.

10. *David*: _____ aussi, je _____ aime beaucoup. Tu es ma copine favorite.

11. *Sara*: Bon, je rentre chez _____. Mes parents _____ attendent.

12. *David*: Viens, je _____ accompagne.

13. *Sara*: _____ veux rentrer et dire bonsoir à mes parents?

14. *David*: Tu peux _____ dire bonsoir de ma part. _____, je suis en retard.

15. *Sara*: Dépêche-_____ alors! À demain!

16. *David*: Téléphone-_____ ce soir!

Exercise 52

C'est mardi. Sara et David continuent leur conversation. *It is Tuesday. Sara and David continue their conversation.* Complete each answer or reply with the correct pronoun (**y** or **en**). The part of the question that needs to be replaced has been underlined for you.

1. *Sara:* Tu as réfléchi à ma question?

   David: Oui, j' _____ ai réfléchi.

2. *Sara:* Tu veux aller au Québec cet été?

   David: Oui, je veux _____ aller.

3. *Sara:* Bon, tu vas m'accompagner chez moi maintenant?

   David: Bien sûr, je vais _____ accompagner.

4. *Sara:* Ta voiture est garée devant le café?

   David: Oui, c'est ça! Elle _____ est.

5. *Sara:* Tu viens du cours d'anglais?

   David: Oui, j'_____ viens tout juste.

6. *Sara:* Tu as faim? Tu voudrais un peu de couscous?

   David: Certainement, j'_____ voudrais un peu.

7. *Sara:* Je voudrais acheter du pain frais pour maman.

   David: D'accord. Achetons-_____!

8. *Sara:* Voilà une boulangerie!

   David: Allons-_____!

9. *Sara:* Bon. Parlons aussi de ce week-end!

   David: OK. Parlons-_____!

10. *Sara:* On va toujours à la party de Marie?

    David: Naturellement qu'on _____ va.

Exercise 53

Qu'est-ce qu'ils ont dit? *What did they say?* Translate the previous conversation into English:

1. *Sara:* _____

   David: _____

2. *Sara:* _____

   David: _____

3. *Sara:* _____

   David: _____

4. *Sara:* _____

   David: _____

5. *Sara:* _____

   David: _____

6. *Sara:* _____

   David: _____

7. *Sara:* _____

   David: _____

8. *Sara:* _____

   David: _____

9. *Sara:* _____

   David: _____

10. *Sara:* _____

   David: _____

Exercise 54

Sara et David sont invités chez Marie. *Sara and David are invited to Marie's house.* Sara and David call their friend Marie to confirm dinner at her house tonight. Complete each answer with the appropriate pronoun (**me, te, nous,** or **vous**). The first one has been done for you.

1. Marie, tu nous as invités pour ce soir! —Bien sûr, je <u>vous</u> ai invités pour ce soir.

2. Qu'est-ce que tu nous fais comme dîner? —Je vais _____ faire un plat italien.

3. Qu'est-ce que nous pouvons t'apporter? —Apportez-_____ une bouteille de vin!

4. D'accord! Et un gâteau peut-être? —Ah non! Ne _____ apportez pas de dessert!

5. On te téléphone avant d'arriver, Marie? —Oui, téléphonez-_____!

Part 6

Possessive, Demonstrative, and Interrogative Pronouns

19

Possessive Pronouns

These pronouns are used to express *mine, yours, his, hers, ours,* and *theirs.* The possessive pronoun reflects the gender (masculine/feminine) and number (singular/plural) of the noun it replaces (that is, the object possessed, never the possessor). The object can be masculine singular, masculine plural, feminine singular, or feminine plural; thus there are four forms of the pronoun *mine.*

	Masculine singular	Masculine plural	Feminine singular	Feminine plural
mine	le mien	les miens	la mienne	les miennes
yours (fam.)	le tien	les tiens	la tienne	les tiennes
his/hers	le sien	les siens	la sienne	les siennes
ours	le nôtre	les nôtres	la nôtre	les nôtres
yours (form./pl)	le vôtre	les vôtres	la vôtre	les vôtres
theirs	le leur	les leurs	la leur	les leurs

Le couteau? C'est **le mien.**	*The knife? It is mine.*
Les couteaux? Ce sont **les miens.**	*The knives? They are mine.*
La fourchette? C'est **la mienne.**	*The fork? It is mine.*
Les fourchettes? Ce sont **les miennes.**	*The forks? They are mine.*

Note that the French possessive pronoun is always preceded by a definite article (**le, la,** or **les**). If the preposition **à** or **de** precedes the article **le** or **les**, the contracted articles **au** or **du** (representing **à le** or **de le**) and **aux** or **des** (representing **à les** or **de les**) must be used.

Je pense souvent **à mes amis.** Et toi? Tu penses **aux tiens?**
*I often think **about my friends.** How about you? Do you think **about yours?***

Exercise 55

Write the correct form of the possessive pronoun to complete each sentence.

Example: Cette robe rouge? C'est <u>la mienne</u>. (*mine*)

1. Ce livre de français? C'est _____. (*mine*)

2. Cette chaise? C'est _____. (*his*)

3. Ce vieil arbre? C'est _____. (*theirs*)

4. Ces beaux crayons de couleur? Ce sont _____. (*ours*)

5. Cette maison blanche? C'est _____. (*ours*)

6. Ces deux gros chiens noirs? Ce sont _____. (*yours, form.*)

7. Cette petite école là-bas? C'est _____. (*ours*)

8. Ces gâteaux au chocolat? Ce sont _____. (*hers*)

9. Ces jolis gants verts? Ce sont _____. (*mine*)

10. Ces bicyclettes? Ce sont _____. (*theirs*)

11. Ce chalet en Suisse? C'est _____? (*yours, fam.*)

12. Cette jolie robe rouge? C'est _____? (*hers*)

13. Ces jouets? Ce sont _____, mes enfants? (*yours*)

14. Ce calendrier? C'est _____, Madame Didi? (*yours*)

15. Ces petits fours? Ce sont _____? (*hers*)

20

Demonstrative Pronouns

These pronouns are used to express *this/that one* and *these/those ones*. They reflect the gender (m/f) and number (s/pl) of the noun they replace. This pronoun has four forms.

Masculine singular	Masculine plural	Feminine singular	Feminine plural
celui *this/that one*	ceux *these/those*	celle *this/that one*	celles *these/those*

Je peux choisir **quel film** on va voir?
—Je veux voir **celui** avec Depardieu.

*Can I choose **what movie** we are going to see?*
*—I want to see **the one** with Depardieu.*

Demonstrative pronouns are never used alone. They are followed by:

- **-ci** or **-là** to distinguish *this one* from *that one*.

  Regarde ces jolies robes!
  Tu veux **celle-ci** ou **celle-là**?

  Look at these pretty dresses!
  *Do you want **this one** or **that one**?*

- a complement introduced by a preposition such as **de/d'** or **en**.

  J'aime les deux tableaux, mais je
  préfère **celui de** Cézanne.

  I like both paintings, but I prefer
  *   **the one by** Cézanne.*

- a relative clause.

  Des deux voitures, j'aime mieux **celle**
  qui consomme le moins d'essence.

  *Of the two cars, I prefer **the one that***
  *   uses the least gasoline.*

Exercise 56

Complete each sentence with the appropriate demonstrative pronoun (**celui, ceux, celle,** or **celles**). Add **-ci** or **-là** when necessary. Then translate each sentence into English.

1. Cet arbre, c'est _____ de mon voisin. Le mien est là-bas.

2. Cette voiture, c'est _____ de Julie. La mienne est dans le garage.

3. Ces plantes vertes, ce sont _____ de ma mère. Les miennes sont dans ma chambre.

4. Cet iPod, c'est _____ de mon frère Jean. Le mien est dans ma voiture.

5. Ces photos-là sont _____ de ma sœur. Les miennes ne sont pas développées.

6. Mes poèmes favoris sont _____ dont j'ai souligné les titres.

7. Ma copine Jeanne, c'est _____ dont tu as fait la connaissance hier soir.

8. Mes plus jolies chaussures de soirée sont _____ que je viens de ranger.

9. Je peux te donner une de mes raquettes. Tu veux _____ou _____?

10. Quel film est-ce qu'on va regarder? _____ ou _____?

11. Le professeur de maths, c'est _____ que tu vois assis derrière son bureau.

12. Laquelle de ces deux robes est la plus belle, _____ ou _____?

13. Tu as besoin d'une cravate? Je peux te prêter _____?

14. Mon émission de radio préférée, c'est _____ de Radio France de 22 h.

15. Le meilleur poème, c'est _____ de Lamartine.

21

Interrogative Pronouns

These pronouns are used to ask *which one(s)*. They reflect the gender (m/f) and number (s/pl) of the noun they replace. This pronoun has four forms.

Masculine singular	Masculine plural	Feminine singular	Feminine plural
lequel	lesquels	laquelle	lesquelles

Voici deux stylos, un rouge et un bleu. **Lequel** est-ce que tu veux?
*Here are two pens, one red and one blue. **Which one** do you want?*

In the above sentence, note that **lequel** replaces **quel stylo**.

J'ai des chaussures noires et des chaussures grises. **Lesquelles** est-ce que je vais mettre?
*I have black shoes and gray shoes. **Which ones** am I going to wear?*

In the above sentence, note that **lesquelles** replaces **quelles chaussures**.

   When **lequel, lesquels,** and **lesquelles** are preceded by the preposition à or de, use the contracted forms.

à + lequel = auquel
à + lesquels = auxquels
à + lesquelles = auxquelles

de + lequel = duquel
de + lesquels = desquels
de + lesquelles = desquelles

Auquel de tes meilleurs amis est-ce
   que tu parles le plus souvent?

*To **which** (one) of your best friends
   do you speak the most often?*

Exercise 57

Complete each sentence with the appropriate interrogative pronoun (**lequel, laquelle, lesquels,** or **lesquelles**). Then translate each sentence into English.

1. J'ai un stylo bleu et un stylo noir. _____ désires-tu?

2. Voici un pull gris et un pull blanc. _____ me va le mieux?

_____

3. J'adore les raisins blancs et les raisins rouges. Et toi? _____ aimes-tu?

_____

4. Je peux servir le vin blanc ou le vin rouge. _____ est le meilleur?

_____

5. J'ai de bonnes pâtes italiennes et de bonnes pâtes allemandes. _____ est-ce

que je vais préparer?

_____

6. Tu veux parler à un employé? —_____?

_____

7. Tu as besoin d'un livre! —_____?

_____

8. Tu veux aller à deux concerts ce mois-ci. —Mais _____?

_____

9. Tu vas donner un cadeau à un de tes copains. _____?

_____

10. Voici deux beaux poulets. _____ vas-tu acheter?

_____

Review 6

Exercise 58

Jeannine pose des questions à son frère François. *Jeannine asks her brother François some questions.* Place the appropriate contracted article (**du, des, au,** or **aux**) before each possessive pronoun. Then translate each exchange into English.

1. **De quel nom** est-ce que tu te moques? —Pas _____ tien, ne t'inquiète pas!

_____

2. **Auxquels** de tes amis est-ce que tu donnes des cadeaux? —_____ meilleurs, bien sûr!

_____

3. Tu parles **de tes vacances** de l'an dernier? —Non, je parle _____ tiennes.

_____

4. **À quels devoirs** penses-tu? —_____ nôtres. Évidemment!

_____

5. **De quel lycée** est-ce qu'ils parlent? —_____ leur.

_____

Exercise 59

Jeannine et François se préparent à aller jouer au tennis. *Jeannine and François are getting ready to go play tennis.* Complete the following conversation with the appropriate pronouns from the list. You may use a word more than once.

> celui   celle   lequel   laquelle   duquel   tienne   mienne

1. *Jeannine:* Dis, François, je ne trouve pas ma raquette de tennis, _____ que je viens d'acheter.
2. *François:* Ah! Je ne sais pas, Jeannine! _____-ci, c'est la _____. Comme tu vois, elle est vieille.
3. *Jeannine:* Bon. Je peux prendre _____ de Catherine. Elle n'en a pas besoin en ce moment.
4. *François:* Moi, mon problème, c'est de décider _____ de mes copains je vais inviter à jouer.

5. *Jeannine:* Invite _____ que tu m'as présenté samedi dernier. Il est sympa.

6. *François:* _____ est-ce que tu parles? Le grand blond ou _____ aux cheveux roux?

7. *Jeannine:* Le grand blond! Remarque, tous tes copains sont toujours gentils avec moi. Mais _____-là est le plus gentil!

8. *François:* _____ des voitures est-ce qu'on prend? La _____ ou la mienne?

Jeannine: Comme tu veux! Mais viens vite. Quel beau temps pour jouer au tennis!

Relative Pronouns

22

The Relative Pronouns *qui* and *que*

Relative pronouns replace a noun antecedent; they introduce a new clause (subject + verb) which gives information about the antecedent.

The pronoun **qui** is the subject of the verb in the relative clause and can replace things or people. It usually translates as *who, that,* or *which* (however, these are often omitted in English).

> La dame **qui parle** est notre professeur de français.
> *The lady **who's speaking** is our French teacher.*

In the above sentence, **qui** is the subject of **parle**.

> L'avion **qui vient de décoller** a pour destination Paris.
> *The plane **that just took off** has Paris as its destination.*

In the above sentence, **qui** is the subject of **vient de décoller**.

The pronoun **que** is the direct object of the verb in the relative clause and can replace things or people. It usually translates as *whom, that,* or *which* (however, these are often omitted in English).

> La dame **que je cherche** vend des parfums.
> *The lady **I'm looking for (for whom I'm looking)** sells perfume.*

In the above sentence, **que** is the direct object of **cherche**, referring back to the antecedent **la dame**.

> L'avion **que je prends** a pour destination Paris.
> *The plane **(that) I am taking** has Paris as its destination.*

In the above sentence, **que** is the direct object of **prends**, referring back to the antecedent **l'avion**.

Exercise 60

Write the appropriate relative pronoun **qui** or **que/qu'** in the space provided.

1. La bicyclette _____ est devant la maison est celle de mon frère.
2. Voici le parfum _____ je préfère.

3. La personne _____ m'envoie le plus de mails, c'est ma copine Suzie.

4. Les devoirs _____ je fais en ce moment sont difficiles.

5. La fenêtre _____ je ne peux pas fermer est cassée.

6. Les gens _____ sont souvent au soleil sont bronzés.

7. C'est Georges _____ je vois là-bas?

8. Montre-moi l'exercice _____ est si facile.

9. J'aime les couleurs _____ ne sont pas trop vives.

10. Le travail _____ je fais est agréable.

11. Le salaire _____ on me paie n'est pas mauvais.

12. La leçon _____ il a apprise lui servira bien.

13. Le cadeau _____ est emballé en papier bleu est pour toi.

14. L'histoire _____ tu nous racontes est improbable.

15. Nous ne faisons pas assez attention aux choses _____ sont les plus importantes.

16. L'hiver est la saison _____ je préfère.

17. Marie est celle _____ arrive toujours en avance.

18. Paris est la ville _____ me fascine depuis toujours.

19. C'est mon frère _____ m'a envoyé ce mail.

20. Ce sont les fleurs _____ je trouve les plus jolies.

23

The Relative Pronouns *qui* and *lequel* After Prepositions

The pronoun **qui** is used after a preposition (**à, pour,** etc.) to replace a person in a relative clause.

Le garçon **à qui** tu parles est mon ami.	*The boy **to whom** you're speaking is my friend.*
La personne **pour qui** tu fais ce travail est là.	*The person **for whom** you're doing this work is here.*

A form of **lequel** is used after a preposition to replace a thing in a relative clause. The form of **lequel** changes according to the gender and number of the noun it replaces.

The four forms of **lequel** are:

Masculine singular	Masculine plural	Feminine singular	Feminine plural
lequel	lesquels	laquelle	lesquelles

Le stylo **avec lequel** tu écris est à moi.	*The pen **with which** you're writing is mine.*
La table **derrière laquelle** il se cache est très petite.	*The table **behind which** he's hiding is very small.*

Remember to use the contracted forms of the prepositions **à** and **de** when they are followed by **lequel, lesquels,** and **lesquelles.**

à + lequel = auquel	de + lequel = duquel
à + lesquels = auxquels	de + lesquels = desquels
à + lesquelles = auxquelles	de + lesquelles = desquelles

Les sociétés **auxquelles** j'envoie mon CV sont toutes à New York.
*The companies **to which** I'm sending my CV are all in New York.*

Irregularities

The rule that states that the pronoun **qui** is used after a preposition to replace a person does not apply when the preposition is **entre, parmi,** or **sans.** A form of **lequel** is used after these prepositions.

Ce sont deux personnes **sans lesquelles** je ne peux pas vivre.

*These are two people **without whom** I cannot live.*

The rule that states that a form of **lequel** is used after a preposition to replace a thing does not apply when the antecedent is vague or when the antecedent is an entire idea. In that case, use the indefinite pronoun **quoi.**

Je me demande **à quoi** tu penses.

*I wonder **what** you are thinking **about**.*

Exercise 61

Write the appropriate relative pronoun **qui** or a form of **lequel** in the space provided. Then translate each sentence into English.

1. La copine avec _____ tu joues au tennis est très sportive.

_____

2. Le monsieur pour _____ tu travailles est généreux.

_____

3. Ta mère est la personne sans _____ tu ne peux pas vivre.

_____

4. Le grand garçon derrière _____ je marche, c'est mon frère.

_____

5. C'est un instrument sans _____ je ne peux pas faire mon travail.

_____

6. Les fleurs devant _____ je me trouve sont vraiment belles.

_____

7. La personne à _____ je pense tout le temps, c'est mon fiancé.

_____

8. La journée à _____ je pense tout le temps, c'est celle de mon mariage.

_____

9. Le moment [à] _____ je pense sans cesse, c'est le moment de dire «oui».

10. C'est la personne avec _____ je veux passer le reste de ma vie.

11. Les choses _____ tu es le plus attachée ne sont que des choses.

12. L'amie sur _____ tu peux compter le plus, c'est moi.

13. J'apprécie les gens sans _____ je ne serais pas où je suis.

14. Le monsieur à côté de _____ tu vas être assis est un artiste connu.

15. Voilà la façade sur _____ est gravé son nom.

16. Je ne sais jamais à _____ tu penses.

17. C'est le bijou pour _____ tu as payé si cher?

18. Est-ce que tu sais par _____ ce poème a été écrit?

19. Dis-moi à _____ tu vas donner ça.

20. À droite de _____ est-ce qu'il sera assis?

24

The Relative Pronouns *où* and *dont*

The pronoun **où** is used to say *where*; it replaces the name of a location.

Voilà la maison **où** j'habitais.   *There is the house **where** I used to live.*

The pronoun **où** is also used to express *when* after expressions such as **au moment, le jour, l'heure,** or **à l'époque.**

J'allais téléphoner **au moment où**   *I was going to call **the moment when***
tu es arrivé.   *you arrived.*

Exercise 62

Translate the italicized part of each sentence into French to complete the sentence.

1. *The day when* you were born was a blessing.

   _____ tu es né était béni.

2. This is *the hotel where* they honeymooned.

   Voici _____ ils ont passé leur lune de miel.

3. Do you remember the *day (when)* you met?

   Tu te souviens du _____ vous vous êtes rencontrés?

4. I was finishing my studies *the month (when)* you arrived.

   Je finissais mes études _____ tu es arrivé.

5. It was at a time *when* I was not seeing anyone.

   C'était à une époque _____ je ne voyais personne.

The pronoun **dont** replaces **de qui** as well as **de +** a form of **lequel.** It stands for things and people. It is often (but not always) translated into English as *of whom* and *whose.* The pronoun **dont** is used:

- with relationships and possession.

La dame **dont** le fils a deux ans ne   *The woman **whose** son is two years old*
travaille pas.   *does not work.*

In the above sentence, the relative pronoun **dont** is necessary because of the relationship: **le fils** *de* **la dame.**

> Appelle l'homme **dont** la voiture est *Call the man **whose** car is in the garage.*
> au garage.

In the above sentence, the relative pronoun **dont** is necessary because of the ownership: **la voiture** *de* **l'homme.**

- when the structure in the relative clause would otherwise include the preposition **de/d'.**

> La chose **dont** j'ai le plus envie, *The thing I crave the most is an ice cream.*
> c'est une glace.

In the above sentence, the relative pronoun **dont** is necessary because it is governed by the structure **avoir envie** *de.*

Here is a list of expressions (originally with **de**) frequently found in such relative clauses:

avoir besoin **de**	to *need*
avoir envie **de**	to *want*
avoir peur **de**	to *be afraid of*
rêver **de**	to *dream of*
parler **de**	to *talk about*
se souvenir **de**	to *remember*
être heureux **de**	to *be happy about*
être fier **de**	to *be proud of*

Exercise 63

Translate each of the following sentences into English. Beware of the varying translations for the pronoun **dont.**

1. Ces dix jours à Tahiti sont les vacances **dont** je me souviendrai toute ma vie.

_____

2. Cette horrible aventure, c'est une chose **dont** je préfère ne pas me souvenir.

_____

3. Mon livre de français, c'est le livre **dont** j'ai besoin tous les jours.

_____

4. Cette Ferrari, c'est la voiture de sport **dont** je rêve depuis toujours.

_____

5. Les rats sont les bêtes **dont** j'ai le plus peur.

_____

6. Ce professeur est celui **dont** j'ai appris le plus.

_____

7. Ce **dont** j'ai envie, c'est un nouveau bracelet.

_____

8. Les personnes **dont** on parle le plus, ce sont les vedettes de cinéma.

_____

9. Ceux **dont** on doit se méfier, ce sont les hypocrites.

_____

10. Voilà le monsieur **dont** la voiture a disparu hier soir.

_____

11. Voilà la jeune fille **dont** on a volé le sac.

_____

12. Tu te souviens du garçon **dont** je t'ai parlé?

_____

13. Regarde! C'est la maison **dont** le toit est couvert de tuiles rouges.

_____

14. C'est le professeur **dont** tout le monde se plaint.

_____

15. Les dates **dont** tu dois te souvenir sont sur ce calendrier.

_____

25

Ce Before *qui*, *que*, and *dont*

In the absence of an antecedent (noun that is being replaced), use **ce** before the relative pronoun.

Ce qui me choque, c'est sa malhonnêteté.	***What** shocks me is his/her dishonesty.*
Ce que tu me dis m'étonne.	***What** you tell me surprises me.*
Ce dont j'ai envie en ce moment, c'est d'une bonne glace.	***What** I really feel like now is a good ice cream.*
Je vais te dire **ce qui** s'est passé.	*I am going to tell you **what** happened.*

Exercise 64

Complete each French sentence with **ce qui, ce que/qu'**, or **ce dont** and translate each sentence into English.

1. Je ne sais pas _____ se passe.

   _____

2. Je ne sais pas encore _____ je vais faire comme études.

   _____

3. Je vais te dire _____ j'ai besoin pour faire le dîner ce soir.

   _____

4. Dis-moi _____ tu as envie.

   _____

5. _____ me fascine, c'est ton imagination.

   _____

6. Je vais te dire _____ j'ai le plus peur.

   _____

7. Devine _____ je veux comme cadeau.

   _____

8. Je peux te dire _____ ne va pas.

_____

9. Je me demande _____ elle veut.

_____

10. Montre-moi _____ est dans la boîte.

_____

Review 7

Exercise 65

Denise est mélancolique aujourd'hui. *Denise is sad today.* Write the appropriate relative pronoun **où**, **dont**, or **quoi** in the space provided, and then translate the sentence into English. You will find out what is making Denise sad today.

1. Tu ne sais pas toujours à _____ je pense.

   _____

2. L'endroit _____ je me sens le mieux, c'est ma maison.

   _____

3. Je vais bientôt revoir la ville _____ je suis née.

   _____

4. La ville _____ je t'ai montré les photos, c'est ma ville natale.

   _____

5. La personne _____ je suis le plus fière, c'est mon père.

   _____

6. Le jour _____ je reverrai ma ville natale, je serai heureuse.

   _____

7. L'ami d'enfance _____ je te parle toujours va venir aujourd'hui.

   _____

8. Nous allons manger, après _____ nous allons nous promener.

   _____

9. Le restaurant _____ nous allons manger est excellent.

   _____

10. Le dessert _____ j'ai envie, c'est la crêpe que faisait ma grand-mère.

    _____

Exercise 66

Une page du journal de Denise. *A page in Denise's diary.* Choose the correct relative pronoun to complete each sentence and find out what Denise wrote in her diary.

1. Ce _____ m'irrite, c'est l'impolitesse. (dont, qui)

2. J'aime ce _____ je fais dans la vie. (qui, que)

3. Voilà la maison _____ je rêve. (dont, lesquelles)

4. Le parc _____ je fais du jogging est près d'ici. (lequel, où)

5. Le musée _____ j'adore est près aussi. (dont, que)

6. Les animaux _____ je préfère sont les chats. (qui, que)

7. Ce _____ j'ai peur, c'est la guerre. (dont, lequel)

8. Ce _____ j'ai le plus besoin, c'est la famille. (que, dont)

9. L'instrument _____ j'adore, c'est le piano. (qui, que)

10. La saison _____ me plaît le mieux, c'est l'été. (qui, que)

11. J'attends le moment _____ je rencontrerai l'homme de ma vie. (que, où)

12. Les hommes _____ me plaisent sont intelligents. (qui, que)

13. L'accident _____ j'ai vu m'est encore à l'esprit. (qui, que)

14. Ce _____ j'ai envie, ce sont des vacances. (que, dont)

15. L'amie _____ je préfère, c'est Maryse. (que, qui)

Exercise 67

Un coup de téléphone de Denise à ses parents. *A phone call from Denise to her parents.* Translate the italicized part of each sentence into French to complete the following sentences. You will discover the big news Denise has for her parents.

1. You are the people *whom* I love most in the world.

   Vous êtes ceux _____ j'aime le plus au monde.

2. *The moment* you arrive, I will take you on a tour of the old town.

   Dès _____ vous arriverez, je vous emmènerai faire le tour de la vieille ville.

3. The house *where* I live is outside of town. I will give you directions.

   La maison _____ j'habite est en dehors de la ville. Je vous donnerai les directions.

4. I have news *which* will be a big surprise to you.

   J'ai des nouvelles _____ vous surprendront.

5. I am going to introduce you to a person (*whom*) you need to know.

   Je vais vous présenter à une personne _____ vous devez connaître.

6. I will show you the building in *which* his studio is.

   Je vous montrerai l'immeuble dans _____ se trouve son studio.

7. Who is the person I am talking *about*?

   Qui est la personne _____ je parle?

8. It is Jean-Paul, the man (*whom*) I am going to marry.

   C'est Jean-Paul, l'homme _____ je vais épouser.

9. It is the moment *of which* I dream every day.

   C'est le moment _____ je rêve tous les jours.

10. This is one person without *whom* I could no longer live.

    C'est la personne sans _____ je ne pourrais plus vivre.

11. That's him! He is the one *that* counts the most in my life.

    C'est lui! C'est celui _____ compte le plus dans ma vie.

12. I know *what* you are thinking.

    Je sais _____ vous pensez.

13. Where is the girl *who* thought only about her career?

    Où est la fille _____ ne pensait qu'à sa carrière?

14. Things change! That's *what* makes life interesting.

    Tout change! C'est _____ rend la vie intéressante.

15. You wonder *what* he does for a living?

    Vous vous demandez _____ il fait dans la vie?

Part 8

Prepositions and Conjunctions

26

Prepositions

Prepositions help situate an element such as a noun or a verb. They may consist of single words or prepositional phrases. Here are some examples:

à	*at, in, to*
à cause de	*because of*
à côté de	*next to*
à propos de	*regarding*
après	*after, afterward*
au centre de	*in the center of*
au lieu de	*instead of*
au milieu de	*in the middle of*
au sujet de	*concerning*
au-dessous de	*underneath*
au-dessus de	*above, over*
avant	*before*
dans	*in*
de	*of, from*
de la part de	*from*
de peur de	*for fear of*
en	*in, of, on*
en face de	*across from*
entre	*between*
grâce à	*thanks to*
jusque	*until*
loin de	*far from*
malgré	*in spite of*
pendant	*during*
pour	*for*
près de	*near*
sans	*without*

sous	under
sur	on
vers	toward

Je ne peux pas sortir à **cause du** mauvais temps.	*I can't go out **because of** the bad weather.*
Accroche ce tableau **au-dessus du** lit.	*Hang this painting **above** the bed.*
J'arrive **de** France.	*I am arriving **from** France.*
J'habite **en face de** l'école.	*I live **across from** the school.*
Je sors **malgré** le mauvais temps.	*I go out **in spite of** the bad weather.*
Je vous écris **de la part de** ma famille.	*I am writing to you **on behalf of** my family.*

Note that, at the end of a prepositional phrase, **de** and **à** contract with **le** or **les** to form **du, des, au,** or **aux.**

Exercise 68

Fill the blank space with the preposition that makes the most sense in the context.

1. Tu es _____ vacances?

2. Écris une carte _____ ton grand-père!

3. Il y a un stylo _____ le bureau.

4. _____ mon absence, ne regarde pas trop la télé!

5. Je vais au bureau _____ métro; c'est plus rapide qu' _____ autobus.

6. Le dentiste est très _____ la pharmacie, à deux minutes de marche.

7. Je vais acheter des médicaments _____ ton frère.

8. Je pense être de retour _____ 3 heures de l'après-midi.

9. Si ton frère se réveille _____ mon retour, appelle-moi.

10. Je ne sais pas ce que je ferais _____ toi!

11. Maman me pose toujours des questions _____ mes amis.

12. Il y a une belle fontaine _____ du village.

13. Je pense que c'est la boutique _____ l'oncle Georges.

14. Sa boutique est _____ la boulangerie et la charcuterie.

15. Je fais les devoirs qu'on m'a donnés _____ demain.

Special meanings of some prepositions

Some prepositions—**à**, **de**, **en**, and **chez**—have special uses and may vary in meaning according to how they are used.

The prepositions **à** and **de** can be used to express possession:

Ce livre est **à moi**.	*This book belongs to me.*
C'est la maison **de Ginette**.	*It is Ginette's house.*

The prepositions **à** and **de** can be used to indicate location or direction:

Ils arrivent à Londres.	*They arrive **in** London.*
Je vais à Paris.	*I am going **to** Paris.*
Va à l'école!	*Go **to** school!*
J'arrive de Paris.	*I am arriving **from** Paris.*
Elle vient de Moscou.	*She is **from** Moscow.*
Paris est la capitale de la France.	*Paris is the capital **of** France.*

The prepositions **à** and **de** can be used to indicate a quality, a use, or how something is done.

la glace **à** la vanille	*vanilla ice cream*
la fille **au** nez retroussé	*the girl with the snub nose*
la boîte **aux** lettres	*the mailbox*
à voix basse	*in a low voice/softly*
paralysé(e) **de** peur	*paralyzed with fear*

The prepositions **à** and **de** can be used to tell time.

à une heure **du** matin	*at one o'clock in the morning*
à trois heures **de** l'après-midi	*at three o'clock in the afternoon*
à six heures trente **du** soir	*at six-thirty in the evening*
de 8 heures à 10 heures	*from 8 to 10 o'clock*
de midi à minuit	*from noon till midnight*
jusqu'à quatorze heures	*until 2:00 P.M.*

The preposition **chez** is used to express *at* or *to* somebody's house or place of business. It is always followed by someone's name or by a stressed pronoun.

Va **chez ta tante**!	*Go to your aunt's house!*
Va **chez elle**!	*Go to her house!*
Va **chez le médecin**!	*Go see the doctor!*

The preposition **en** is used with transportation.

en voiture	*by car*
en autobus	*by bus*
en bateau	*by boat*
en chemin de fer/en train	*by rail/train*
en avion	*by plane*
en métro	*by subway*

The preposition **en** is used with materials.

en soie	*(out of) silk*
en laine	*(out of) wool, woollen*
en bois	*(out of) wood, wooden*
en fer	*(out of) iron*
en acier	*(out of) steel*
en porcelaine	*(out of) ceramic*

Exercise 69

Choose the correct preposition (**à, au, aux, de, pour, chez,** or **en**) to complete each sentence in the following exchanges.

1. *Rémy*: J'arriverai _____ Reims à 14 h. Viens me chercher.

   Dara: D'accord. Je t'emmènerai visiter la cathédrale _____ Reims.

2. *Rémy*: À quelle heure tu arrives _____ Lyon?

   Dara: À 8 h. Mais je pars immédiatement _____ Paris.

3. *Rémy*: Tu restes _____ tes grands-parents samedi soir?

   Dara: Oui, mais dimanche je dormirai _____ tante Irma.

4. *Rémy*: Tu voyageras _____ avion?

   Dara: Naturellement! Sûrement pas _____ train.

5. *Rémy*: Parle _____ voix basse; maman dort.

   Dara: Tu sais bien que je ne parle jamais _____ voix haute!

6. *Rémy:* Quelle jolie tasse _____ porcelaine!

   Dara: J'aime bien aussi celle _____ verre de Venise.

7. *Rémy:* Passe-moi les photos _____ Pierre, s'il te plaît!

   Dara: D'accord. Mais où sont celles _____ Joanne?

8. *Rémy:* La fille _____ cheveux longs, c'est Irène.

   Dara: Et celle _____ cheveux courts, c'est ma sœur.

9. *Rémy:* Ce billet de 20 euros est _____ moi.

   Dara: Je croyais qu'il était _____ moi.

10. *Rémy:* Cette statue _____ acier est moderne.

    Dara: Et cette statue _____ marbre. Qu'en penses-tu?

11. *Rémy:* Est-ce que cette robe est _____ soie?

    Dara: Je crois qu'elle est _____ laine.

12. *Rémy:* J'ai laissé mon livre _____ ma copine. Zut alors!

    Dara: Tu n'en as pas un exemplaire _____ toi?

13. *Rémy:* Tu voudrais une glace _____ la fraise?

    Dara: Je préfère la glace _____ chocolat.

14. *Rémy:* La mousse _____ chocolat est mon dessert favori.

    Dara: Et pour moi, le soufflé _____ la vanille.

15. *Rémy:* Donne-moi aussi un bonbon _____ la menthe.

    Dara: Voilà avec un bonbon _____ citron.

Idiomatic use of prepositions in English and French

In both English and French some verbs are automatically followed by a certain preposition. In some cases the preposition is required as part of the verb in one language, but not in the other. These verbs can easily confuse the language learner.

Note that the following verbs are followed by a preposition in English but not in French.

chercher; *to look for*
Il **cherche** la femme idéale.

*He looks (is looking) **for** the ideal woman.*

attendre; *to wait for*
Elle **attend** le Prince Charmant.

*She waits (is waiting) **for** Prince Charming.*

regarder; *to look at*
On **regarde** le ciel.   *We look (are looking)* **at** *the sky.*

écouter; *to listen to*
On **écoute** les nouvelles.   *We listen* **to the news.**

demander; *to ask for*
On **demande** l'addition.   *We ask* **for the check.**

payer; *to pay for*
Tu **paies** mon café.   *You pay* **for my coffee.**

Note that while many conjugated French verbs are followed directly by an infinitive verb (**J'aime** *dormir*), others require the use of a specific preposition before the infinitive verb that follows.

Some commonly used verbs followed by the preposition **à** are:

J'**aide** maman **à** faire la vaisselle.   *I help Mom do the dishes.*
Je **m'amuse à** dessiner.   *I have fun drawing.*
J'**apprends à** parler le français.   *I learn to speak French.*
Je **commence à** écrire.   *I begin to write.*
Je **réussis à** faire l'exercice.   *I manage to do the exercise.*

Some commonly used verbs followed by the preposition **de/d'** are:

Je **cesse de** parler.   *I stop talking.*
Je **décide de** partir.   *I decide to leave.*
Je **demande à** mon prof **de** m'aider.   *I ask my teacher to help me.*
Je **dis à** maman **de** venir.   *I tell Mom to come.*
Je **finis de** manger.   *I finish eating.*
J'**oublie** toujours **de** fermer la porte.   *I always forget to close the door.*

Exercise 70

Complete each French sentence; use the object pronoun **te/t'** to express *you*.

1. I am looking for paper. _____ du papier.

2. I listen to my mother! _____ ma mère!

3. I ask for my book! _____ mon livre!

4. I am watching a movie. _____ un film.

5. I am waiting for my friends. _____ mes amis.

6. I pay for my dinner. _____ mon dîner.

7. I begin to speak. _____ parler.

8. I forget to write. _____ écrire.

9. I help you do your homework. _____ faire tes devoirs.

10. I am learning to drive. _____ conduire.

11. I decide to stay. _____ rester.

12. I ask for forgiveness. _____ pardon.

13. I ask you to forgive me. _____ me pardonner.

14. I tell you to hurry. _____ te dépêcher.

15. I stop working. _____ travailler.

27

Geographical Expressions

Geographical expressions encompass cities, regions, countries, continents, and natural features of land and sea. Like other French nouns, most of these expressions have a gender and are preceded by an article.

The definite article before place names

Cities are not preceded by an article in French:

Londres	*London*
Montréal	*Montreal*
New York	*New York*
Paris	*Paris*
Rome	*Rome*

A notable exception is **la Nouvelle-Orléans** (*New Orleans*).

Countries are preceded by a definite article (**le/la/l'/les**) in French. (See Chapter 1 to review genders of nouns.)

l'Algérie (f)	*Algeria*
l'Angleterre (f)	*England*
l'Argentine (f)	*Argentina*
l'Espagne (f)	*Spain*
l'Italie (f)	*Italy*
la Belgique	*Belgium*
la Chine	*China*
la Colombie	*Colombia*
la France	*France*
la Russie	*Russia*
la Suisse	*Switzerland*

la Tunisie	*Tunisia*
le Brésil	*Brazil*
le Canada	*Canada*
le Chili	*Chile*
le Danemark	*Denmark*
le Guatemala	*Guatemala*
le Japon	*Japan*
le Maroc	*Morocco*
le Mexique	*Mexico*
le Nicaragua	*Nicaragua*
le Portugal	*Portugal*
le Sénégal	*Senegal*
le Venezuela	*Venezuela*

Note that *the United States* is **les États-Unis** (masculine plural).

Continents are preceded by a definite article in French and they are all feminine nouns.

l'Afrique (f)	*Africa*
l'Amérique du Nord (f)	*North America*
l'Amérique du Sud (f)	*South America*
l'Asie (f)	*Asia*
l'Australie (f)	*Australia*
l'Europe (f)	*Europe*

Regions, provinces, rivers, and mountains are preceded by the definite article in French.

la Normandie	*Normandy*
le Québec	*Quebec (province)*
le Saint-Laurent	*the Saint Lawrence river*
les Alpes (fpl)	*the Alps*

Islands are treated like cities (**Haïti**) or like regions (**la Guadeloupe**):

Cuba	*Cuba*
Hawaï	*Hawaii*
la Corse	*Corsica*
la Jamaïque	*Jamaica*
la Martinique	*Martinique*
Tahiti	*Tahiti*

Oceans are masculine and seas are feminine.

l'(océan) Arctique (m)	*the Arctic Ocean*
l'(océan) Atlantique (m)	*the Atlantic Ocean*
l'/le (océan) Pacifique (m)	*the Pacific Ocean*
l'océan Indien (m)	*the Indian Ocean*
la (mer) Baltique	*the Baltic Sea*
la (mer) Méditerranée	*the Mediterranean*
la mer Rouge	*the Red Sea*
la/l' (mer) Adriatique (f)	*the Adriatic Sea*

Exercise 71

Write the correct definite article before each place name. If the article is **l'** or **les,** specify the gender of the noun by indicating (m) or (f). If no article is necessary, write X.

1. _____ Baltique _____
2. _____ Angleterre _____
3. _____ Saint-Laurent _____
4. _____ Maroc _____
5. _____ Londres _____
6. _____ Guadeloupe _____
7. _____ Espagne _____
8. _____ Chine _____
9. _____ Allemagne _____
10. _____ Tahiti _____
11. _____ États-Unis _____
12. _____ Haïti _____
13. _____ Japon _____
14. _____ Miami _____
15. _____ Afrique _____
16. _____ Alpes _____
17. _____ Méditerranée _____
18. _____ Suisse _____
19. _____ Nouvelle-Orléans _____
20. _____ Asie _____

Prepositions before place names

The preposition used before a place name to express *in* and *to* varies according to the nature of the place.

Only cities and some islands are not preceded by an article. Use the preposition **à** to say *in/to* before cities:

Je vais **à** Hong Kong.   *I am going **to** Hong Kong.*

The article before a place name changes according to gender (m/f) and number (s/pl). Use the preposition **en** to say *in* or *to* before feminine place names and the preposition **au(x)** to say *in* or *to* before masculine place names.

Je vais **en** Normandie.   *I am going **to** Normandy.*
Je vais **au** Canada.   *I am going **to** Canada.*
Je vais **aux** États-Unis.   *I am going **to** the United States.*

The preposition used before a place name to express *from* and *of* varies as above. Use the preposition:

- **de/d'** to say *from* or *of* before cities.

    Je suis **de** Hong Kong.   *I am **from** Hong Kong.*

- **de/d'** to say *from* or *of* before feminine place names.

    Je suis **de** Normandie.   *I am **from** Normandy.*

- **du** and **des** to say *from* or *of* before masculine place names.

    Je suis **du** Canada.   *I am **from** Canada.*
    Voilà une carte **des** États-Unis.   *Here is a map **of** the United States.*

Exercise 72

Write the correct preposition (**à, en, au,** or **aux**) to tell in which country or city each person was born and lives.

1. Juan est né _____ Bogota.

2. Il habite _____ Colombie.

3. Inès est née _____ Madrid.

4. Elle habite _____ Espagne.

5. John est né _____ Londres.

6. Il habite _____ Angleterre.

7. Inge est née _____ Bonn.

8. Elle habite _____ Allemagne.

9. Monique est née _____ Nice.

10. Elle habite _____ France.

11. Jérôme est né _____ Montréal.

12. Il habite _____ Canada.

13. Harold est né _____ Boston.

14. Il habite _____ États-Unis.

15. Josiane est née _____ Lausanne.

16. Elle habite _____ Suisse.

17. Danielle est née _____ Brasilia.

18. Elle habite _____ Brésil.

19. Myriam est née _____ Marrakech.

20. Elle habite _____ Maroc.

Exercise 73

Write the correct preposition or contraction (**de/d'**, **du**, or **des**) before each country or city.

1. Juan vient _____ Colombie.

2. Inès vient _____ Espagne.

3. John vient _____ Angleterre.

4. Inge vient _____ Allemagne.

5. Monique vient _____ France.

6. Jérôme vient _____ Canada.

7. Harold vient _____ États-Unis.

8. Josiane vient _____ Suisse.

9. Danielle vient _____ Brésil.

10. Myriam vient _____ Maroc.

11. Thomas vient _____ Belgique.

12. Luigi vient _____ Italie.

13. Ali vient _____ Algérie.

14. Jorg vient _____ Danemark.

15. Juan vient _____ Guatemala.

16. José vient _____ Mexique.

17. Manuel vient _____ Portugal.

18. Maria vient _____ Argentine.

19. Luisa vient _____ Chili.

20. Anna vient _____ Russie.

Exercise 74

Un tour du monde. *Around the world.* Write the correct preposition or contraction before each country's name. You will learn the capital cities of many countries.

1. Londres est la capitale _____ Angleterre.

2. Ottawa est la capitale _____ Canada.

3. Paris est la capitale _____ France.

4. Washington, D.C., est la capitale _____ États-Unis.

5. Port-au-Prince est la capitale _____ Haïti.

6. Rome est la capitale _____ Italie.

7. Oslo est la capitale _____ Norvège.

8. Mexico est la capitale _____ Mexique.

9. Alger est la capitale _____ Algérie.

10. Rabat est la capitale _____ Maroc.

11. Copenhague est la capitale _____ Danemark.

12. Tunis est la capitale _____ Tunisie.

13. Bogotá est la capitale _____ Colombie.

14. Madrid est la capitale _____ Espagne.

15. Moscou est la capitale _____ Russie.

16. Berlin est la capitale _____ Allemagne.

17. Tokyo est la capitale _____ Japon.

18. Beijing est la capitale _____ Chine.

19. Caracas est la capitale _____Venezuela.

20. Berne est la capitale _____ Suisse.

28

Prepositional Expressions and Idioms

Some prepositions are an integral part of idiomatic (fixed) expressions and do not carry their own original meaning within those expressions. Here are some frequently used expressions grouped according to the preposition included in them. Whenever possible they center around a common theme.

À idioms

Here are several groups of commonly used idiomatic expressions that include the preposition **à** or the contracted form **au.**

Expressions of time

à bientôt	*see you soon*
à ce soir	*see you tonight*
à cet après-midi	*see you this afternoon*
à demain	*see you tomorrow*
à l'avenir	*in the future*
à l'heure	*on time*
à la fois	*at the same time*
à plus tard	*see you later*
à samedi	*see you Saturday*
à temps	*in time*
à tout à l'heure	*see you in a while*
au printemps	*in (the) spring*
au revoir	*good-bye*

Je dois partir. **À ce soir!**	*I have to leave. **See you tonight!***
Tu arrives juste **à temps** pour manger.	*You're getting here just **in time** to eat.*
À l'avenir, tâche de faire ton travail!	***In the future,** try to do your work!*
Tu écris et tu écoutes **à la fois?**	*You're writing and listening **at the same time?***

Expressions of direction

à côté de	*next to*
à deux kilomètres d'ici	*two kilometers from here*
à droite de	*to the right of*
à gauche de	*to the left of*
à la fin de	*at the end of* (with time)
à la page...	*on page . . .*
à travers	*across*
à un mètre de hauteur	*one meter up*
au bas de	*at the bottom of*
au bout de	*at the end of* (with distance)
au coin de	*at the corner of*
au fond de	*at the bottom of*
au milieu de	*in the middle of*
au pied de	*at the foot of*
au sommet de	*at the top/summit of*
au-dessous de	*beneath/below*
au-dessus de	*on top of/above*
loin de	*far from*
près de	*near*

À **la fin** de l'histoire, tout est bien.	*At **the end** of the story, all is well.*
Le bistrot est **au coin de** la rue.	*The bistro is **at the corner of** the street.*
La poste est **au bout de** l'avenue.	*The post office is **at the end of** the avenue.*
Ma bague est tombée **au fond du** lac.	*My ring fell **to the bottom of** the lake.*

Expressions of place

à l'école	*at school*
à l'étranger	*abroad*
à la campagne	*in the country*
à la maison	*at home*
à la montagne	*in the mountains*
à la plage	*at the beach*

Un chalet **à la montagne**, c'est chouette!	*A cabin **in the mountains**, that's great!*
Elle fait un voyage **à l'étranger**.	*She is traveling **abroad**.*

Here are some additional common prepositional phrases:

à cause de	*because of*
à haute voix	*aloud/out loud*
à l'aide!	*Help!*
à l'improviste	*unexpectedly*
à la longue	*in the long run*
à la rigueur	*if need be*
à peine	*barely*
à perte de vue	*as far as you can see*
à propos de	*concerning/about*
à voix basse	*in a low voice*
au contraire	*on the contrary*
au lieu de	*instead of*
au maximum	*to the maximum/at most*
au secours!	*help! to the rescue!*

Un incendie! **À l'aide!** (**Au secours!**)	*Fire! **Help!***
J'ai **à peine** pu finir.	*I could **barely** finish.*
Étudie **au lieu de** jouer!	*Study **instead of** playing!*

Exercise 75

Complete each sentence with an appropriate prepositional phrase.

1. Je ne suis pas parfaite. _____ je fais pas mal de fautes.

2. Fais ton travail _____ t'amuser.

3. C'est _____ que je suis punie.

4. Mon oncle est arrivé _____. Quelle surprise!

5. La station-service n'est pas à droite. Elle est _____.

6. L'eau est si claire qu'on peut voir _____ de l'océan.

7. Tu es venue juste _____ pour me voir courir.

8. Il faut lire _____ pour qu'on entende.

9. Je ne crois pas pouvoir chanter. _____ je simulerai.

10. Si tu es malade, reste _____!

11. Je dois partir. _____!

12. Il revient de France. Il a été _____ pendant très longtemps.

13. _____ il faudra faire attention de ne pas refaire cette erreur.

14. Tu peux écouter la radio et regarder la télé _____?

15. J'ai _____ assez d'argent pour payer le cinéma.

De idioms

Here are several groups of commonly used idiomatic expressions that include the preposition **de/d'** or the contracted form **du**.

Expressions of time and frequency

d'abord	*(at) first*
de bonne heure	*early*
de jour	*by day*
de jour en jour	*from day to day*
de nouveau	*again*
de nuit	*by night*
de plus en plus	*more and more*
de temps en temps	*from time to time*

D'abord je vais faire les courses.	***First**, I am going to do the shopping.*
Tu es **de nouveau** en retard.	*You are late **again**.*
De nuit je ne peux rien voir.	*At **night** I can't see anything.*

Musical instruments following the verb *jouer*

de l'orgue	*organ*
de la flûte	*flute*
de la guitare	*guitar*
de la trompette	*trumpet*
du piano	*piano*
du saxophone	*saxophone*
du violon	*violin*
du violoncelle	*cello*

Je joue **du piano**.	*I play **the piano**.*
Louis Armstrong jouait **de la trompette**.	*Louis Armstrong played **the trumpet**.*

Other frequently used expressions with **de** are:

de bon appétit	*with a good appetite*
de bon cœur	*gladly*
de bonheur	*from happiness*
de fatigue	*from fatigue*
de grâce	*for heaven's sake*
de large	*wide*
de long	*long*
de long en large	*back and forth*
de peur	*from fear*
de rien	*you're welcome*
de rigueur	*compulsory/necessary*

Je mange toujours **de bon appétit**.	*I always eat **with a good appetite**.*
Merci, madame. —**De rien**, monsieur!	*Thank you, ma'am. —**You're welcome**, sir!*
De grâce, ne vous blessez pas!	***For heaven's sake**, don't hurt yourself!*

Exercise 76

Complete each sentence with a phrase from the following list: **de grâce, de rien, de bon cœur, du violon, d'abord, de rigueur, de la trompette, de long, de jour, de fatigue.**

1. J'aime les instruments à corde. Alors j'apprends à jouer _____.

2. Je travaille depuis hier. Je tombe _____.

3. Je veux bien t'accompagner. Mais _____ laisse-moi finir de manger.

4. La cravate est _____ au bureau.

5. J'adore entendre Louis Armstrong jouer _____.

6. Ce bateau fait trente pieds _____.

7. Je ne peux pas dormir ni _____ ni de nuit.

8. Je te remercie d'être venu. _____! C'est un plaisir.

9. Moi, je rends toujours service _____.

10. _____, ne me donnez plus de dessert. Je vais éclater.

Exercise 77

Complete each sentence with the appropriate prepositional phrase from the list below:

de rien	de plus en plus	à voix basse
à droite	à travers	au lieu de
à l'heure	à peine	à temps
de bon cœur	à propos	à la montagne
au bas	à la fois	à l'improviste
à la fin	de bon appétit	à perte de vue
au contraire	d'abord	au revoir
à la maison	au bout	de l'orgue
au fond		

1. Je comprends _____ de mots français.

2. Est-ce que la poste est _____ après le café?

3. Si tu pars maintenant, tu peux encore arriver _____.

4. Merci madame! — _____, monsieur.

5. Tu peux me rendre ce service? — _____, chéri!

6. Signe ton nom _____ de cette lettre.

7. Où est-ce que j'écris le numéro? — _____ de la page.

8. Ma cousine est arrivée _____ sans s'annoncer.

9. Je commence à jouer _____ pour mon église.

10. Parle _____. Le bébé dort.

11. Reste _____ puisque tu es malade.

12. Il faut s'amuser quelquefois _____ travailler.

13. J'ai très faim. Je vais manger _____.

14. Tu peux sortir mais _____ il faut laver la vaisselle.

15. Cet hiver on va _____ faire du ski.

16. Il a fallu passer _____ les Alpes pour arriver en Italie.

17. Je peux chanter et danser _____.

18. Tu veux manger? J'ai _____ commencé le rôti.

19. Il ne m'a rien dit _____ de l'accident.

20. J'ai reçu mon passeport _____ pour mon voyage.

Exercise 78

Translate the following sentences into English to recreate the adventures of a couple in the Alps.

1. De temps en temps, mon époux est très casse-cou.

_____

2. L'an dernier nous sommes allés dans les Alpes où l'alpinisme est de rigueur.

_____

3. D'abord j'ai participé de bon cœur.

_____

4. À la longue je me suis fatiguée de marcher.

_____

5. Je dois dire que la vue sur la plaine est très belle de jour.

_____

6. Mais quand j'ai vu Henri arriver au sommet de la montagne, j'ai tremblé de peur.

_____

7. Je marchais de long en large parce que j'étais nerveuse.

_____

8. Il a planté un grand drapeau de deux mètres de long sur deux mètres de large.

_____

9. Il était à cinq cents mètres de hauteur.

_____

10. Il n'était pas fatigué du tout, lui; au contraire il était plein d'énergie.

_____

29

Conjunctions

Conjunctions are words such as *and, or,* and *however.* They are used to connect ideas from one sentence to the next as well as from one clause to the next within a sentence.

Coordinating conjunctions

These are used to join groups of words and make transitions.

ainsi	*thus*
donc	*so/then*
et	*and*
mais	*but*
ou	*or*
par contre	*on the other hand*
pourtant	*however*
surtout	*especially*

J'aime celui-ci, **mais** pas l'autre.	*I like this one, **but** not the other one.*
Tu n'aimes pas cette couleur?	*You don't like this color?*
Pourtant elle te va bien.	***However,** it looks good on you.*

Exercise 79

Choose the conjunction from the list which makes the most sense in each sentence.

surtout   et   par contre   ou   pourtant

1. Sa mère est très gentille; _____ son père est sévère.

2. Toi _____ moi, nous allons à la fête ensemble.

3. Je ne sais pas si je dois tourner à droite _____ à gauche ici.

4. Denise n'est pas là? _____ c'est la bonne adresse!

5. J'adore les fêtes, _____ chez une bonne copine.

Subordinating conjunctions

These are used to join clauses in a sentence. Each clause has its own subject and verb.

alors que	*while/when/whereas*
aussitôt que	*as soon as*
bien que	*although* (+ subjunctive)
car	*for*
comme	*like/as*
dès que	*as soon as*
lorsque	*when*
malgré que	*although* (+ subjunctive)
parce que	*because*
pendant que	*while*
puisque	*since*
quand	*when*
quoique	*although* (+ subjunctive); *whatever* (+ subjunctive)
tandis que	*while* (contrast)

Je travaille toute la journée **tandis que** toi, tu t'amuses.	*I work all day long **while** you are having fun.*
Je reste à la maison **parce que** je suis malade.	*I stay at home **because** I am sick.*
Quoique je fasse, tu n'es pas content!	***Whatever** I do, you are not happy!*

Since several subordinating conjunctions require use of the subjunctive in the dependent clause, see the subjunctive mode and tenses in Chapter 35.

Exercise 80

Write the French conjunction of similar or identical meaning to the one in italics. Then translate each sentence into English.

1. La grammaire est difficile pour toi *quoique* tu étudies beaucoup. _____

_____

2. Va dormir *aussitôt que* tu arriveras. _____

_____

3. Je vais t'aider à apprendre le français *puisque* je le parle bien. _____

_____

4. *Lorsque* tu parleras bien, tu viendras en France avec moi. _____

_____

5. Je fais la cuisine *tandis que* tu regardes la télé _____

_____

6. *Quand* je suis fatigué, je vais dormir. _____

_____

7. Je rentre à la maison *car* il est tard. _____

_____

8. *Dès que* tu m'aideras, je finirai l'exercice. _____

_____

9. Tu joues toujours *pendant que* ton frère travaille. _____

_____

10. Tu réussis à tes examens *bien qu*'ils soient difficiles. _____

_____

Conjunctions derived from prepositions

Many conjunctions are composed of a preposition followed by *que*.

Prepositions		Conjunctions	English
après	*after*	après que	*after*
avant	*before*	avant que (+ subjunctive)	*before*

de peur de	*for fear of*	de peur que (+ subjunctive)	*for fear that*
jusqu'à	*until*	jusqu'à ce que (+ subjunctive)	*until*
pendant	*while*	pendant que	*while*
pour	*for*	pour que (+ subjunctive)	*so that/in order that*
sans	*without*	sans que (+ subjunctive)	*without*

Je reste au bureau **jusqu'à** 7 heures.   *I'm staying at the office **until** 7 o'clock.*

Reste là-bas **jusqu'à ce que** j'arrive!   *Stay there **until** I arrive!*

Since several of the above-listed conjunctions require use of the subjunctive in the dependent clause, see the subjunctive mode and tenses in Chapter 35.

Exercise 81

Decide what is needed in each sentence: the preposition or the conjunction.

1. J'ai un système d'alarme à la maison _____ voleurs. (de peur des, de peur que)

2. Je ne veux pas de maison _____ alarme. (sans, sans que)

3. _____ l'orage est passé, on ira dehors. (après, après que)

4. J'attendrai _____ tu reviennes. (jusqu'à, jusqu'à ce que)

5. Je te donne de l'argent _____ les provisions. (pour, pour que)

6. _____ ton absence, moi, je fais le ménage. (pendant, pendant que)

7. Il faut préparer les hors-d'œuvre _____ l'arrivée des invités. (avant, avant que)

8. Cette table n'est pas jolie _____ chandelles. (sans, sans que)

9. Je préfère que tu restes à la maison _____ tu te perdes. (de peur de, de peur que)

10. Finissons les préparatifs _____ tout soit prêt! (pour, pour que)

11. Il me faut un stylo rouge _____ corriger ces fautes. (pour, pour que)

12. Je vais laver la vaisselle _____ tu passes l'aspirateur. (pendant, pendant que)

13. Je prends vite une douche _____ ils n'arrivent. (avant, avant qu')

14. _____ le dîner, on boit un cognac. (après, après que)

15. Je resterai ici _____ 11 heures. (jusqu'à, jusqu'à ce que)

Review 8

Exercise 82

Pierre parle à sa copine Corinne avant de partir en voyage. *Pierre speaks to his friend Corinne before leaving on a trip.* In the following conversation between Pierre and Corinne, restore all prepositions and conjunctions that have been omitted. Choose them from the following list:

mais	à	puisque	surtout	et	pour
sur	de	pourtant	pendant	pour que	

1. *Pierre:* Salut Corinne. Ça va? Quoi _____ neuf?

2. *Corinne:* Ça va bien, merci. _____ toi?

3. *Pierre:* La vie est super! Je vais _____ Paris demain.

4. *Corinne:* Quelle chance! Tu pars _____ combien de temps?

5. *Pierre:* Je reste deux mois pour étudier. _____ après, je vais passer quelques jours à Èze.

6. *Corinne:* Èze est _____ la Côte d'Azur, non?

7. *Pierre:* Oui, c'est ça! C'est bien connu. _____ c'est tout petit.

8. *Corinne:* Tu prendras beaucoup de photos _____ ton voyage.

9. *Pierre:* Bien sûr! Et _____ tu es ma meilleure amie, je t'apporterai une tour Eiffel miniature.

10. *Corinne:* C'est bien sympa. Envoie-moi _____ de belles photos _____ je puisse partager tes aventures.

Exercise 83

Corinne parle à sa copine après le retour de Pierre. *Corinne is talking to her girlfriend after Pierre's return.* Complete each French sentence to provide a translation of the corresponding English sentence.

1. This gift is *for me.*

   Ce cadeau est _____.

2. My friend brought it back *from Paris*.

   Mon ami l'a rapporté _____.

3. He was there *during* the month of July.

   Il y était _____ le mois de juillet.

4. I was very lonely *without him*.

   J'étais très seule _____.

5. He was there *for* his French studies.

   Il y était _____ ses études de français.

6. *However*, he spoke it well already.

   _____, il le parlait déjà bien.

7. *Thanks to* his good grades, he got a scholarship.

   _____ ses bonnes notes, il a eu une bourse.

8. *So* he took classes at the Sorbonne.

   _____ il a suivi des cours à la Sorbonne.

9. His apartment was *close to* the Sorbonne.

   Son appartement était _____ la Sorbonne.

10. My days were long *until* his return.

    Mes journées étaient longues _____ son retour.

Part 9

Basic Verbal Structures

30

The Present Participle, Present Tense, and Imperative

French verbs that have regular present-tense conjugations can be classified into three groups according to the endings of their infinitive form.

> parler (*to speak*)
> finir (*to finish*)
> vendre (*to sell*)

In English, the infinitive form of the verb is preceded by *to*. In French, the infinitive form is identified by its ending (usually **-er**, **-ir**, or **-re**).

The infinitive

The infinitive form of a verb must be used after prepositions (with the exception of **après**, which is followed by a past infinitive; see Chapter 34). The infinitive must also be used after conjugated verb forms.

Use the infinitive form of the verb:

- after prepositions regardless of the structure that follows in the English equivalent.

Je chante **pour exprimer** ma joie.	*I sing **to express** my joy.*
Je le ferai **sans attendre** un moment de plus.	*I will do it **without waiting** a moment longer.*

- after conjugated verb forms.

J'aime **danser**.	*I like to dance.*
Nous **allons manger**.	*We are going to eat.*

- after the conjugated form of **faire** to express that one is *having something done*.

Elle **fait réparer** le toit.	*She **is having** the roof **repaired**.*
Je **fais bâtir** une maison.	*I **am having** a house **built**.*
Il me **fait descendre** l'escalier.	*He **is having** me **go down** the stairs.*

The present participle

The present participle, or **-ant** form, of French verbs is translated by the English *-ing* form. The preposition **en** (*while, on, upon, by, in, when*) governs the present participle form of French verbs. The preposition **en** may however be omitted while still implied.

The present participle of all French verbs ends in **-ant**. The stem is obtained by replacing the **-ons** ending of the **nous** form of the present indicative with **-ant**.

(nous) **parl**ons	**parl**ant
(nous) **finiss**ons	**finiss**ant
(nous) **vend**ons	**vend**ant
(nous) **fais**ons	**fais**ant

Il prend des risques **en plongeant** si profondément.	*He takes risks **by diving** so deep.*
En entendant les nouvelles, elle s'est évanouie.	*Upon hearing the news, she fainted.*
En voyant l'accident, elle a eu un choc.	*Upon seeing the accident, she got a shock.*
Brûlant de fièvre, il a appelé l'ambulance.	*Burning up with fever, he called the ambulance.*

Only the following verbs have irregular present participles:

être: étant (*being*)
avoir: ayant (*having*)
savoir: sachant (*knowing*)

Exercise 84

Complete the following sentences with the present participle of the verb in parentheses. Then translate each sentence into English.

1. On réussit dans la vie en _____ dans ses efforts. (persister)

_____

2. On ne réussit pas en _____ paresseux. (être)

_____

3. C'est en _____ qu'on fait des progrès. (pratiquer)

_____

4. En _____, je me suis rendu compte que j'avais tort. (réfléchir)

_____

5. _____ à toi, j'étais émue. (penser)

_____

6. Il est tombé en _____ à bicyclette. (rouler)

_____

7. _____ beaucoup de patience, je suis bon professeur. (avoir)

_____

8. Je ne fais jamais mes devoirs en _____ la télé. (regarder)

_____

9. J'ai vu Suzie en _____ vers la boulangerie ce matin. (marcher)

_____

10. En _____ le bus, nous bavardons. (attendre)

_____

11. En _____ devant le parc, j'ai rencontré une copine. (passer)

_____

12. En _____ silencieux, on ne dérange pas les gens. (rester)

_____

13. En _____ attention, on évite les accidents. (faire)

_____

14. En _____ bien ses amis, on montre son bon sens. (choisir)

_____

15. En _____ être d'accord, il est hypocrite. (prétendre)

_____

16. On ne gagne pas sa vie en _____. (dormir)

_____

17. L'appétit vient en _____. (manger)

_____

18. C'est en _____ qu'on devient forgeron. (forger)

_____

19. C'est en _____ qu'on apprend. (enseigner)

_____

20. C'est en _____ qu'on devient voyageur. (voyager)

_____

The present tense

The present tense is used to tell what is happening or what happens at the present moment or habitually. You conjugate a regular verb in the present tense by using its stem (obtained by dropping the last two letters from the infinitive form) and the appropriate ending for that group of words.

	-er endings	*-ir* endings	*-re* endings
je	-e	-is	-s
tu	-es	-is	-s
il/elle/on	-e	-it	(stem)
nous	-ons	-issons	-ons
vous	-ez	-issez	-ez
ils/elles	-ent	-issent	-ent

J'étudie le français en ce moment.   *I **am studying** French right now.*
D'habitude je **finis** mon travail.   *Usually I **finish** my work.*
Elle **vend** sa maison.   *She **is selling** her house.*

The imperative

These forms serve to give instructions or orders. They are the same forms as the **tu, nous,** and **vous** forms of the present tense.

Parle plus fort!   *Speak louder!* (to a familiar person)

Note that for **-er** verbs only, this ending is **-e** instead of **-es.**

Fin**issez!**   *Finish!* (to a person formally or to several people)

Vend**ons!**   *Let's sell!*

Exercise 85

Identify the infinitive form by indicating INF, the imperative form by indicating IMP, and the conjugated present tense form by indicating CP. Then translate each verb into English.

1. choisir _____

2. parler _____

3. nous parlons _____

4. Finissez! _____

5. finir _____

6. on parle _____

7. tu finis _____

8. Étudie! _____

9. ils parlent _____

10. étudier _____

11. ils finissent _____

12. Parle! _____

13. je parle _____

14. elle vend _____

15. Vendez! _____

Commonly used regular -er verbs

The great majority of French verbs fall into the category of regular -er verbs. Here is a list of typical -er verbs:

accompagner	*to accompany*
aider	*to help*
aimer	*to like/love*
ajouter	*to add*
apporter	*to bring*
bavarder	*to chat*
briller	*to shine*
brosser	*to brush*
cacher	*to hide*
cesser	*to cease*
chanter	*to sing*
chercher	*to look for*
commander	*to order*
compter	*to count*
coûter	*to cost*
danser	*to dance*
déjeuner	*to have lunch*
demander	*to ask*
désirer	*to desire*
dîner	*to have dinner*
donner	*to give*
écouter	*to listen*
embrasser	*to kiss*
entrer	*to enter*
épouser	*to marry*
étudier	*to study*
expliquer	*to explain*
féliciter	*to congratulate*
fermer	*to close*
jouer	*to play*
laver	*to wash*
manquer	*to miss*
marcher	*to walk*
mériter	*to deserve*

monter	*to go up*
montrer	*to show*
oublier	*to forget*
pardonner	*to forgive*
parler	*to speak*
passer	*to pass by*
peigner	*to comb*
penser	*to think*
porter	*to carry*
présenter	*to present*
prêter	*to lend*
quitter	*to leave*
raconter	*to tell*
regretter	*to regret*
remercier	*to thank*
rencontrer	*to meet*
rester	*to stay*
souhaiter	*to wish*
téléphoner	*to call*
terminer	*to finish*
tomber	*to fall*
travailler	*to work*
tromper	*to deceive*
trouver	*to find*

All regular -er verbs have the same pattern of conjugation. The stem of the verb is obtained by removing the -er ending of the infinitive verb. The conjugated form of the verb is obtained by adding the appropriate ending to this stem.

fermer/ferm

je ferme	*I close/I am closing*
tu fermes	*you close/you are closing (fam.)*
il/elle/on ferme	*he, she, one closes/he, she, one is closing*
nous fermons	*we close/we are closing*
vous fermez	*you close/you are closing (form. or pl)*
ils/elles ferment	*they close/they are closing*
Ferme!	*Close! (to a familiar person)*
Fermez!	*Close! (to one person formally or to several people)*
Fermons!	*Let's close!*

Exercise 86

Write all conjugated forms for the following -er verbs in the present tense. Use the stem of the verb in bold print and add the appropriate ending.

1. **présenter**

je _____

tu _____

il/elle/on _____

nous _____

vous _____

ils/elles _____

2. **oublier**

j' _____

tu _____

il/elle/on _____

nous _____

vous _____

ils/elles _____

Exercise 87

Add the correct endings to the stem of each -er verb; then translate each phrase into English.

1. tu chant_____

2. je parl_____

3. nous écout_____

4. vous cherch_____

5. on port_____

6. ils apport_____

7. j'ador_____

8. elles rest_____

9. Paul dans_____

10. mes parents arriv_____

11. Écout_____, Marie! _____

12. Regard_____, mes enfants! _____

13. Chers amis, félicit_____ les mariés! _____

14. Embrass_____-vous! _____

15. Dîn_____, toi et moi, Paul! _____

Commonly used regular *-ir* verbs

Here is a list of commonly used -ir verbs.

applaudir	*to applaud*
bâtir	*to build*
choisir	*to choose*
désobéir	*to disobey*
finir	*to finish*
grandir	*to grow*
guérir	*to heal*
nourrir	*to nourish*
obéir	*to obey*
punir	*to punish*
ravir	*to delight*
réfléchir	*to reflect/think*
remplir	*to fill (out)*
réussir	*to succeed*
rougir	*to blush*
saisir	*to seize*

All regular **-ir** verbs have the same pattern of conjugation. The stem of the verb is obtained by removing the **-ir** ending of the infinitive verb. The conjugated form of the verb is obtained by adding the appropriate ending for each subject to that stem.

obéir/obé	
j'obéis	*I obey/I am obeying*
tu obéis	*you obey/you are obeying (fam.)*
il/elle/on obéit	*he, she, one obeys/he, she, one is obeying*
nous obéissons	*we obey/we are obeying*
vous obéissez	*you obey/you are obeying (form. or pl)*
ils, elles obéissent	*they obey/they are obeying*
Obéis!	*Obey!* (to a familiar person)
Obéissez!	*Obey!* (to one person formally or to several people)
Obéissons!	*Let's obey!*

Exercise 88

Write all conjugated forms for the following -ir verbs in the present tense. Use the stem of the verb in bold print and add the appropriate ending.

1. **chois**ir

je _____

tu _____

il/elle/on _____

nous _____

vous _____

ils/elles _____

2. **fin**ir

je _____

tu _____

il/elle/on _____

nous _____

vous _____

ils/elles _____

Exercise 89

Add the correct endings to each -ir verb stem; then translate that phrase into English.

1. tu réuss_____

2. je roug_____

3. nous grand_____

4. vous guér_____

5. elle rav_____

6. ils réfléch_____

7. Chois_____ ton métier! _____

8. Mes amis, sais_____ l'occasion! _____

9. Paul, ne roug_____ pas! _____

10. Obéiss_____ à nos parents! _____

Commonly used regular *-re* verbs

Here is a list of commonly used -re verbs.

attendre	*to wait*
défendre	*to defend*
descendre	*to go down*
entendre	*to hear*
perdre	*to lose*
rendre	*to give back*
répondre	*to answer*
vendre	*to sell*

All regular -re verbs have the same pattern of conjugation. Remove the **-re** ending of the infinitive to obtain the stem. Then add the appropriate ending for each subject.

vendre/vend

je vend**s**	*I sell/I am selling*
tu vend**s**	*you sell/you are selling*
il/elle/on vend	*he, she, one sells/ he, she, one is selling*
nous vend**ons**	*we sell/we are selling*
vous vend**ez**	*you sell/you are selling*
ils/elles vend**ent**	*they sell/they are selling*

Attend**s**!	*Wait!* (to a familiar person)
Attend**ez**!	*Wait!* (to one person formally or to several people)
Attend**ons**!	*Let's wait!*

See Chapter 39 for the present-tense conjugations of a number of common irregular verbs.

Exercise 90

Write all conjugated forms for the following -re verbs in the present tense. Use the stem of the verb in bold print and add the appropriate ending.

1. **répond**re

je _____

tu _____

il/elle/on _____

nous _____

vous _____

ils/elles _____

2. **attend**re

j' _____

tu _____

il/elle/on _____

nous _____

vous _____

ils/elles _____

Exercise 91

Add the correct ending to the stem of each -re verb; then translate each phrase into English.

1. tu attend_____

2. je défend_____

3. nous perd_____

4. vous entend_____

5. elle répond_____

6. ils vend_____

7. Descend_____ de l'échelle, Paul! _____

8. Mes amis, ne perd_____ pas patience! _____

9. Luc, répond_____-moi! _____

10. Attend_____ nos copains! _____

31

The Near Future, Simple Future, Future Perfect, and Present Conditional

The near future is used to talk about what is going to happen. Similarly, the simple future talks about what will happen. Both tenses refer to future events. However, the near future is more frequently used in familiar conversation while the simple future is more formal. The future perfect, found less frequently in familiar conversation, is used to say that something will be done by the time something else happens.

The present conditional is used to express wishes such as *I would like . . .*, to make polite requests such as *Could you . . .*, and to draw conclusions based on hypothetical situations such as *I would travel if I had money.*

The near future

The near future (**le futur proche**) is formed by using the conjugated form of the verb **aller** and an infinitive verb form.

je vais déjeuner	*je vais réussir*	*je vais vendre*
I am going to eat lunch	*I am going to succeed*	*I am going to sell*
tu vas déjeuner	tu vas réussir	tu vas vendre
il/elle/on va déjeuner	il/elle/on va réussir	il/elle/on va vendre
nous allons déjeuner	nous allons réussir	nous allons vendre
vous allez déjeuner	vous allez réussir	vous allez vendre
ils/elles vont déjeuner	ils/elles vont réussir	ils/elles vont vendre

Exercise 92

Write the *near future* of the verb in the person indicated by the subject pronoun.

1. je (regarder) _____

2. vous (punir) _____

3. on (entendre) _____

4. nous (danser) _____

5. tu (chercher) _____

6. elles (choisir) _____

7. ils (attendre) _____

8. je (répondre) _____

9. elle (rougir) _____

10. nous (écouter) _____

11. je (faire) _____

12. tu (apprendre) _____

13. vous (mettre) _____

14. ils (être) _____

15. on (avoir) _____

The simple future

The simple future tense (**le futur simple**) is formed by adding the endings **-ai, -as, -a, -ons, -ez, -ont** to the infinitive form of a verb. If the infinitive verb ends in **-e,** drop the final **-e** before adding the appropriate ending.

parler	*finir*	*vendre*
je parlerai	je finirai	je vendrai
I will speak	*I will finish*	*I will sell*
tu parleras	tu finiras	tu vendras
il/elle/on parlera	il/elle/on finira	il/elle/on vendra
nous parlerons	nous finirons	nous vendrons
vous parlerez	vous finirez	vous vendrez
ils/elles parleront	ils/elles finiront	ils/elles vendront

The future tense, or **futur simple,** in French expresses future time as it does in English. In addition, it is used after **quand/lorsque** (*when*) or **dès que/aussitôt que** (*as soon as*) when the verb that follows refers to the future. (Note that in English the present tense is required in this clause.)

Je te parlerai **dès que je rentrerai.**   *I will speak to you **as soon as I come home.***

See Chapter 39 for the future stems of a number of common irregular verbs.

Write the *simple future* of the verb in the person indicated by the pronoun.

1. *I will bring*   j' (apporter) _____
2. *you will prefer* vous (préférer) _____
3. *one will defend* on (défendre) _____
4. *we will count*   nous (compter) _____
5. *you will look for* tu (chercher) _____
6. *they will choose* elles (choisir) _____
7. *they will wait*   ils (attendre) _____
8. *I will answer*   je (répondre) _____
9. *she will blush*   elle (rougir) _____
10. *we will comb*   nous (peigner) _____
11. *you will succeed* tu (réussir) _____
12. *they will think*   ils (penser) _____
13. *she will come*   elle (venir) _____
14. *I will wash*   je (laver) _____
15. *we will take*   nous (prendre) _____
16. *you will study*   vous (étudier) _____
17. *he will decide*   il (décider) _____
18. *she will please*   elle (plaire) _____
19. *they will forbid* ils (défendre) _____
20. *I will laugh*   je (rire) _____

The future perfect

The future perfect (or **futur antérieur**) is used to express that something will have happened before another action occurs in the future. It is often found before the terms **quand, lorsque, dès que,** and **aussitôt que.**

J'aurai fini mes devoirs quand tu rentreras à la maison.

I will have finished my homework when you come home.

The future perfect consists of the conjugated future form of the helping (auxiliary) verb **avoir** or **être** plus the past participle of the verb (see Chapter 32). The past participle of regular verbs is formed by adding **-é** for **-er** verbs, **-i** for **-ir** verbs, and **-u** for **-re** verbs to the stem of the verb.

j'aurai lavé	*je serai descendu(e)*
I will have washed	*I will have come down*
tu auras lavé	tu seras descendu(e)
il/elle/on aura lavé	il/elle/on sera descendu(e)
nous aurons lavé	nous serons descendus (es)
vous aurez lavé	vous serez descendu (e, s, es)
ils/elles auront lavé	ils/elles seront descendus (es)

For **avoir** verbs, there is agreement of the past participle only in the presence of a preceding direct object. In that case, the past participle agrees with the preceding direct object in gender and number. For further explanation, see Chapter 32.

For verbs conjugated with **être**, the past participle agrees in gender and number with the subject of the verb. For further explanation, see Chapter 32.

Exercise 94

Change each verb from the future to the future perfect (**futur antérieur**).

1. il répondra _____
2. nous accompagnerons _____
3. tu saisiras _____
4. vous bâtirez _____
5. je commanderai _____
6. ils ajouteront _____
7. on présentera _____
8. je guérirai _____
9. cela ravira _____
10. je chanterai _____
11. tu arriveras _____

12. elle naîtra _____

13. il mourra _____

14. nous irons _____

15. vous retournerez _____

The present conditional

The present conditional (or **présent du conditionnel**) is used to express what one would do, given certain circumstances. The present conditional is conjugated by adding the endings **-ais, -ais, -ait, -ions, -iez, -aient** to the infinitive form of the verb. If the infinitive form ends in **-e**, the final **-e** is dropped before adding the appropriate ending.

parler	*finir*	*vendre*
je parlerais	je finirais	je vendrais
I would speak	*I would finish*	*I would sell*
tu parlerais	tu finirais	tu vendrais
il/elle/on parlerait	il/elle/on finirait	il/elle/on vendrait
nous parlerions	nous finirions	nous vendrions
vous parleriez	vous finiriez	vous vendriez
ils/elles parleraient	ils/elles finiraient	ils/elles vendraient

Verbs that have irregular stems in the future tense have the same irregular stems for the conditional. See Chapter 39.

Exercise 95

Write the conditional form of the verb in the person indicated by the pronoun.

1. *I would chat*   je (bavarder) _____

2. *you would hide*   vous (cacher) _____

3. *one would hear*   on (entendre) _____

4. *we would feed*   nous (nourrir) _____

5. *you would merit*   tu (mériter) _____

6. *they would cease*   elles (cesser) _____

7. *they would wait*   ils (attendre) _____

8. *I would come down*   je (descendre) _____

9. *she would think over*   elle (réfléchir) _____

10. *we would give back*   nous (rendre) _____

11. *she would give*   elle (donner) _____

12. *I would say*   je (dire) _____

13. *they would write*   ils (écrire) _____

14. *we would meet*   nous (rencontrer) _____

15. *you would eat*   tu (manger) _____

16. *he would teach*   il (enseigner) _____

17. *you would wait*   vous (attendre) _____

18. *I would learn*   j'(apprendre) _____

19. *they would arrive*   elles (arriver) _____

20. *you would sing*   tu (chanter) _____

Exercise 96

Translate the italicized part of each sentence into French using the appropriate tense and form (near future, simple future, future perfect, or conditional).

1. *I am going to speak* French today.

   _____ le français aujourd'hui. (parler)

2. *I will answer* Grandma's letter tomorrow.

   _____ la lettre de mamie demain. (répondre)

3. Paul, *you are going to wait*, right?

   Paul, _____, n'est-ce pas? (attendre)

4. *You will meet* my friend Lucie today.

   _____ mon amie Lucie aujourd'hui. (faire la

   connaissance de)

5. *She is going to arrive* at 2 P.M.

   _____ à deux heures de l'après-midi. (arriver)

6. *I will introduce you*, Paul.

_____, Paul. (présenter)

7. Look, these people *are going to miss* their train.

Regarde, ces gens _____ leur train. (rater)

8. *They will have waited* in vain.

_____ en vain. (attendre)

9. *They are going to walk* to get home.

_____ pour rentrer. (marcher)

10. Well, *we are going to have lunch* now.

Bon, _____ maintenant. (déjeuner)

11. *We will have finished* by the time she arrives.

_____ quand elle arrivera. (finir)

12. *She is going to be* here soon now.

_____ maintenant. (ne plus tarder)

13. *She would stay* if we asked.

_____ si on lui demandait. (rester)

14. *You would not be sorry.*

_____. (ne pas le regretter)

15. I know for sure *you would like her.*

Je suis sûre qu' _____. (plaire)

32

Imparfait and passé composé

The **imparfait** is used to give background information and describe inherent traits and characteristics of things or people. This tense helps relate actions that were ongoing in the past or that were not completed within the context of the narrative. The **passé composé** is used to relate activities that were completed or occurred at a specific point of time in the narrative.

Imparfait

The **imparfait** is formed by adding **-ais, -ais, -ait, -ions, -iez, -aient** to the stem of the verb. The stem of the **imparfait** verb is obtained by dropping **-ons** from the **nous** form of the present tense.

parler	nous parlons	**parl**
finir	nous finissons	**finiss**
vendre	nous vendons	**vend**

je parlais	*I was speaking, I used to speak*
tu finissais	*you were finishing, you used to finish*
elle vendait	*she was selling, she used to sell*

The only verb for which the stem must be memorized is the irregular verb **être.**

j'<u>é</u>tais	*I was*

Exercise 97

Write the **imparfait** form of the verb in parentheses and translate each phrase into English.

1. vous (rencontrer) _____

2. je (souhaiter) _____

3. ils (perdre) _____

4. j' (épouser) _____

5. tu (remplir) _____

6. nous (applaudir) _____

7. on (regretter) _____

8. vous (remercier) _____

9. elle (tromper) _____

10. nous (quitter) _____

11. tu (brosser) _____

12. j' (expliquer) _____

13. elle (désobéir) _____

14. ils (travailler) _____

15. elle (punir) _____

16. nous (écrire) _____

17. vous (dire) _____

18. elle (choisir) _____

19. tu (tomber) _____

20. je (retourner) _____

Passé composé

The **passé composé** is one of two past tenses frequently used in conversation and in non-literary writing. The other past tense is the **imparfait**; the two have different uses. The **passé composé**, a compound tense, is formed with the present tense of the auxiliary verb **avoir** or **être** plus the past participle of the verb being conjugated.

The **passé composé** is the tense used for

- a completed action that took place at a specific point in time or for an action that occurred a specific number of times.
- a succession of completed past actions.

The past participle of regular verbs is formed by adding, to the stem of the verb -**é** for -**er** verbs, -**i** for -**ir** verbs, and -**u** for -**re** verbs.

fermer	fermé
finir	fini
attendre	attendu

In the **passé composé** most French verbs are conjugated with the auxiliary verb **avoir.** Only the form of **avoir** changes throughout the conjugation. The past participle does not change unless the conjugated verb in the **passé composé** is preceded by a direct object. See the next section in this chapter.

écouter	*obéir*	*attendre*
j'ai écouté	j'ai obéi	j'ai attendu
I listened, I have listened,	*I obeyed, I have*	*I waited, I have*
I did listen	*obeyed, I did obey*	*waited, I did wait*
tu as écouté	tu as obéi	tu as attendu
il/elle/on a écouté	il/elle/on a obéi	il/elle/on a attendu
nous avons écouté	nous avons obéi	nous avons attendu
vous avez écouté	vous avez obéi	vous avez attendu
ils/elles ont écouté	ils/elles ont obéi	ils/elles ont attendu

See Chapter 39 for irregular past participles of some common verbs.

Exercise 98

Write the verb in parentheses in the **passé composé** using the subject given.

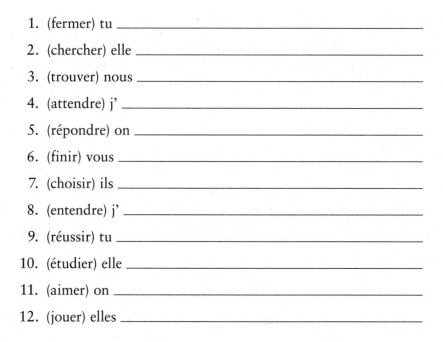

1. (fermer) tu _____

2. (chercher) elle _____

3. (trouver) nous _____

4. (attendre) j' _____

5. (répondre) on _____

6. (finir) vous _____

7. (choisir) ils _____

8. (entendre) j' _____

9. (réussir) tu _____

10. (étudier) elle _____

11. (aimer) on _____

12. (jouer) elles _____

13. (perdre) nous _____

14. (désobéir) tu _____

15. (donner) j' _____

16. (bâtir) vous _____

17. (parler) ils _____

18. (regarder) on _____

19. (téléphoner) nous _____

20. (vendre) j' _____

Agreement of past participle with preceding direct object

The past participle agrees with the direct object of the verb (1) if there is a direct object in the sentence and (2) if the direct object is placed before the verb in the same sentence.

> Annie a acheté **une voiture bleue**.   *Annie bought **a blue car**.*

In the above sentence, the past participle **acheté** does not change. Even though there is a feminine direct object (**une voiture bleue**), it is not placed before the verb.

> **La voiture que** j'ai achetée est bleue.   ***The car (that)** I bought is blue.*

In the above sentence, the past participle changed from **acheté** to **achetée** because **que** is the direct object of the verb **acheter**, replacing the feminine noun **voiture**. The pronoun **que** is the direct object placed before the verb. Therefore the feminine ending -e must be added to the past participle **acheté**.

> La voiture bleue? Je **l'**ai achetée hier.   *The blue car? I bought **it** yesterday.*

In the above sentence, the past participle changed from **acheté** to **achetée** because **l'** is the direct object of the verb **acheter**, replacing the feminine noun **voiture**. The pronoun **l'** is the direct object placed before the verb. Therefore the feminine ending -e must be added to the past participle **acheté**.

Similarly, the ending -s must be added to the past participle to create a masculine plural agreement, and the ending -es must be added to the past participle to create the feminine plural agreement with the preceding direct object. Examples:

> **Les légumes que** j'ai achetés sont frais.   ***The vegetables (that)** I bought are fresh.*
> **Les pêches?** Je **les** ai achetées hier.   ***The peaches?** I bought **them** yesterday.*

Exercise 99

Add the appropriate ending (-e, -s, or -es) to the past participle to make the past participle agree with the preceding direct object, which has been underlined. (Do not add anything to the past participle when the underlined object is masculine singular.)

1. J'aime beaucoup <u>la chanson que</u> tu as **chanté**_____.

2. Je veux voir <u>les meilleurs devoirs que</u> tu as **fait**_____.

3. Montre-moi <u>la jolie plante que</u> tu as **acheté**_____.

4. Le petit chat blanc? Je ne <u>l</u>'ai pas **vu**_____.

5. Les vieux journaux? Je <u>les</u> ai **jeté**_____.

6. La tarte aux fruits? Nous <u>l</u>'avons **mangé**_____.

7. Donne-moi <u>le stylo bleu que</u> je t'ai **prêté**_____.

8. Passe-moi <u>les nouvelles assiettes que</u> j'ai **sorti**_____.

9. Les beaux arbres devant la maison? Oui, je <u>les</u> ai **vu**_____.

10. La carte d'anniversaire? Je <u>l</u>'ai **lu**_____.

Exercise 100

If there is a direct object placed before the verb, underline it, and then add the appropriate ending (-e, -s, or -es) to the past participle when necessary.

1. J'ai **écouté**_____ la radio.

2. Cette musique que tu as **joué**_____ dans la voiture est très belle.

3. Nous avons **entendu**_____ la sonnette.

4. Les films que vous avez **regardé**_____ hier soir sont très vieux.

5. La vieille dame que tu as **aidé**_____ était très aimable.

6. Les exercices de français? Moi, je les ai déjà **fini**_____.

7. Tu as **lu**_____ le même livre que moi.

8. Ils ont **porté**_____ leurs lunettes de soleil.

9. La réponse que tu m'as **donné**_____ est bonne.

10. Tes vêtements? Je les ai **lavé**_____. Ils étaient sales.

Passé composé of être verbs

The following verbs are conjugated with **être**. Note that the past participle of an **être** verb behaves like an adjective. It agrees in gender and number with the subject of the verb. Also note that many of these verbs are easier to remember in pairs as they are often opposites.

aller	*to go*
arriver	*to arrive*
entrer	*to enter*
rentrer	*to come back (in)*
monter	*to go up*
descendre	*to go down/to get off*
rester	*to stay*
sortir	*to go out*
partir	*to leave*
retourner	*to go back*
venir	*to come*
revenir	*to come back*
tomber	*to fall*
devenir	*to become*
naître	*to be born*
mourir	*to die*

aller	*sortir*
je suis allé(e)	je suis sorti(e)
I went, I have gone, I did go	*I went out, I have gone out, I did go out*
tu es allé(e)	tu es sorti(e)
il/on est allé	il/on est sorti
elle est allée	elle est sortie
nous sommes allés/allées	nous sommes sortis/sorties
vous êtes allé/allée/allés/allées	vous êtes sorti/sortie/sortis/sorties
ils sont allés	ils sont sortis
elles sont allées	elles sont sorties

The following verbs conjugated with **être** have irregular past participles:

mourir	**mort**
naître	**né**
venir	**venu**

Exercise 101

Complete each sentence by writing the verb in parentheses in the **passé composé** with the subject given.

1. Elle _____ au cinéma hier soir. (sortir)

2. Tu _____ à l'école, Marie? (aller)

3. On _____ à 9 heures du matin. (arriver)

4. Nous _____ au premier étage. (descendre)

5. Je _____ dans la salle de classe. (entrer)

6. Vous _____ avant la fin du concert, monsieur. (partir)

7. Ils _____ de France il y a un mois. (venir)

8. Tu _____ de ta bicyclette, Sandrine? (tomber)

9. Je _____ avant la nuit. (rentrer)

10. Ils _____ en 1860. (mourir)

11. Monique _____ au parc. (aller)

12. Luc et Marc _____ à la maison. (retourner)

13. Elle _____ le 30 novembre. (naître)

14. Elle _____ très belle. (devenir)

15. Les enfants _____ à l'école. (rester)

Exercise 102

Write the verbs in the **passé composé.** Be sure to make the distinction between **avoir** and **être** verbs.

1. je (brosser) _____

2. tu (finir) _____

3. vous (répondre) _____

4. nous (rencontrer) _____

5. il (tomber) _____

6. elle (arriver) _____

7. on (attendre) _____

8. ils (monter) _____

9. tu (aller) _____

10. nous (sortir) _____

11. j' (oublier) _____

12. on (présenter) _____

13. tu (défendre) _____

14. vous (rougir) _____

15. elle (venir) _____

Verbs conjugated with either *avoir* or *être*

The following verbs are conjugated in the **passé composé** with the auxiliary verb **être** when they do not have a direct object.

monter	Marc est monté en haut.	*Marc went upstairs.*
descendre	Marc est descendu en bas.	*Marc went downstairs.*
rentrer	Marc est rentré.	*Marc went home.*
sortir	Marc est sorti.	*Marc went out.*
passer	Marc est passé.	*Marc came by.*

The same verbs are conjugated with the auxiliary verb **avoir** when they have a direct object. Notice how the meaning of the verb changes when it has a direct object.

monter	Marc a monté la valise en haut.	*Marc took the suitcase upstairs.*
descendre	Marc a descendu la valise en bas.	*Marc took the suitcase downstairs.*
rentrer	Marc a rentré la voiture.	*Marc took the car in.*
sortir	Marc a sorti la poubelle.	*Marc took the garbage can out.*
passer	Marc a passé un examen.	*Marc took an exam.*

Exercise 103

Complete the following sentences in the **passé composé** using the verbs suggested in parentheses.

1. Élise _____ devant notre maison tout à l'heure. (passer)

2. Nous _____ nos gants de la valise car il fait froid. (sortir)

3. Ils _____ ce matin à 9 h. (sortir)

4. Vous _____ une semaine à Paris! (passer)

5. Il _____ très vite du train. (descendre)

6. Nous _____ les marches de l'escalier à toute vitesse. (monter)

7. Dis, Jean, tu _____ la petite table du premier étage? (descendre)

8. Tu _____ la vieille chaise au grenier? (monter)

9. Ils _____ le chien ce matin. (sortir)

10. Elle _____ un bon moment avec ses cousins. (passer)

11. Les nouveaux voisins _____ dire bonjour. (passer)

12. Je/J'_____ le courrier de la boîte aux lettres. (sortir)

13. Nous _____ les pots de fleurs à cause du froid. (rentrer)

14. Voilà! Elle _____ dans l'avion. Elle part. (monter)

15. Les filles _____ très tôt! (rentrer)

Imparfait *and* passé composé

The **passé composé** refers to a completed past action or a succession of past events. It contrasts with the **imparfait** used for ongoing, customary, or habitual actions and descriptive settings. Both tenses may be used in the same sentence.

J'**étais** encore fatigué quand le réveil **a sonné**.	*I was still tired when the alarm clock rang.*
Nous **parlions** des devoirs au moment où tu **as téléphoné**.	*We were talking about homework (at the moment) when you called.*

Exercise 104

Write the following sentences in French using the **passé composé** and the **imparfait** appropriately.

1. He was studying when the teacher came in.

_____

2. She blushed when he spoke.

_____

3. They were speaking French.

_____

4. I used to study a lot.

_____

5. She invited her friend.

_____

6. She kissed her mother.

_____

7. I watched television every day.

_____

8. When you arrived, I was eating dinner.

_____

9. We went up and played cards.

_____

10. We were playing when Lisa called.

_____

33

Imparfait and *conditionnel*

The **imparfait** and **conditionnel** are used concurrently in a sentence to express what would happen (**conditionnel**) if a certain condition were realized (**imparfait**).

> La plante **grandirait** si tu l'**arrosais** tous les jours.

> *The plant **would grow** if you **watered** it every day.*

Two other tenses used concurrently are the pluperfect and past conditional. In this type of sentence, you express what would have happened if a certain condition had been realized in the past. Both tenses are compound tenses requiring a helping (auxiliary) verb and a past participle. In the pluperfect, the helping verb is in the **imparfait**. In the past conditional, the helping verb is in the **conditionnel**.

> La plante **aurait grandi** si tu l'**avais arrosée.**

> *The plant **would have grown** if you **had watered** it.*

Exercise 105

Express the following conditions and results using the combination **imparfait** and **conditionnel**. Use **vous** for *you.*

1. If you met the president, you would not forget that day. (rencontrer le président/oublier ce jour)

_____

2. If you spoke more languages, you would travel more. (parler plus de langues/voyager plus)

_____

3. If you finished now, you would watch television. (finir/regarder la télé)

_____

4. If I asked a question, would you answer? (poser une question/répondre)

_____

5. If we walked a lot, we would lose weight. (marcher/maigrir)

_____

6. If she loved him, she would wait for him. (aimer/l'attendre)

_____

7. If you played against me, I would win. (jouer/gagner)

_____

8. If she listened, she would hear. (écouter/entendre)

_____

9. If I were there, I would explain. (être là/expliquer)

_____

10. If you lost the ball, we would look for it. (perdre/la chercher)

_____

34

The Past Infinitive

The past infinitive is used after doing or having done something, although the English translation may vary. Note the two translations for the following French sentence.

> Après **avoir fait** les courses, nous sommes rentrés.
> *After doing the shopping, we went home.*
> *After we did the shopping, we went home.*

The past infinitive is a verbal construction that consists of the auxiliary verb **avoir** or **être** in its infinitive form followed by a past participle. See Chapter 32 to review which verbs use the auxiliary verb **être** in compound tenses.

The past participle follows the same rules of agreement outlined for **passé composé.** In the following sentence, the past participle agrees with the subject of the verb. Note that the verb **sortir** is in the past infinitive (with the auxiliary **être**).

> **Après être sorties** de la maison, **elles** ont vu que leur voiture n'était plus là.
> *After leaving their house, they saw that their car was no longer there.*

The past participle agrees with the preceding direct object in the following sentence. Note that the verb **chercher** is in the past infinitive (with the auxiliary **avoir**).

Après les avoir cherchées, les garçons ont emmené **les filles** au cinéma.	*After picking them up, the boys took the girls to the movies.*
Elle a regardé les informations **après être rentrée** du travail.	*She watched the news after coming home from work.*
Après avoir gagné le match de foot, ils étaient vraiment fatigués mais heureux.	*After winning the soccer game, they were really tired but happy.*

The past infinitive is also used after adjectives of feeling. In these cases, the subject of the past infinitive is the same as the subject of the verb in the main clause, and the action expressed in the past infinitive occurred before the action expressed in the main verb.

> Je suis **heureux d'avoir fait** votre connaissance.

> *I am happy to have made your acquaintance.*

> Ils sont **désolés d'être arrivés** en retard.

> *They are sorry they arrived late.*

Exercise 106

Complete each French sentence with the *past infinitive* form of the verb in parentheses.

1. After they got home, they ate dinner.

   Après _____, ils ont dîné. (rentrer)

2. After singing, we bowed.

   Après _____, nous avons fait la révérence. (chanter)

3. After winning the prize, she was elated.

   Après _____ le prix, elle était transportée de joie. (gagner)

4. After you heard the news, you ran out.

   Après _____ la nouvelle, tu es parti en courant. (entendre)

5. After they built the school, they got a lot of work.

   Après _____ l'école, ils ont eu beaucoup de travail. (bâtir)

6. He is sad that he lost his job.

   Il est triste d'_____ son emploi. (perdre)

7. We are delighted we gave a good impression.

   Nous sommes enchantés d'_____ une bonne impression. (faire)

8. She is tired after walking so much.

   Elle est fatiguée après _____ autant. (marcher)

9. They are sorry they missed the train.

   Ils sont désolés d'_____ le train. (rater)

10. They are happy they left earlier.

    Elles sont contentes d'_____ plus tôt. (partir)

11. He is surprised that he came in first.

    Il est surpris d'_____ en premier. (arriver)

12. He paid the driver after he got off.

    Il a payé le chauffeur après _____. (descendre)

13. We are disgusted that we made such a big mistake.

    Nous sommes dégoûtés d'_____ une si grosse faute. (faire)

14. She is horrified that she forgot.

    Elle est horrifiée d'_____. (oublier)

15. They are sorry they left before the end.

    Ils sont désolés d'_____ avant la fin. (sortir)

16. After she came home, she went to bed.

    Après _____ à la maison, elle s'est couchée. (rentrer)

17. After they washed the dog, they dried him.

    Après _____ le chien, ils l'ont séché. (laver)

18. After they went out, the boys picked up their friend.

    Après _____, les garçons ont cherché leur copain. (sortir)

19. After she went upstairs, she calmed down.

    Après _____, elle s'est calmée. (monter)

20. I am shocked that I passed the exam.

    Je suis ahurie d'_____ à l'examen. (réussir)

Review 9

Exercise 107

Faites la connaissance de Marie! *Meet Marie!* Translate the following sentences into English.

1. J'adore jouer à la balle avec mes amis.

_____

2. Mais j'aime aussi discuter.

_____

3. Quand je parle, c'est pour exprimer mes pensées.

_____

4. J'essaie de finir un exercice.

_____

5. Le soir j'étudie.

_____

6. Ma copine reste ici pour m'aider.

_____

7. Elle me rend service.

_____

8. Maman fait réparer la voiture.

_____

9. Le mécanicien la fait attendre.

_____

10. Nous dînons à huit heures.

_____

Exercise 108

C'est samedi. *It is Saturday.* Marie accompanies her mother to the hair salon on Saturdays. Translate the italicized parts of each sentence into French. Be sure to change the infinitive form (in parentheses) to the correct conjugated form of the verb.

1. *I accompany* my mother to the hair salon. (accompagner)

    _____ ma mère au salon de coiffure.

2. *We like* having our hair styled weekly. (aimer)

    _____ nous faire coiffer chaque semaine.

3. Yvonne *washes and styles* our hair beautifully. (laver/coiffer)

    Yvonne _____ nos cheveux à merveille.

4. She often *tells* funny stories *while working.* (raconter/travailler)

    _____ souvent des histoires drôles en _____.

5. Mom and I *chat.* (bavarder)

    Maman et moi, _____.

6. Afterward *we go back home.* (rentrer)

    Après, _____.

7. Everybody *admires* our stylish cuts. (admirer)

    Tout le monde _____ nos coupes à la mode.

8. The family *has lunch* at the restaurant. (déjeuner)

    La famille _____ au restaurant.

9. *I* usually *eat* a big salad. (manger)

    Moi, d'habitude, _____ une grande salade.

10. Is this how *you spend* your Saturday? (passer)

    C'est ainsi que _____ votre samedi?

Exercise 109

Une page du journal de Marie. *A page in Marie's diary.* Translate the italicized parts of each sentence into French. Be sure to change the infinitive form (in parentheses) to the correct conjugated form of the verb when necessary.

1. *They are building* a new movie theater in the neighborhood. (bâtir)

    _____ un nouveau cinéma dans le quartier.

2. My friends and I *are waiting* for it to open. (attendre)

   Mes amis et moi, _____ qu'il ouvre.

3. On Saturdays, people *fill* the old movie theater. (remplir)

   Le samedi, les gens _____ le vieux cinéma.

4. That's because our town *is growing*. (grandir)

   C'est parce que notre ville _____.

5. When they finish *building* it, we can *choose* between the two theaters. (bâtir/choisir)

   Quand on finira de le _____, nous pourrons _____

   entre les deux cinémas.

6. *I hear* that it is going to be ready soon. (entendre)

   _____ dire qu'il sera bientôt prêt.

7. My parents *forbid* me to go to the movies. (défendre)

   Mes parents me _____ d'aller au cinéma.

8. If *I disobey*, they are going *to punish* me. (désobéir/punir)

   Si je _____, ils vont me _____.

9. I do not want *to lose* their trust in me. (perdre)

   Je ne veux pas _____ leur confiance en moi.

10. So *while waiting* to be older, I *obey*. (attendre/obéir)

    Alors en _____ d'être plus âgée, j' _____.

Exercise 110

La soirée de Marie. *Marie's evening.* Marie spent some time with Chloé's family last night and tells her mom about it. Write the following sentences in French using the **passé composé** and the **imparfait**.

1. The family was finishing dinner when I arrived. (finir le dîner/arriver)

   _____

2. But Chloé was speaking on the phone when I came in. (parler au téléphone/entrer)

   _____

3. She was speaking French. It was probably her French cousin. (parler français/être sûrement)

   _____

4. She said good-bye to her when she saw me. (dire au revoir/voir)

   _____

5. She invited me to have dessert. (inviter/prendre le dessert)

_____

6. I stayed a little bit. (rester un peu)

_____

7. I even spoke some French with Chloé. (parler français avec Chloé)

_____

8. I spent a nice moment with her. (passer un bon moment)

_____

9. When I left, the family was still at the table. (partir/être à table)

_____

10. I took the bus at 8 P.M. (prendre le bus)

_____

Exercise 111

Marie parle de son frère Marc. _Marie talks about her brother Marc._ Complete each of her sentences with the appropriate form and the appropriate tense of the verb in parentheses (**passé composé, imparfait,** or **conditionnel**) to find out what Marie has to say about her big brother.

1. Avant-hier Marc _____ sa leçon pendant deux heures. (étudier)

2. Moi, j'attendais toujours quand il _____ sa leçon. (terminer)

3. Quand il était petit, il _____ être astronaute. (souhaiter)

4. À l'école il _____ le premier ses devoirs de maths. (finir)

5. Tous les jours, il _____ ses livres d'aéronautique. (lire)

6. Marc _____ à l'examen de physique hier matin. (réussir)

7. S'il était à la maison, je le _____. (féliciter)

8. J'étais ravie quand son prof _____ la nouvelle. (annoncer)

9. Moi, s'il m'aidait, je _____ mon petit exercice d'algèbre. (finir)

10. J'_____, moi aussi, réussir à mon examen demain. (aimer)

Exercise 112

Marie a passé une très bonne soirée au cinéma. *Marie spent a very good evening at the movies.* Fill in each blank with the *past infinitive* form of the verb in parentheses and find out why Marie had such a nice evening.

1. Après _____ très dur toute la semaine, j'ai donné rendez-vous à mon copain Marc à 18 h chez moi. (travailler)

2. J'étais triste de ne pas lui _____ toute la semaine. (parler)

3. Il est arrivé à l'heure. Après _____ quelques moments, nous avons décidé d'aller voir un film. (bavarder)

4. Je suis encore surprise de l' _____ d'aller voir un film romantique. Ce n'est pas son genre. (persuader)

5. En fin de compte, Marc m'a remerciée de lui _____ ce film. Il l'a beaucoup aimé. (conseiller)

6. Nous étions tous les deux contents d' _____ au cinéma à la séance de 19 h. (aller)

7. Nous avons eu le temps d'aller au café. Après _____ du film, nous sommes rentrés en métro. (discuter)

8. Je suis heureuse _____ une si bonne soirée avec Marc. (passer)

Part 10

Other Verbal Structures

35

The Present and Past Subjunctive

The present subjunctive is formed by adding **-e, -es, -e, -ions, -iez, -ent** to the stem of the verb. The stem is obtained by dropping the **-ent** ending of the third-person plural in the present tense.

Ils parlent	**parl**
Ils finissent	**finiss**
Ils vendent	**vend**

parler	*finir*	*vendre*
que je **parle**	que je **finisse**	que je **vende**
that I may speak	*that I may finish*	*that I may sell*
que tu **parles**	que tu **finisses**	que tu **vendes**
qu'il/elle/on **parle**	qu'il/elle/on **finisse**	qu'il/elle/on **vende**
que nous **parlions**	que nous **finissions**	que nous **vendions**
que vous **parliez**	que vous **finissiez**	que vous **vendiez**
qu'ils/elles **parlent**	qu'ils/elles **finissent**	qu'ils/elles **vendent**

Note that subjunctive endings are the same for all verbs except for **avoir** and **être**.

avoir	*être*
que j'**aie**	que je **sois**
that I may have	*that I may be*
que tu **aies**	que tu **sois**
qu'il/elle/on **ait**	qu'il/elle/on **soit**
que nous **ayons**	que nous **soyons**
que vous **ayez**	que vous **soyez**
qu'ils/elles **aient**	qu'ils/elles **soient**

See Chapter 39 for stems and conjugations of other common French verbs that are irregular in the subjunctive.

In contrast with the indicative mood, which indicates facts or certainty, the subjunctive mood (present and past tenses) indicates subjectivity and uncertainty. The subjunctive is found in subordinate clauses starting with **que** and introduced by verbs or adjectives expressing:

feelings	je regrette que, je suis content(e) que,...
advice	je suggère que, je recommande que,...
wishes	je voudrais que, j'aimerais que,...
commands	je veux que, j'ordonne que,...
necessity	il faut que, il est nécessaire que,...
doubt	je doute que, je ne suis pas sûr(e) que,...
uncertainty	il semble que, il n'est pas certain que,...

Je suis triste qu'elle **ait** tant de problèmes.	*I am sad that she has so many problems.*
Je voudrais que tu **sois** plus patient.	*I would like you to be more patient.*
Il faut que je **finisse** mes devoirs.	*I have to finish my homework.*

The subjunctive is also found in subordinate clauses introduced by the following conjunctions:

afin que/pour que	*in order that*
avant que	*before*
bien que/malgré que/quoique	*although*
jusqu'à ce que	*until*
pourvu que	*provided that*
sans que	*without*

Je vous envoie en France **pour que** vous **pratiquiez** le français.	*I am sending you to France so that you will practice French.*
Attendez **jusqu'à ce que** nous vous **trouvions** une famille d'accueil.	*Wait until we find you a host family.*

The present subjunctive

The action of the verb in the present subjunctive (in the subordinate clause) occurs at the same time as, or later than, the action expressed by the verb in the main clause. The subject of the subordinate clause must differ from the subject of the main clause. Note that the English equivalents are sometimes worded differently from the French. The word *that* (**que**) is not always used in English.

Il veut **que tu** vendes ton vieil ordinateur.	*He wants you to sell your old computer.*
Il sera ravi **que tu** obéisses.	*He will be delighted that you obey.*

Exercise 113

Write the present subjunctive forms using the pronoun given.

1. (choisir) que je _____
2. (aimer) que nous _____
3. (rencontrer) que vous _____
4. (rendre) qu'elle _____
5. (être) que tu _____
6. (avoir) qu'on _____
7. (saisir) qu'ils _____
8. (répondre) que je _____
9. (remplir) qu'elles _____
10. (vendre) que tu _____
11. (expliquer) que j' _____
12. (raconter) que vous _____
13. (nourrir) qu'elles _____
14. (souhaiter) qu'on _____
15. (chanter) que nous _____
16. (réfléchir) que je _____
17. (descendre) que nous _____
18. (monter) que tu _____
19. (peigner) que je _____
20. (attendre) qu'on _____

The past subjunctive

The past subjunctive is a compound tense formed with the present subjunctive of the auxiliary verb **avoir** or **être** and the past participle of the verb.

parler	finir	vendre
que j'aie parlé	que j'aie fini	que j'aie vendu
that I spoke	*that I finished*	*that I sold*
que tu aies parlé	que tu aies fini	que tu aies vendu
qu'il/elle/on ait parlé	qu'il/elle/on ait fini	qu'il/elle/on ait vendu
que nous ayons parlé	que nous ayons fini	que nous ayons vendu
que vous ayez parlé	que vous ayez fini	que vous ayez vendu
qu'ils/elles aient parlé	qu'ils/elles aient fini	qu'ils/elles aient vendu

venir

que je sois venu(e)

that I came

que tu sois venu(e)

qu'il/elle/on soit venu(e)

que nous soyons venu(e)s

que vous soyez venu(e)(s)

qu'ils/elles soient venu(e)s

The past subjunctive is used in subordinate clauses following the same expressions as the present subjunctive. It shows that the action or situation in the subordinate clause (after **que**) happened *prior* to the action or situation in the main clause.

Je regrette qu'elle *soit arrivée* en retard.	*I am sorry that she arrived late.*
Il est douteux qu'elle *ait fini* son travail.	*It is doubtful that she finished her work.*

Exercise 114

Write the past subjunctive form of each verb, using the subject provided.

1. Je suis désolé qu'elle _____ sa maison. (vendre)

2. Pourvu qu'il _____, nous le trouverons. (attendre)

3. Je suis contente que tu _____ la bonne réponse. (donner)

4. Elle est en première place bien qu'elle _____ son dernier match. (perdre)

5. Il est incroyable que vous _____ si vite. (guérir)

6. Nous doutons qu'elle _____ à notre lettre. (répondre)

7. Je ne vais pas la laisser partir sans qu'elle _____ son livre. (trouver)

8. Je n'étais pas sûre qu'elle _____. (dîner)

9. Tu regrettes qu'elle _____ avant ton arrivée. (partir)

10. Nous sommes contents qu'il _____ cette jeune fille. (rencontrer)

11. J'ai peur que tu _____. (échouer)

12. Bien qu'elle _____ de l'argent, elle était avare. (obtenir)

13. Malgré que tu _____ en retard, on t'a admis. (être)

14. Il est possible que nous _____ les clefs. (perdre)

15. Il est injuste qu'on vous _____ l'admission. (refuser)

16. Il se peut que vous _____ à cet examen-ci. (réussir)

17. Je suis si triste qu'elle _____ pendant mon absence. (passer)

18. J'aurais mieux aimé qu'ils _____ à l'université. (aller)

19. Je doute qu'elle _____ à l'heure. (arriver)

20. Je suis ravie que nous _____ tout le monde. (rencontrer)

36

Reflexive Verbs and the Passive Voice

In reflexive verbs (including idiomatic reflexives, presented in Chapter 40) the action is performed by the subject on or to itself. These verbs are therefore accompanied by reflexive (object) pronouns.

Se laver (to wash oneself) present indicative and imperative

je **me** lave	*I wash (am washing) myself*
tu **te** laves	*you wash (are washing) yourself*
il/elle/on **se** lave	*he/she/one washes (is washing) himself/herself/oneself*
nous **nous** lavons	*we wash (are washing) ourselves*
vous **vous** lavez	*you wash (are washing) yourself/yourselves*
ils/elles **se** lavent	*they wash (are washing) themselves*
Lave-**toi!**	*Wash yourself!*
Lavons-**nous!**	*Let's wash ourselves!*
Lavez-**vous!**	*Wash yourself/yourselves!*

Note that

- the -e of **me**, **te**, and **se** is dropped before a vowel or a mute **h**; they become **m'**, **t'**, and **s'**.

  Il **s'habille** vite.   *He dresses himself quickly.*

- **-toi** is used instead of **te** in the imperative affirmative of the familiar *you* form.

  Habille-**toi!**   *Dress yourself!*

Agreement of the past participle in reflexive verbs

The verb **être** is always used as the auxiliary verb with reflexive verbs in compound tenses such as the **passé composé**.

Ils **se** <u>sont</u> habillés.   *They dressed (got dressed).*

In compound tenses with reflexive verbs, the past participle agrees in gender and number with the preceding direct object (it is the same person as the subject). In the earlier example, the past participle agrees with the direct object pronoun **se** (same person as **ils**).

The reflexive pronoun (**me, te, se, nous, vous, se**) is the preceding direct object except in sentences where the direct object follows the reflexive verb.

> Ils se sont lavé **la figure**. *They washed their faces.*

In the sentence above, the word **la figure** is the direct object, and **se** has the function of the indirect object. Therefore, the past participle does not agree; it remains masculine singular, or neuter.

Here is a list of commonly used reflexive verbs:

s'amuser	*to have fun, have a good time*
s'appeler	*to be named, called*
s'approcher	*to approach*
s'arrêter	*to stop*
s'asseoir	*to sit (down)*
s'en aller	*to go away*
s'endormir	*to fall asleep*
s'ennuyer	*to get bored*
s'entendre	*to get along*
s'épiler	*to tweeze*
s'habiller	*to get dressed*
se baigner	*to bathe/take a bath/swim*
se brosser les dents	*to brush one's teeth*
se coiffer	*to style/brush one's hair*
se coucher	*to go to bed/lie down*
se dépêcher	*to hurry*
se fâcher	*to get mad/angry*
se laver	*to wash (oneself)*
se lever	*to get up*
se marier	*to get married*
se perdre	*to get lost*
se promener	*to take a walk*
se raser	*to shave*
se rencontrer	*to meet (each other)*
se reposer	*to rest*
se réveiller	*to wake up*

se souvenir de	*to remember*
se taire	*to be quiet/silent*
se tromper	*to make a mistake*

Exercise 115

Conjugate the verb **s'amuser** in the present tense.

1. je _____
2. tu _____
3. il/elle/on _____
4. nous _____
5. vous _____
6. ils/elles _____

Exercise 116

Conjugate the verb **se fâcher** in the future tense (simple future).

1. je _____
2. tu _____
3. il/elle/on _____
4. nous _____
5. vous _____
6. ils/elles _____

Exercise 117

Conjugate the verb **se reposer** in the **imparfait**.

1. je _____
2. tu _____
3. il/elle/on _____
4. nous _____
5. vous _____
6. ils/elles _____

Exercise 118

Conjugate the verb **se promener** in the **passé composé**.

1. je _____

2. tu _____

3. il/elle/on _____

4. nous _____

5. vous _____

6. ils/elles _____

Transitive verbs in nonreflexive or reflexive structures

A transitive verb, in French, is a verb that admits an object, direct or indirect. Any transitive verb can be used reflexively.

Nous promenons **le chien**.	*We walk the dog.*

In the sentence above, **le chien** is the *direct* object.

Nous **nous** promenons.	*We take a walk.*

In the sentence above, **nous** is the *direct* object.

Ils parlent **à des amis**.	*They speak to friends.*

In the sentence above, **à des amis** is the *indirect* object.

Ils **se** parlent.	*They speak to each other.*

In the sentence above, **se** is the *indirect* object.

    Remember to use the auxiliary verb **être** when you conjugate a verb reflexively in a compound tense such as the **passé composé**. Compare the following two sentences; note the use of the auxiliary **avoir** when the verb is used nonreflexively and the use of the auxiliary verb **être** when the same verb is used reflexively.

J'**ai** perdu mes clefs.   *I lost my keys.*
Je **me suis** perdu(e).   *I got lost. (i.e., I lost myself)*

Exercise 119

Translate the following sentences into English, paying attention to whether the verbs are used reflexively or nonreflexively.

1. Nous rencontrons des copines.

_____

2. Nous nous rencontrons au square.

_____

3. Ils perdent toujours leurs affaires.

_____

4. Ils se perdent dans cette grande ville.

_____

5. J'ai épilé les sourcils de ma sœur.

_____

6. Je me suis épilé les sourcils.

_____

7. Maman a couché le bébé.

_____

8. Maman s'est couchée.

_____

9. Le téléphone l'a réveillé.

_____

10. Il s'est réveillé à 8 heures.

_____

11. Un juge les a mariés.

_____

12. Ils se sont mariés devant un juge.

_____

13. Ce clown amusera bien les enfants.

_____

14. Les enfants s'amuseront bien avec ce clown.

_____

15. Rase ta barbe, papa!

_____

16. Papa va se raser.

_____

17. Renée a promené le chien ce matin.

_____

18. Renée s'est promenée ce matin.

_____

19. Jacqueline a baigné le petit Luc.

_____

20. Jacqueline s'est baignée.

_____

The passive voice

In the active voice, the subject performs the action of the verb. In the passive voice, the subject receives the action.

Active voice	Un acteur **raconte** l'histoire.	_An actor tells the story._
Passive voice	L'histoire **est racontée** par un acteur.	_The story is told by an actor._

The passive voice consists of the appropriate form of the verb **être** (in any tense) followed by the past participle of the verb. The past participle agrees in gender and number with the subject of **être**.

Ma maison **a été construite** par un architecte.	_My house was built by an architect._
Les rôles **étaient joués** par des amateurs.	_The roles were performed by amateurs._
Le gâteau **sera coupé** par la mariée.	_The cake will be cut by the bride._

French has several structures that can be used instead of the passive voice. They include active third-person singular verb forms with the subject **on** (*people, we, they, one*), third-person verb forms with the reflexive pronoun **se**, as well as other constructions.

On a annoncé l'heure du départ.	*The departure time was announced.*
L'anglais **se parle** partout.	*English is spoken everywhere.*
Cela me plaît.	*I am pleased/I like that.*

Exercise 120

Translate the following sentences into English.

1. La porte s'ouvre facilement.

_____

2. On prépare ce plat de cette façon.

_____

3. L'apéritif se boit avant le repas.

_____

4. «Bon voyage» se dit dans beaucoup de langues.

_____

5. Ce livre se vend dans toutes les librairies.

_____

6. On casse les œufs pour faire une omelette.

_____

7. L'exercice sera bientôt terminé.

_____

8. Ce président était aimé de tous.

_____

9. Le vrai bonheur se trouve rarement.

_____

10. Ici on parle français.

_____

37

Negations

A negative statement may consist of a single word such as **non** (*no*), **jamais** (*never*), **rien** (*nothing*) or a short phrase such as **pas ici** (*not here*), **jamais plus** (*never again*), and so on. Frequently, however, a negative statement includes a negative structure that centers around a verb, such as **Nous n'allons pas...** (*We are not going . . .*) or **Je ne dors jamais tard...** (*I never sleep late . . .*).

Simple negations

A verb is made negative by placing **ne** before the verb and **pas** after it. The -e of **ne** is dropped before a vowel or a silent (mute) **h**.

Elle **ne** dormait **pas**.	*She was not sleeping.*
Tu **n'**écoutes **pas**.	*You do not listen/You are not listening.*

In compound tenses (**passé composé, plus-que-parfait, futur antérieur**), **n'** is placed before the form of the auxiliary verb (**avoir** or **être**) and **pas** after it.

Je **n'**ai **pas** répondu.	*I did not answer.*
Vous **n'**étiez **pas** rentrés à la maison.	*You had not come home.*

Exercise 121

Translate the following sentences into French.

1. He does not play.

_____

2. We are not applauding.

_____

3. They have not sold the house.

_____

4. We did not obey.

_____

5. I will not wait.

_____

6. She was not listening.

_____

7. He has not answered.

_____

8. You were not there.

_____

9. I did not wish this.

_____

10. These plants have not turned yellow.

_____

Complex negations

To make negative statements other than _I do not_, _she does not_, and so on, use the following expressions in the same way that you use **ne... pas**.

ne... jamais	_never_
ne... rien	_nothing_
ne... pas encore	_not yet_

Tu **ne** reviens **jamais**.	_You never come back._
Il n'a **rien** fait.	_He did not do anything._

In compound tenses, do not place **personne, nulle part,** or **que** after the auxiliary verb, but rather after the past participle.

ne... personne	_nobody_
ne... nulle part	_nowhere_
ne... que	_only_

Il **n**'a invité **personne**.	*He invited **nobody**/He did **not** invite **anybody**.*
Elle **n**'est allée **nulle part**.	*She went **nowhere**/She did **not** go **anywhere**.*
Elle **n**'a choisi **que** les fruits.	*She **only** chose the fruit.*

Do not combine **pas** with any other negative word, such as **plus** or **jamais**. However, you may combine the other negative words with each other: **plus jamais** (*never again*), **plus personne** (*nobody else*), **plus rien** (*nothing more*), **jamais personne** (*never anybody*), or **jamais rien** (*never anything*).

| Je n'invite **plus personne**. | *I am **not** inviting **anyone else**.* |
| Ils **n**'ont **jamais** rien dit. | *They **never** said **anything**.* |

Exercise 122

Translate the following into French.

1. She never thinks (reflects).

_____

2. I don't want any more.

_____

3. We never say anything.

_____

4. He wears only black.

_____

5. They never like anything.

_____

6. I will never again disobey.

_____

7. You did not hear anybody?

_____

8. She does not dance anywhere anymore.

_____

9. I do not go down yet.

_____

10. We never go up anymore.

_____

38

The Interrogative

The French interrogative is formed in a variety of ways

- with intonation (word order does not change).

  Tu vas au cinéma?   *Are you going to the movies?*

- by placing **est-ce que** before the statement.

  Est-ce que tu danses bien?   *Do you dance well?*

- by placing the subject pronoun after the verb (pronoun and verb joined by a hyphen); this is called *inversion*.

  Chantent-**ils**?   *Are they singing?*

Inversion

In the inverted form with **il** and **elle**, a **-t-** is placed (and pronounced) between the verb and the pronoun, surrounded by closed-up hyphens, unless the conjugated verb form itself ends in **-t** or **-d**.

Joue-t-il?	*Is he playing?*
Réussit-il?	*Is he succeeding?*
Répond-elle?	*Is she answering?*

Inversion is not used with the pronoun je except in a few rare cases such as:

Suis-je?	*Am I?*
Puis-je?	*May I?*

In compound tenses, the inversion affects only the subject pronoun and the helping (auxiliary) verb. If the sentence has a noun subject, it remains in its original position and the corresponding subject pronoun is inserted in the inverted form.

Sommes-nous arrivés?	*Did we arrive?*
A-t-elle étudié?	*Did she study?*
Giselle est-elle arrivée?	*Did Giselle get here?*

Exercise 123

Translate the following sentences into French. Use *inversion* except for questions whose subject is **je**.

1. Did he go up?

_____

2. Are you listening? (**tu**)

_____

3. Is she wearing a dress?

_____

4. Do they speak French?

_____

5. Did I succeed?

_____

6. Did we help?

_____

7. Is she waiting?

_____

8. Are you going down? (**vous**)

_____

9. Do I dance well?

_____

10. Does he like French movies?

_____

11. Do you hear? (**vous**)

_____

12. Did we arrive?

_____

13. Did they go out?

_____

14. Is he here?

_____

15. Are the children studying?

_____

16. Do I look good?

_____

17. Did Rachelle like the music?

_____

18. Do we go up?

_____

19. Did your (**tes**) parents stay?

_____

20. Are you finishing? (**tu**)

_____

Interrogative words involving intonation, _est-ce que_, or inversion

Interrogative words such as _how_ (**comment**) or _why_ (**pourquoi**) can be used to ask questions in three different ways. You are asking or hearing a question when

- the subject pronoun appears before the verb and the pitch of the voice goes up on the last syllable (intonation). This is a colloquial way of speaking.

    Comment tu vas?   _How are you?_

- **est-ce que** appears after the interrogative word and before the subject pronoun.

    Comment est-ce que tu vas?   _How are you?_

- the subject pronoun appears after the verb with a hyphen between verb and subject (inversion).

Comment vas-tu?	*How are you?*

Common interrogative words

combien	*how many*
comment	*how*
lequel/laquelle/lesquels/lesquelles	*which one(s)* (replaces noun)
où	*where*
pourquoi	*why*
quand	*when*
que	*what*
quel/quelle/quels/quelles	*which* (adjective used before a noun)
qui	*who*
quoi	*what* (used alone or after a preposition)

Exercise 124

Find the answer to each question and write the corresponding letter before each question.

1. _____ Comment allez-vous?   a. Pas beaucoup.

2. _____ Quel temps fait-il?   b. Ma mère.

3. _____ Où est l'épicerie?   c. Mes copains.

4. _____ Combien d'argent tu as?   d. L'équipe de Paris.

5. _____ Quand est la fête? Ce soir? e. Pas très loin d'ici.

6. _____ Qui est-ce que tu invites?   f. Un match de foot.

7. _____ Que regardes-tu à la télé?   g. Non, je déteste ça.

8. _____ Qui prépare à manger?   h. Oui, à huit heures.

9. _____ Quoi? Tu n'aimes pas ça?   i. Bien, merci.

10. _____ Laquelle est-ce que tu préfères? j. Il pleut.

39

Stem-Changing and Irregular Verbs

Many verbs have irregular present-tense conjugations. Most of these verbs also have irregular past participles (used in compound tenses such as the **passé composé**, **plus-que-parfait**, and **futur antérieur**). They may also have irregular imperative (command) forms and/or irregular present subjunctive conjugations.

In this chapter, verbs that have similar patterns have been grouped for easier assimilation.

Stem-changing regular *-er* verbs

Several groups of regular -er verbs have predictable stem changes affecting the spelling of conjugated forms. These changes exist largely to retain consistent pronunciation.

Verbs with the letter *c* in the stem

The letter **c** in the stem of these verbs gains a cedilla (-ç-) before the letter **a** or **o** in conjugated forms. This serves to retain the soft **c** sound (equivalent to the **s** sound). The endings of these verbs are regular.

Note the following forms/tenses:

Commencer (to start, begin)

Présent de l'indicatif	*Imparfait*
nous commençons	je commençais
	tu commençais
	il/elle/on commençait
	ils/elles commençaient

Here is a list of verbs like **commencer**:

annoncer	*to announce*
avancer	*to advance*
prononcer	*to pronounce*
renoncer	*to give up*

Verbs with the letter *g* in the stem

Verbs ending in **-ger** gain a silent **-e-** after the letter **g**, before the letter **a** or **o**, to retain the soft **g** sound. The endings of these verbs are regular. Note the following forms/tenses where this occurs:

Changer (to change)

Présent de l'indicatif	*Imparfait*
nous changeons	je changeais
	tu changeais
	il/elle/on changeait
	ils/elles changeaient

Here is a list of verbs like changer:

corriger	*to correct*
manger	*to eat*
nager	*to swim*
neiger	*to snow*
partager	*to share*
plonger	*to dive*
voyager	*to travel*

Verbs with the letter *y* in the stem

In verbs ending in **-yer** (such as **employer**), the y may be changed to **i** before a silent **e**. (Note that usage has made this particular spelling rule optional in French.) The endings of these verbs are regular. Note the following forms/tenses:

Employer (to use, employ)

Présent de l'indicatif, *Présent du subjonctif*	*Futur*	*Conditionnel*
j'emploie	j'emploierai	j'emploierais
tu emploies	tu emploieras	tu emploierais
il/elle/on emploie	il/elle/on emploiera	il/elle/on emploierait
ils/elles emploient	nous emploierons	nous emploierions
	vous emploierez	vous emploieriez
	ils/elles emploieront	ils/elles emploieraient

However, in verbs ending -**ayer** (such as **essayer**), this rule is optional: the y may be used throughout the conjugation, or the y may change to i in all conjugated froms but the **nous** and **vous** forms.

Here is a list of verbs ending in -**yer**. Ones with an optional y to i change include:

essayer	*to try*
payer	*to pay*

The mandatory **y** to **i** change include:

ennuyer	*to annoy/to bore*
essuyer	*to wipe*
nettoyer	*to clean*
employer	*to use/to employ*

Verbs with a silent -*e* in the syllable preceding the ending

In verbs that have a silent -e- in the stem before the consonant + -er ending, change the silent -e- to -è- if the following syllable in the conjugated form contains another silent e. The endings of these verbs are regular. Note the following forms/tenses where this occurs:

Acheter (to buy)

Présent de l'indicatif, *Présent du subjonctif*	*Futur*	*Conditionnel*
j'achète	j'achèterai	j'achèterais
tu achètes	tu achèteras	tu achèterais
il/elle/on achète	il/elle/on achètera	il/elle/on achèterait
ils/elles achètent	nous achèterons	nous achèterions
	vous achèterez	vous achèteriez
	ils/elles achèteront	ils/elles achèteraient

Here is a list of verbs like **acheter**:

amener	*to bring along*
emmener	*to take along*
geler	*to freeze*
lever	*to raise/lift*
mener	*to lead*

Verbs with *é* in the syllable preceding the ending

In verbs that have an -é- in the stem before the consonant + -er ending, change the -é- to -è- only before the endings **-e, -es,** and **-ent** in forms of the present indicative and the present subjunctive. The endings of these verbs are regular.

Espérer (to hope)

Présent de l'indicatif, présent du subjonctif
j'espère
tu espères
il/elle/on espère
ils/elles espèrent

Other verbs like **espérer** are **répéter** (*to repeat*) and **préférer** (*to prefer*).

Verbs that double a consonant

Verbs such as **appeler** double the consonant that precedes their -er ending in some conjugated forms. The endings of these verbs are regular. Note the following forms/tenses:

Appeler (to call)

Présent de l'indicatif, Présent du subjonctif	**Futur**	**Conditionnel**
j'appelle	j'appellerai	j'appellerais
tu appelles	tu appelleras	tu appellerais
il/elle/on appelle	il/elle/on appellera	il/elle/on appellerait

ils/elles appellent	nous appellerons	nous appellerions
	vous appellerez	vous appelleriez
	ils/elles appelleront	ils/elles appelleraient

Here is a list of verbs like **appeler**:

jeter	*to throw*
rappeler	*to remind*
rejeter	*to reject*
s'appeler	*to be named*
se rappeler	*to recall, remember*

Exercise 125

Conjugate each of the following verbs with the subject pronouns given in the tenses needed to indicate what used to be in the past (**imparfait**), what is happening now (**présent de l'indicatif**), and what happened yesterday (**passé composé**).

Ce qui se passait (Imparfait)	Ce qui se passe (Présent de l'indicatif)	Ce qui s'est passé (Passé composé)

1. je (préférer) _____

2. tu (s'appeler) _____

3. elle (jeter) _____

4. ils (espérer) _____

5. j' (acheter) _____

6. ils (payer) _____

7. il (neiger) _____

8. il (geler) _____

9. on (annoncer) _____

10. je (lever) _____

Exercise 126

Conjugate each of the following ten verbs with the subject pronouns given in the tenses needed to indicate what would be today (**conditionnel**) and what will be tomorrow (**futur simple**).

	Ce qui se passerait (Conditionnel)	Ce qui se passera (Futur simple)

1. je (préférer) _____
2. tu (s'appeler) _____
3. elle (jeter) _____
4. nous (espérer) _____
5. vous (acheter) _____
6. ils (payer) _____
7. il (neiger) _____
8. il (geler) _____
9. on (annoncer) _____
10. je (lever) _____

Irregular verbs

Many irregular verbs must simply be memorized or learned through sheer practice. However, even among irregular verbs, some groupings have regular patterns that can be learned. Here are some groups of the most commonly used irregular verbs.

Auxiliary verbs

The verbs **avoir** and **être** are helping verbs for compound tense conjugations such as the **passé composé.** The verb **aller** is an auxiliary verb for the **futur proche** (**aller** + infinitive), and the verb **faire** is a helping verb in the **faire causatif** (**faire faire**) structure. Each of these verbs should be memorized in the tenses that follow.

Aller (to go)

Présent de l'indicatif	Présent du subjonctif
je vais	que j'aille
tu vas	que tu ailles
il/elle/on va	qu'il/elle/on aille
nous allons	que nous allions
vous allez	que vous alliez
ils/elles vont	qu'ils/elles aillent

Imparfait: j'allais
Futur/Conditionnel: j'irai/j'irais
Passé composé: je suis allé(e)
Passé du subjonctif: que je sois allé(e)
Impératif: va, allons, allez

Avoir (to have)

Présent de l'indicatif	Présent du subjonctif
j'ai	que j'aie
tu as	que tu aies
il/elle/on a	qu'il/elle/on ait
nous avons	que nous ayons
vous avez	que vous ayez
ils/elles ont	qu'ils/elles aient

Imparfait: j'avais
Futur/Conditionnel: j'aurai/j'aurais
Passé composé: j'ai eu
Passé du subjonctif: que j'aie eu
Impératif: aie, ayons, ayez

Être (to be)

Présent de l'indicatif	Présent du subjonctif
je suis	que je sois
tu es	que tu sois
il/elle/on est	qu'il/elle/on soit
nous sommes	que nous soyons
vous êtes	que vous soyez
ils/elles sont	qu'ils/elles soient

Imparfait: j'étais

Futur/Conditionnel: je serai/je serais

Passé composé: j'ai été

Passé du subjonctif: que j'aie été

Impératif: sois, soyons, soyez

Faire (to do)

Présent de l'indicatif	*Présent du subjonctif*
je fais	que je fasse
tu fais	que tu fasses
il/elle/on fait	qu'il/elle/on fasse
nous faisons	que nous fassions
vous faites	que vous fassiez
ils/elles font	qu'ils/elles fassent

Imparfait: je faisais

Futur/Conditionnel: je ferai/je ferais

Passé composé: j'ai fait

Passé du subjonctif: que j'aie fait

Impératif: fais, faisons, faites

Exercise 127

In this exercise, you will practice the **présent** (P), the **imparfait** (I), the **futur simple** (F), the **futur antérieur** (future perfect) (FA), and the **présent du subjonctif** (S). Write the corresponding French verb form next to each English phrase.

1. I am doing (P) _____

2. she is going (P) _____

3. we are (P) _____

4. you (**tu**) have (P) _____

5. they have (P) _____

6. I was doing (I) _____

7. she was going (I) _____

8. we were (I) _____

9. you (**vous**) had (I) _____

10. they had (I) _____

11. I will do (F) _____

12. she will go (F) _____

13. we will be (F) _____

14. you (**tu**) will have (F) _____

15. they will have (F) _____

16. I will have done (FA) _____

17. she will have gone (FA) _____

18. we will have been (FA) _____

19. you (**vous**) will have had (FA) _____

20. they will have had (FA) _____

21. I must do (**Il faut que** + S) _____

22. she must go (**Il faut qu'** + S) _____

23. we must be (**Il faut que** + S) _____

24. you (**tu**) must have (**Il faut que** + S) _____

25. they must have (**Il faut qu'** + S) _____

Verbs ending in *-ire*

These verbs follow similar patterns of conjugation. Note however that the verb **dire** breaks the pattern in the **vous** form of the present tense (**vous dites**); the verb **lire** breaks the pattern in the form of the past participle (**lu**).

Lire (to read)

Présent de l'indicatif	*Présent du subjonctif*
je lis	que je lise
tu lis	que tu lises
il/elle/on lit	qu'il/elle/on lise
nous lisons	que nous lisions
vous lisez	que vous lisiez
ils/elles lisent	qu'ils/elles lisent

Imparfait: je lisais
Futur/Conditionnel: je lirai/je lirais

Passé composé: j'ai **lu**

Passé du subjonctif: que j'aie **lu**

Impératif: lis, lisons, lisez

Dire (to say/to tell)

Présent de l'indicatif	*Présent du subjonctif*
je dis	que je dise
tu dis	que tu dises
il/elle/on dit	qu'il/elle/on dise
nous disons	que nous disions
vous dites	que vous disiez
ils/elles disent	qu'ils/elles disent

Imparfait: je **dis**ais

Futur/Conditionnel: je **dir**ai/je **dir**ais

Passé composé: j'ai **dit**

Passé du subjonctif: que j'aie **dit**

Impératif: dis, disons, dites

Écrire (to write)

Présent de l'indicatif	*Présent du subjonctif*
j'écris	que j'écrive
tu écris	que tu écrives
il/elle/on écrit	qu'il/elle/on écrive
nous écrivons	que nous écrivions
vous écrivez	que vous écriviez
ils/elles écrivent	qu'ils/elles écrivent

Imparfait: j'écrivais

Futur/Conditionnel: j'écrirai/j'écrirais

Passé composé: j'ai écrit

Passé du subjonctif: que j'aie écrit

Impératif: écris, écrivons, écrivez

Conduire (to drive)

Présent de l'indicatif	*Présent du subjonctif*
je conduis	que je conduise
tu conduis	que tu conduises
il/elle/on conduit	qu'il/elle/on conduise

nous conduisons   que nous conduisions

vous conduisez   que vous conduisiez

ils/elles conduisent   qu'ils/elles conduisent

Imparfait: je **conduis**ais

Futur/Conditionnel: je **conduir**ai/je **conduir**ais

Passé composé: j'ai **conduit**

Passé du subjonctif: que j'aie **conduit**

Impératif: conduis, conduisons, conduisez

Exercise 128

In this exercise, you will practice the **présent** (P), the **passé composé** (PC), the **imparfait** (I), the **futur simple** (F), the **futur antérieur** (future perfect) (FA), and the **présent du subjonctif** (S). Write the corresponding French verb form next to each English phrase.

1. I am reading (P) _____

2. you (**vous**) are reading (P) _____

3. she read (PC) _____

4. they read (PC) _____

5. we were reading (I) _____

6. I was reading (I) _____

7. you (**tu**) will read (F) _____

8. they will read (F) _____

9. she will have read (FA) _____

10. I must read (**Il faut que** + S) _____

11. they must read (**Il faut qu'** + S) _____

12. I must say (**Il faut que** + S) _____

13. she said (PC) _____

14. he was saying (I) _____

15. we will say (F) _____

16. you (**tu**) are writing (P) _____

17. they were writing (I) _____

18. he wrote (PC) _____

19. he will have written (FA) _____

20. she must write (**Il faut qu'** + S) _____

21. she is driving (P) _____

22. I drove (PC) _____

23. we must drive (**Il faut que** + S) _____

24. they will drive (F) _____

25. they were driving (I) _____

Verbs ending in -*vre*

The verbs **vivre** and **suivre** have similar patterns of conjugation. The present tense indicative stem of these verbs is obtained by dropping the last three letters (**-vre**) from the infinitive form. Note however that their past participles follow a different pattern.

Vivre (to live)

Présent de l'indicatif	*Présent du subjonctif*
je vis	que je vive
tu vis	que tu vives
il/elle/on vit	qu'il/elle/on vive
nous vivons	que nous vivions
vous vivez	que vous viviez
ils/elles vivent	qu'ils/elles vivent

Imparfait: je vivais
Futur/Conditionnel: je vivrai/je vivrais
Passé composé: j'ai vécu
Passé du subjonctif: que j'aie vécu
Impératif: vis, vivons, vivez

Suivre (to follow)

Présent de l'indicatif	*Présent du subjonctif*
je suis	que je suive
tu suis	que tu suives
il/elle/on suit	qu'il/elle/on suive

nous suivons   que nous suivons

vous suivez   que vous suiviez

ils/elles suivent   qu'ils/elles suivent

Imparfait: je **suivais**

Futur/Conditionnel: je **suivrai**/je **suivrais**

Passé composé: j'ai **suivi**

Passé du subjonctif: que j'aie **suivi**

Impératif: suis, suivons, suivez

Exercise 129

In this exercise, you will practice the **présent** (P), the **passé composé** (PC), the **imparfait** (I), the command forms/imperative (C), the **présent du subjonctif** (S), and the **passé du subjonctif** (SP). Write the corresponding French verb form next to each English phrase.

1. I am following (P) _____

2. they are following (P) _____

3. she followed (PC) _____

4. we followed (PC) _____

5. you (**vous**) were following (I) _____

6. Follow (singular)! (C) _____

7. Let's follow! (C) _____

8. she must follow (**Il faut qu'** + S) _____

9. Too bad he followed (**Dommage qu'** + SP) _____

10. they live (P) _____

11. Let's live! (C) _____

12. Live! (singular) (C) _____

13. Live! (plural) (C) _____

14. we were living (I) _____

15. I lived (PC) _____

16. he lived (PC) _____

17. I must live (**Il faut que** + S) _____

18. they must live (**Il faut qu'** + S) _____

19. It is good she lived (**Il est bon qu'** + SP) _____

20. It is good they lived (**Il est bon qu'** + SP) _____

Verbs like *prendre*

In the present tense indicative, **prendre** verbs differ from regular **-re** verbs since they lose the letter **d** from the stem in the plural form (**nous, vous, ils/elles**) of the present indicative and in all the forms of the present subjunctive. They also have unique though similar past participles. Note that the verbs **apprendre** (*to learn*), **comprendre** (*to understand*), and **surprendre** (*to surprise*) are conjugated like **prendre,** since they are composed of the verb **prendre** plus a prefix.

Prendre (to take)

Présent de l'indicatif	*Présent du subjonctif*
je prends	que je prenne
tu prends	que tu prennes
il/elle/on prend	qu'il/elle/on prenne
nous prenons	que nous prenions
vous prenez	que vous preniez
ils/elles prennent	qu'ils/elles prennent

Imparfait: je prenais

Futur/Conditionnel: je prendrai/je prendrais

Passé composé: j'ai pris

Passé du subjonctif: que j'aie pris

Impératif: prends, prenons, prenez

Exercise 130

In this exercise, you will practice the **présent** (P), the **passé composé** (PC), the **imparfait** (I), the command forms/imperative (C), the **présent du subjonctif** (S), the **passé du subjonctif** (SP), and the **conditionnel** (CL). Write the corresponding French verb form next to each English phrase.

1. I understand (P) _____

2. they are learning (P) _____

3. we surprise (P) _____

4. you (**tu**) are taking (P) _____

5. I understood (PC) _____

6. they learned (PC) _____

7. they were taking (I) _____

8. Take! (singular) (C) _____

9. Take! (plural) (C) _____

10. Let's take! (C) _____

11. she must take (**Il faut qu'** + S) _____

12. we must take (**Il faut que** + S) _____

13. too bad I took (**Dommage que** + SP) _____

14. too bad you (**tu**) surprised (**Dommage que** + SP) _____

15. It's good he understood (**Il est bon qu'** + SP) _____

16. I would learn (CL) _____

17. they would learn (CL) _____

18. I would take (CL) _____

19. they would surprise (CL) _____

20. she would understand (CL) _____

Verbs like *mettre*

The stem of the verb **mettre** in the present indicative is obtained by dropping the last three letters from its infinitive form for the singular forms (**je, tu, il, elle, on**) and the last two letters only for the plural forms (**nous, vous, ils, elles**). Note that **permettre** (*to allow*) and **promettre** (*to promise*) are conjugated like **mettre** since they are composed of the verb **mettre** plus a prefix.

Mettre (to put/to put on)

Présent de l'indicatif	*Présent du subjonctif*
je mets	que je mette
tu mets	que tu mettes
il/elle/on met	qu'il/elle/on mette
nous mettons	que nous mettions
vous mettez	que vous mettiez
ils/elles mettent	qu'ils/elles mettent

Imparfait: je mett**ais**

Futur/Conditionnel: je mett**rai**/je mett**rais**

Passé composé: j'ai **mis**

Passé du subjonctif: que j'aie **mis**

Impératif: mets, mettons, mettez

Exercise 131

In this exercise, you will practice the **présent** (P), the **passé composé** (PC), the **imparfait** (I), the command forms/imperative (C), the **présent du subjonctif** (S), the **passé du subjonctif** (SP), and the **conditionnel** (CL). Write the corresponding French verb form next to each English phrase.

1. I put (P) _____

2. we put (P) _____

3. they put (P) _____

4. I was putting (I) _____

5. I promised (PC) _____

6. they promised (PC) _____

7. they allowed (PC) _____

8. Put! (singular) (C) _____

9. Let's put . . . ! (C) _____

10. we have to allow (**Il faut que** + S) _____

11. she has to allow (**Il faut qu'** + S) _____

12. we have to promise (**Il faut que** + S) _____

13. it is good she promised (**Il est bon qu'** + SP) _____

14. it is good he allowed (**Il est bon qu'** + SP) _____

15. I would allow (CL) _____

16. they would allow (CL) _____

17. you (**vous**) would promise (CL) _____

18. I used to promise (I) _____

19. she used to put (I) _____

20. I used to allow (I) _____

Verbs ending in -aire

The verbs **plaire** and **se taire** follow similar patterns in the present indicative and have similar past participles. Note that the verb **se taire** is reflexive.

Plaire (to please)

Présent de l'indicatif	Présent du subjonctif
je plais	que je plaise
tu plais	que tu plaises
il/elle/on plaît	qu'il/elle/on plaise
nous plaisons	que nous plaisions
vous plaisez	que vous plaisiez
ils/elles plaisent	qu'ils/elles plaisent

Imparfait: je **plais**ais
Futur/Conditionnel: je **plair**ai/je **plair**ais
Passé composé: j'ai **plu**
Passé du subjonctif: que j'aie **plu**
Impératif: plais, plaisons, plaisez

Se taire (to be quiet)

Présent de l'indicatif	Présent du subjonctif
je me tais	que je me taise
tu te tais	que tu te taises
il/elle/on se tait	qu'il/elle/on se taise
nous nous taisons	que nous nous taisions
vous vous taisez	que vous vous taisiez
ils/elles se taisent	qu'ils/elles se taisent

Imparfait: je me **tais**ais
Futur/Conditionnel: je me **tair**ai/je me **tair**ais
Passé composé: je me suis **tu**(e)
Passé du subjonctif: que je me sois **tu**(e)
Impératif: tais-toi, taisons-nous, taisez-vous

Exercise 132

In this exercise, you will practice the **présent** (P), the **passé composé** (PC), the command forms/imperative (C), the **présent du subjonctif** (S), and the **futur simple** (F). Write the corresponding French verb form next to each English phrase.

1. they please (P) _____
2. we please (P) _____
3. he is quiet (P) _____
4. you (**vous**) are quiet (P) _____
5. they pleased (PC) _____
6. he became quiet (PC) _____
7. you (**tu**) became quiet (PC) _____
8. I will be quiet (F) _____
9. I must please (**Il faut que** + S) _____
10. Let's be quiet! (C) _____

Verbs like *dormir*

These verbs have two different stems in the present tense indicative. The stem of the verb is obtained by dropping the last three letters from its infinitive for the singular forms (**je, tu, il, elle, on**) and the last two letters only for the plural forms (**nous, vous, ils, elles**). Note that the verb **endormir** (*to put to sleep*) is conjugated like **dormir**.

Dormir (to sleep)

Présent de l'indicatif	*Présent du subjonctif*
je dors	que je dorme
tu dors	que tu dormes
il/elle/on dort	qu'il/elle/on dorme
nous dormons	que nous dormions
vous dormez	que vous dormiez
ils/elles dorment	qu'ils/elles dorment

Imparfait: je dormais
Futur/Conditionnel: je dormirai/je dormirais
Passé composé: j'ai dormi

Passé du subjonctif: que j'aie **dormi**
Impératif: dors, dormons, dormez

Partir (to leave)

Présent de l'indicatif	*Présent du subjonctif*
je pars	que je parte
tu pars	que tu partes
il/elle/on part	qu'il/elle/on parte
nous partons	que nous partions
vous partez	que vous partiez
ils/elles partent	qu'ils/elles partent

Imparfait: je **part**ais
Futur/Conditionnel: je **partir**ai/je **partir**ais
Passé composé: je suis **parti**(e)
Passé du subjonctif: que je sois **parti**(e)
Impératif: pars, partons, partez

Sortir (to go out/to leave)

Présent de l'indicatif	*Présent du subjonctif*
je sors	que je sorte
tu sors	que tu sortes
il/elle/on sort	qu'il/elle/on sorte
nous sortons	que nous sortions
vous sortez	que vous sortiez
ils/elles sortent	qu'ils/elles sortent

Imparfait: je **sort**ais
Futur/Conditionnel: je **sortir**ai/je **sortir**ais
Passé composé: je suis **sorti**(e)
Passé du subjonctif: que je sois **sorti**(e)
Impératif: sors, sortons, sortez

Servir (to serve)

Présent de l'indicatif	*Présent du subjonctif*
je sers	que je serve
tu sers	que tu serves

il/elle/on sert	qu'il/elle/on serve
nous servons	que nous servions
vous servez	que vous serviez
ils/elles servent	qu'ils/elles servent

Imparfait: je servais
Futur/Conditionnel: je servirai/je servirais
Passé composé: j'ai servi
Passé du subjonctif: que j'aie servi
Impératif: sers, servons, servez

Mentir (to lie, tell a lie)

Présent de l'indicatif	*Présent du subjonctif*
je mens	que je mente
tu mens	que tu mentes
il/elle/on ment	qu'il/elle/on mente
nous mentons	que nous mentions
vous mentez	que vous mentiez
ils/elles mentent	qu'ils/elles mentent

Imparfait: je mentais
Futur/Conditionnel: je mentirai/je mentirais
Passé composé: j'ai menti
Passé du subjonctif: que j'aie menti
Impératif: mens, mentons, mentez

Exercise 133

In this exercise, you will practice the **présent** (P), the **passé composé** (PC), the **imparfait** (I), the command forms/imperative (C), and the **présent du subjonctif** (S). Write the corresponding French verb form next to each English phrase.

1. I serve (P) _____
2. we serve (P) _____
3. they lie (P) _____
4. you (**tu**) lie (P) _____
5. I am going out (P) _____

6. he is going out (P) _____

7. he is sleeping (P) _____

8. we are leaving (P) _____

9. you (plural) are leaving (P) _____

10. I served (PC) _____

11. we slept (PC) _____

12. we served (PC) _____

13. they lied (PC) _____

14. she went out (PC) _____

15. we went out (P) _____

16. I left (P) _____

17. they were leaving (I) _____

18. I was lying (I) _____

19. he was lying (I) _____

20. I was sleeping (I) _____

21. Leave! (plural) (C) _____

22. Let's serve! (C) _____

23. Let's sleep! (C) _____

24. you (**tu**) must sleep (**Il faut que** + S) _____

25. It is good we sleep. (**Il est bon que** + S) _____

Verbs with -*oi* in the stem

These verbs are spelled with -ois, -ois, -oit in the singular forms (**je, tu, il, elle, on**) of the present indicative. However, note that their plural forms (**nous, vous, ils, elles**) differ. They also have similar past participles.

Voir (to see)

Présent de l'indicatif	*Présent du subjonctif*
je vois	que je voie
tu vois	que tu voies
il/elle/on voit	qu'il/elle/on voie

nous voyons	que nous voyions
vous voyez	que vous voyiez
ils/elles voient	qu'ils/elles voient

Imparfait: je voyais
Futur/Conditionnel: je verrai/je verrais
Passé composé: j'ai vu
Passé du subjonctif: que j'aie vu
Impératif: vois, voyons, voyez

Croire (to believe)

Présent de l'indicatif	*Présent du subjonctif*
je crois	que je croie
tu crois	que tu croies
il/elle/on croit	qu'il/elle/on croie
nous croyons	que nous croyions
vous croyez	que vous croyiez
ils/elles croient	qu'ils/elles croient

Imparfait: je croyais
Futur/Conditionnel: je croirai/je croirais
Passé composé: j'ai cru
Passé du subjonctif: que j'aie cru
Impératif: crois, croyons, croyez

Recevoir (to receive)

Présent de l'indicatif	*Présent du subjonctif*
je reçois	que je reçoive
tu reçois	que tu reçoives
il/elle/on reçoit	qu'il/elle/on reçoive
nous recevons	que nous recevions
vous recevez	que vous receviez
ils/elles reçoivent	qu'ils/elles reçoivent

Imparfait: je recevais
Futur/Conditionnel: je recevrai/je recevrais
Passé composé: j'ai reçu

Passé du subjonctif: que j'aie **reçu**

Impératif: reçois, recevons, recevez

Devoir (to have to/must)

Présent de l'indicatif	Présent du subjonctif
je dois	que je doive
tu dois	que tu doives
il/elle/on doit	qu'il/elle/on doive
nous devons	que nous devions
vous devez	que vous deviez
ils/elles doivent	qu'ils/elles doivent

Imparfait: je **devais** (*I was obliged to/I was supposed to*)

Futur/Conditionnel: je **devrai** (*I will have to*)/je **devrais** (*I should*)

Passé composé: j'ai **dû** (*I had to*)

Passé du subjonctif: que j'aie **dû**

Exercise 134

In this exercise, you will practice the **présent** (P), the **passé composé** (PC), the **imparfait** (I), and the **futur simple** (F). Write the corresponding French verb form next to each English phrase.

1. I see (P) _____

2. you (**vous**) see (P) _____

3. they believe (P) _____

4. I believe (P) _____

5. I must (P) _____

6. they must (P) _____

7. we have to (P) _____

8. you (**tu**) receive (P) _____

9. she receives (P) _____

10. they receive (P) _____

11. I saw (PC) _____

12. you (**vous**) saw (PC) _____

13. they believed (PC) _____

14. I believed (PC) _____

15. I had to (PC) _____

16. they had to (PC) _____

17. we received (PC) _____

18. they received (PC) _____

19. I was supposed to (I) _____

20. they were supposed to (I) _____

21. I was receiving (I) _____

22. we were receiving (I) _____

23. I will see (F) _____

24. they will receive (F) _____

25. I will have to (F) _____

Verbs like *ouvrir*

The **ouvrir** verbs are conjugated like regular -er verbs in the present indicative. The verbs **couvrir** (*to cover*) and **découvrir** (*to discover*) are conjugated like the verb **ouvrir**. Note also that they have similar but unique past participles.

Ouvrir (to open)

Présent de l'indicatif	*Présent du subjonctif*
j'ouvre	que j'ouvre
tu ouvres	que tu ouvres
il/elle/on ouvre	qu'il/elle/on ouvre
nous ouvrons	que nous ouvrions
vous ouvrez	que vous ouvriez
ils/elles ouvrent	qu'ils/elles ouvrent

Imparfait: j'ouvrais

Futur/Conditionnel: j'ouvrirai/j'ouvrirais

Passé composé: j'ai **ouvert**

Passé du subjonctif: que j'aie **ouvert**

Impératif: ouvre, ouvrons, ouvrez

Offrir (to offer)

Présent de l'indicatif	Présent du subjonctif
j'offre	que j'offre
tu offres	que tu offres
il/elle/on offre	qu'il/elle/on offre
nous offrons	que nous offrions
vous offrez	que vous offriez
ils/elles offrent	qu'ils/elles offrent

Imparfait: j'offrais
Futur/Conditionnel: j'offrirai/j'offrirais
Passé composé: j'ai **offert**
Passé du subjonctif: que j'aie **offert**
Impératif: offre, offrons, offrez

Exercise 135

In this exercise, you will practice the **présent** (P), the **passé composé** (PC), the **imparfait** (I), the command forms/imperative (C), the **présent du subjonctif** (S), the **passé du subjonctif** (SP), and the **conditionnel** (CL). Write the corresponding French verb form next to each English phrase.

1. I am opening (P) _____
2. they open (P) _____
3. you (**tu**) offer (P) _____
4. we offer (P) _____
5. he covers (P) _____
6. they covered (PC) _____
7. we offered (PC) _____
8. he discovered (PC) _____
9. she was offering (I) _____
10. they were covering (I) _____
11. Open! (singular) (C) _____
12. Let's open! (C) _____
13. Cover! (plural) (C) _____
14. I must open (**Il faut que** + S) _____

15. It is good he discovered (**Il est bon qu' + SP**) _____

16. Too bad she covered (**Dommage qu' + SP**) _____

17. we would cover (CL) _____

18. they would open (CL) _____

19. I would offer (CL) _____

20. you (**tu**) would offer (CL) _____

The verbs *pouvoir* and *vouloir*

These two verbs have similar but unique conjugations in the present tense indicative.

Vouloir (to want)

Présent de l'indicatif	*Présent du subjonctif*
je veux	que je veuille
tu veux	que tu veuilles
il/elle/on veut	qu'il/elle/on veuille
nous voulons	que nous voulions
vous voulez	que vous vouliez
ils/elles veulent	qu'ils/elles veuillent

Imparfait: je **voul**ais
Futur/Conditionnel: je **voudr**ai/je **voudr**ais (*I would like*)
Passé composé: j'ai **voulu**
Passé du subjonctif: que j'aie **voulu**
Impératif: veuillez (formal address used to say *please*)

Pouvoir (to be able to)

Présent de l'indicatif	*Présent du subjonctif*
je peux	que je puisse
tu peux	que tu puisses
il/elle/on peut	qu'il/elle/on puisse
nous pouvons	que nous puissions
vous pouvez	que vous puissiez
ils/elles peuvent	qu'ils/elles puissent

Imparfait: je pouv**ais**
Futur/Conditionnel: je pourr**ai**/je pourr**ais**
Passé composé: j'ai **pu**
Passé du subjonctif: que j'aie **pu**

Exercise 136

In this exercise, you will practice the **présent** (P), the **passé composé** (PC), the **imparfait** (I), the **présent du subjonctif** (S), the **passé du subjonctif** (SP), and the **conditionnel** (CL). Write the corresponding French verb form next to each English phrase.

1. he wants (P) _____

2. we want (P) _____

3. I want (P) _____

4. you (**vous**) can (P) _____

5. they can (P) _____

6. I am able to (P) _____

7. I have been able to (PC) _____

8. I wanted (PC) _____

9. they wanted (PC) _____

10. we could (I) _____

11. she could (I) _____

12. I wanted (I) _____

13. they wanted (I) _____

14. you (**tu**) would like (CL) _____

15. we would like (CL) _____

16. they would like (CL) _____

17. I would be able to (CL) _____

18. he would be able to (CL) _____

19. they would be able to (CL) _____

20. I must want (**Il faut que** + S) _____

21. we must want (**Il faut que** + S) _____

22. she must be able to (**Il faut qu'** + S) _____

23. they must be able to (**Il faut qu'** + S) _____

24. It is good we were able to (**Il est bon que** + SP) _____

25. It is good that we wanted (**Il est bon que** + SP) _____

Verbs like *venir* and *tenir*

The plural forms of these verbs have regular stems, obtained by dropping the last two letters of the infinitive. However, their singular forms have unique stems.

Note that **retenir** (*to hold back*) is conjugated like **tenir**. **Revenir** (*to come back*), **devenir** (*to become*), and **se souvenir** (*to remember*) are conjugated like **venir**. Don't forget that the verbs **venir**, **revenir**, **devenir**, and **se souvenir** are conjugated with the auxiliary verb **être** in the **passé composé**.

Tenir (to hold)

Présent de l'indicatif	*Présent du subjonctif*
je tiens	que je tienne
tu tiens	que tu tiennes
il/elle/on tient	qu'il/elle/on tienne
nous tenons	que nous tenions
vous tenez	que vous teniez
ils/elles tiennent	qu'ils/elles tiennent

Imparfait: je tenais

Futur/Conditionnel: je tiendrai/je tiendrais

Passé composé: j'ai **tenu**

Passé du subjonctif: que j'aie **tenu**

Impératif: tiens, tenons, tenez

Venir (to come)

Présent de l'indicatif	*Présent du subjonctif*
je viens	que je vienne
tu viens	que tu viennes
il/elle/on vient	qu'il/elle/on vienne
nous venons	que nous venions
vous venez	que vous veniez
ils/elles viennent	qu'ils/elles viennent

Imparfait: je ven**ais**
Futur/Conditionnel: je vien**dr**ai/je vien**dr**ais
Passé composé: je suis **venu**(e)
Passé du subjonctif: que je sois **venu**(e)
Impératif: viens, venons, venez

Exercise 137

In this exercise, you will practice the **présent** (P), the **passé composé** (PC), the **imparfait** (I), the command forms/imperative (C), the **présent du subjonctif** (S), the **passé du subjonctif** (SP), and the **conditionnel** (CL). Write the corresponding French verb form next to each English phrase.

1. I hold (P) _____
2. she is holding (P) _____
3. he is coming (P) _____
4. we are coming (P) _____
5. you (**tu**) are becoming (P) _____
6. they are becoming (P) _____
7. I come back (P) _____
8. I held (PC) _____
9. you (**vous**) held back (PC) _____
10. they became (PC) _____
11. she came back (PC) _____
12. we were holding (I) _____
13. you (**tu**) were holding (I) _____
14. they were coming (I) _____
15. she was coming back (I) _____
16. Come back! (singular) (C) _____
17. Let's hold! (C) _____
18. Come! (plural) (C) _____
19. She must come back (**Il faut qu'** + S) _____
20. They must hold back (**Il faut qu'** + S) _____
21. Too bad we became (**Dommage que** + SP) _____

22. Too bad I came back (**Dommage que** + SP) _____

23. I would remember (CL) _____

24. they would remember (CL) _____

25. she would remember (CL) _____

The verbs *savoir* and *connaître*

These two verbs mean *to know* but are used differently. Savoir means *to know a fact*, whereas **connaître** means *to be familiar with*.

Savoir (to know a fact)

Présent de l'indicatif	*Présent du subjonctif*
je sais	que je sache
tu sais	que tu saches
il/elle/on sait	qu'il/elle/on sache
nous savons	que nous sachions
vous savez	que vous sachiez
ils/elles savent	qu'ils/elles sachent

Imparfait: je sav**ais**

Futur/Conditionnel: je saur**ai**/je saur**ais**

Passé composé: j'ai **su**

Passé du subjonctif: que j'aie **su**

Impératif: sache, sachons, sachez

Connaître (to know/to be familiar with)

Présent de l'indicatif	*Présent du subjonctif*
je connais	que je connaisse
tu connais	que tu connaisses
il/elle/on connaît	qu'il/elle/on connaisse
nous connaissons	que nous connaissions
vous connaissez	que vous connaissiez
ils/elles connaissent	qu'ils/elles connaissent

Imparfait: je **connaissais**
Futur/Conditionnel: je **connaîtrai**/je **connaîtrais**
Passé composé: j'ai **connu**
Passé du subjonctif: que j'aie **connu**

Exercise 138

In this exercise, you will practice the **présent** (P), the **passé composé** (PC), the **imparfait** (I), the command forms/imperative (C), the **présent du subjonctif** (S), the **passé du subjonctif** (SP), and the **futur simple** (F). Translate each sentence from English into French. Use the verb **savoir**.

1. I know what time it is. (P) _____

2. They know my name. (P) _____

3. One knows the truth. (P) _____

4. She knows the answer. (P) _____

5. We know how to count. (P) _____

6. You (**tu**) know how to play. (P) _____

7. He knows how to sing. (P) _____

8. I found out/realized it was a lie. (PC) _____

9. She found out/realized that I was there. (PC) _____

10. I knew how to sing. (I) _____

11. Know that . . . ! (singular) (C) _____

12. Know that . . . ! (plural) (C) _____

13. We knew how to speak French. (I) _____

14. I must know. (**Il faut que** + S) _____

15. They must know. (**Il faut que** + S) _____

16. Too bad you found out. (**Dommage que** + SP) _____

17. It is good we found out. (**Il est bon que** + SP) _____

18. I will know that name. (F) _____

19. You (**vous**) will know it. (F) _____

20. They will know how to do it. (F) _____

Exercise 139

In this exercise, you will practice the **présent** (P), the **passé composé** (PC), the **imparfait** (I), the **présent du subjonctif** (S), the **passé du subjonctif** (SP), and the **futur simple** (F). Translate each sentence from English into French. Use the verb **connaître**.

1. They know the city. (P) _____

2. I know your teacher. (P) _____

3. We know lots of people. (P) _____

4. I knew her for a little while. (PC) _____

5. They knew my uncle. (I) _____

6. You (**vous**) knew him. (I) _____

7. We will recognize him. (F) _____

8. They will know everybody. (F) _____

9. He must recognize me. (**Il faut qu'** + S) _____

10. It is good you (**tu**) recognized me. (**Il est bon que** + SP) _____

Impersonal verbs

Because of their meaning, these verbs can only be conjugated in the third-person singular with the singular impersonal subject **il**.

Falloir (to be necessary/must)

Présent: il faut (*It is necessary*)
Imparfait: il fallait
Futur/Conditionnel: il faudra/Il faudrait
Passé composé: il a **fallu**
Présent du subjonctif: qu'il faille

Pleuvoir (to rain)

Présent: il pleut (*it rains, it's raining*)
Imparfait: il pleuvait
Futur/Conditionnel: il pleuvra/il pleuvrait
Passé composé: il a **plu**
Présent du subjonctif: qu'il pleuve

Neiger (to snow)

Présent: il neige (*it snows, it's snowing*)
Imparfait: il neigeait
Futur/Conditionnel: il **neiger**a/il **neiger**ait
Passé composé: il a **neigé**
Présent du subjonctif: qu'il neige

Exercise 140

In this exercise, you will practice the **présent** (P), the **passé composé** (PC), the **imparfait** (I), the **futur simple** (F), and the **conditionnel** (CL). Translate each sentence from English into French.

1. It is snowing now. (P) _____

2. It is raining at the moment. (P) _____

3. We must listen. (**falloir**) (P) _____

4. It rained yesterday. (PC) _____

5. It snowed yesterday. (PC) _____

6. We had to listen. (**falloir**) (PC) _____

7. It was raining an hour ago. (I) _____

8. It was snowing. (I) _____

9. We had to leave. (**falloir**) (I) _____

10. It will rain tomorrow. (F) _____

11. It will snow soon. (F) _____

12. It will be necessary to forget. (F) _____

13. It would be necessary to go. (CL) _____

14. It would rain. (CL) _____

15. It would snow. (CL) _____

40

Verbal Expressions and Idioms

Every language has its unique idiomatic structures. Thus, French has many verbal expressions that cannot be translated word for word from French to English. It is best to learn the whole expression as an entity. Many verbal expressions use the verbs **avoir**, **être**, and **faire**. See the previous chapter, on irregular verbs, for their conjugations.

Avoir

Numerous idiomatic expressions use the verb **avoir**. Many are translated as *to be* + an adjective. They include expressions of feeling, thought, and sensation.

avoir besoin de	*to need*
avoir bonne mine	*to look healthy*
avoir chaud	*to be hot* (a person)
avoir de l'allure	*to have presence*
avoir de l'esprit	*to be witty*
avoir de la chance	*to be lucky*
avoir du courage	*to have courage*
avoir envie de	*to feel like*
avoir faim	*to be hungry*
avoir froid	*to be cold* (a person)
avoir honte (de)	*to be ashamed (of)*
avoir l'air (+ adjective)	*to look* (+ adjective)
avoir l'habitude de	*to be used to*
avoir l'intention de	*to intend to*
avoir la parole	*to have the floor*
avoir le temps de	*to have the time to*
avoir lieu	*to take place*
avoir mal (à)	*to ache, hurt*
avoir mauvaise mine	*to look sickly*

avoir peur (de)	*to be afraid (of)*
avoir raison	*to be right*
avoir soif	*to be thirsty*
avoir sommeil	*to be sleepy*
avoir tort	*to be wrong*
avoir... ans	*to be . . . years old*
Il y a...	*. . . ago*
Il y avait une fois...	*Once upon a time . . .*
Qu'est-ce qu'il y a?	*What's wrong?*

Exercise 141

Complete each sentence with an expression from the above list. Be sure to use the appropriate present indicative form of the verb **avoir** unless the infinitive or **il y avait** is required. (See Chapter 39 to review various conjugations of **avoir**.)

1. Aujourd'hui j' _____ d'un manteau. Il fait froid.

2. En ce moment Paul _____ de voir un bon film.

3. C'est moi qui parle d'abord. Après, toi, tu _____.

4. Mes amis et moi, nous _____ d'aller aux cours ensemble.

5. _____, Annie? Tu es malade?

6. Avec sa belle physionomie et sa magnifique voix, elle _____.

7. Vous venez de gagner la loterie? Vous _____.

8. Pour sortir plus souvent, il faut _____ et le désir.

9. Cette fille _____ sérieuse.

10. Il faut aller chez le dentiste si tu _____ aux dents.

11. Les enfants _____ des monstres.

12. Les pompiers et les agents de police _____.

13. Tu peux voter cette année puisque tu _____ dix-huit _____.

14. Quand est-ce qu'il _____, le mariage?

15. _____ une jeune fille nommée Cendrillon.

Être

There are a variety of fixed expressions that use **être**; most are translated as *to be*. **Être** is used in expressions of time and dates, but it is generally not used to describe the weather (see below under faire).

C'en est trop!	*That's too much!*
Ça y est!	*That's it!*
être de bonne humeur	*to be in a good mood*
être de garde	*to be on call/on duty*
être de mauvaise humeur	*to be in a bad mood*
être de retour	*to be back*
Il est des nôtres.	*He is/belongs with us.*
Il est deux heures.	*It is two o'clock.*
Il est une heure.	*It is one o'clock.*
J'en suis.	*I am game (ready to be involved).*
J'y suis.	*I understand/I get it.*
Nous sommes le 1er mai.	*It is May first.*
Quelle heure est-il?	*What time is it?*

Exercise 142

Complete each sentence with an expression from the above **être** list. Be sure to use the appropriate present indicative form of the verb unless the infinitive is required. See Chapter 39 to review conjugations of **être**.

1. Tu as fini tes devoirs, Marc? Oui, _____!

2. Est-ce que _____ le 1er novembre aujourd'hui? —Oui, c'est ça!

3. Papa _____ à l'hôpital.

4. Il va _____ à 7 heures ce soir.

5. Marc, tu _____ ce soir pour dîner. D'accord?

6. Volontiers, mais _____? —Il est 5 heures!

7. Bon, si maman _____, elle me donnera la permission de rester.

8. Tu vois, c'est comme ça qu'on jette la balle! Ah oui, _____!

9. _____ une heure et demie. Allons-y!

10. Ça ne va pas? Tu es vraiment de _____!

Faire

The following weather-related expressions use the verb **faire**.

Il fait beau.	*It is nice.*
Il fait brumeux.	*It is misty/foggy.*
Il fait chaud.	*It is hot.*
Il fait doux.	*It is mild.*
Il fait du brouillard.	*It is foggy.*
Il fait du soleil.	*It is sunny.*
Il fait du vent.	*It is windy.*
Il fait frais.	*It is cool.*
Il fait froid.	*It is cold.*
Il fait jour.	*It is daytime.*
Il fait lourd.	*It is sultry.*
Il fait mauvais.	*It is bad out/bad weather.*
Il fait nuageux.	*It is cloudy.*
Il fait nuit.	*It is nighttime.*
Il fait orageux.	*There is a storm in the air.*
Il fait pluvieux.	*It is rainy.*
Quel temps fait-il?	*What's the weather like?*

Here are some other commonly used expressions with **faire**:

faire attention (à)	*to watch out for*
faire de son mieux	*to do one's best*
faire des achats	*to go shopping*
faire des courses	*to run errands*
faire des emplettes	*to go shopping*
faire des progrès	*to make progress*
faire du français	*to learn French*
faire du sport	*to practice/do sports*
faire la bise	*to give (someone) a kiss (greeting or farewell)*
faire la connaissance de	*to meet, make the acquaintance of*
faire mal (à)	*to hurt (someone)*
faire peur (à)	*to frighten/scare*
faire sa toilette	*to groom oneself*
faire ses adieux	*to bid good-bye*

faire un tour	*to go for a stroll*
faire un voyage	*to take a trip*
faire une promenade	*to take a walk/ride*

Reflexive verbs

Here are some commonly used expressions that use reflexive verbs.

s'en aller	*to go away*
se casser la jambe (le bras...)	*to break a leg (an arm . . .)*
se faire du souci	*to worry*
se faire mal (à)	*to hurt oneself*
se mettre à	*to begin*
se rappeler	*to remember*
se servir de	*to use*
se souvenir de	*to remember*

Exercise 143

Complete each sentence with an appropriate expression from the list.

fait des courses	fait un tour	se sert
fait de son mieux	fait mal	se casse
fait la connaissance	fait des progrès	s'en va
fait des voyages	fait attention	se rappelle
fait la bise	fait sa toilette	fait du sport

1. Elle _____ à sa mère tous les jours.

2. Elle _____ tout de suite après s'être levée.

3. Elle _____ du sèche-cheveux.

4. Elle _____ pour ne pas être en retard.

5. Elle _____ vers 8 heures.

6. Elle _____ de nouveaux clients chaque jour.

7. Après le travail, elle _____ au supermarché.

8. Le samedi elle _____ au parc avec son chien.

9. Elle _____ en traversant la rue principale.

10. Après ses matchs de tennis, l'épaule droite lui _____.

11. Elle _____ assez rarement.

12. Elle n'aime pas le ski parce qu'on _____ facilement un bras ou une jambe.

13. L'été elle _____ en France avec ses parents.

14. Elle _____ en français.

15. Elle _____ toujours d'écrire des cartes postales.

Review 10

Exercise 144

Un bon ami. *A good friend.* Translate the following sentences into French, using the present or past subjunctive (as appropriate) in the subordinate clause.

1. I am sorry Monique is sick. (être désolée/être malade)

   _____

2. I am not sure that her husband got my message. (être sûre/recevoir mon message)

   _____

3. Provided that he got the message, he will be here soon. (recevoir le message/être bientôt là)

   _____

4. I am happy that she called me. (être heureuse/téléphoner)

   _____

5. I wish she would get better quickly. (souhaiter/guérir)

   _____

6. The doctor wanted her to sleep. (vouloir/dormir)

   _____

7. I doubt that she listened to him. (douter/l'écouter)

   _____

8. I am going to stay here even though it may not be necessary. (rester ici/être nécessaire)

   _____

9. She must be patient. (Il faut/être patiente)

   _____

10. It is time that I eat something. (être temps/manger)

   _____

Exercise 145

Une histoire d'amour. *A love story.* To find out how Chloé's parents met, complete each sentence with the correct form of the verb in parentheses in the tense indicated.

1. Cette histoire _____ il y a vingt ans. (se passer/*passé composé*)

2. Mes parents _____ très bien de ce jour. (se souvenir/*présent*)

3. Ils _____ le long de la Seine. (se promener/*imparfait*)

4. Mon père _____ de ma mère. (s'approcher/*passé composé*)

5. Il lui a demandé comment elle _____. (s'appeler/*présent*)

6. Elle _____. (s'arrêter/*passé composé*)

7. Ils _____ longtemps. (se parler/*passé composé*)

8. Après cela, ils sont sortis ensemble. Ils _____ toujours beaucoup. (s'amuser/*imparfait*)

9. Ils _____ (se marier/*passé composé*) un an plus tard.

10. Je suis sûre qu'ils _____ toute leur vie. (s'aimer/*futur*)

Exercise 146

Proverbs and sayings are often expressed with structures such as the passive voice, reflexive verbs, and impersonal structures because they are general and universal in nature. Translate the following proverbs into English.

1. On est aisément dupé par ce qu'on aime. (Molière)

_____

2. Si tu veux être apprécié, meurs ou voyage. (Proverbe persan)

_____

3. L'éloge des absents se fait sans flatterie. (Gresset)

_____

4. Celui qui ne sait pas se fâcher est un sot, mais celui qui ne veut pas se fâcher est un sage. (W. Scarborough)

_____

5. Ce que l'on craint arrive plus facilement que ce qu'on espère. (Publilius)

_____

6. La loi nous oblige à faire ce qui est dit et non ce qui est juste. (Hugo Grotius)

_____

Exercise 147

Une soirée au concert. *An evening at a concert.* Put the following sentences into the correct order by using the numbers 1 through 10 to reconstitute Chloé's evening at the concert. The first one has been done for you.

_____1._____ J'ai un très bon copain qui s'appelle Jean-Claude.

_____ Je sais que je me rappellerai cette soirée toute ma vie.

_____ Lui et moi, nous nous sommes donné rendez-vous chez moi aujourd'hui à 18 h.

_____ Cet après-midi je me suis coiffé les cheveux pendant des heures.

_____ Je n'étais encore jamais allée au concert. Alors j'étais excitée!

_____ Ensuite je me suis habillée trois fois différemment juste avant son arrivée.

_____ Un bon concert ne se voit pas tous les jours. C'est très spécial!

_____ Enfin, mon copain est arrivé.

_____ Surtout ce concert-ci, les billets se vendaient très cher.

_____ On l'avait annoncé il y a des mois.

Exercise 148

Maman n'est pas contente. *Mom is not happy.* Chloé brings a friend home to study but her mom is not happy. Translate the following conversation among the three of them into English to find out why.

1. *Maman:* Pourquoi es-tu en retard, Chloé?

   Chloé: Je suis allée à la bibliothèque de l'école.

2. *Maman:* À quelle heure es-tu partie de l'école?

   Chloé: Vers quatre heures et demie.

3. *Maman:* Pourquoi est-ce que tu n'as pas téléphoné?

   Chloé: On ne peut pas utiliser le téléphone à la bibliothèque.

4. *Maman:* Qui est avec toi?

   Chloé: C'est mon copain Jean qui va m'aider avec mes devoirs.

5. *Maman:* Et qui va m'aider à préparer le gâteau d'anniversaire de papa?

   Chloé: Oh! J'ai oublié, maman.

6. *Maman:* Quoi! Comment est-ce que tu peux oublier quelque chose de si important?

   Chloé: Je suis vraiment désolée, maman.

7. *Maman:* Ton copain peut-il venir étudier avec toi samedi ou dimanche?

   Chloé: Quel jour est-ce que tu peux revenir, Jean?

8. *Jean:* Moi, ça va samedi ou dimanche. Qu'est-ce que tu préfères?

   Chloé: Viens samedi!

9. *Jean:* À quelle heure?

   Chloé: À 14 heures.

10. *Jean:* Est-ce que tu me garderas un morceau de gâteau?

    Chloé: Naturellement!

1. _____

_____

2. _____

_____

3. _____

_____

4. _____

_____

5. _____

_____

6. _____

_____

7. _____

_____

8. _____

_____

9. _____

_____

10. _____

_____

Exercise 149

Chloé bavarde avec son petit frère. *Chloé chats with her little brother.* Find the replies that Chloé's brother makes to his sister's statements and write the letter corresponding to the correct reply next to each statement.

1. _____ Ne mens pas; je sais que tu n'as pas fait tes devoirs.

2. _____ Ce n'est pas possible; je ne peux pas le croire.

3. _____ Il s'est bien moqué de toi! Tu vas le laisser faire?

4. _____ Tu crois que tu pourras lire ce long roman?

5. _____ Grand-père devrait faire du jogging.

6. _____ Maman et papa m'ont offert un cadeau qui me plaît beaucoup.

7. _____ Tu passes trop de temps à la maison. Il faut sortir.

8. _____ Je dors trop et je mange trop. Alors je grossis.

9. _____ Si tu m'avais envoyé une note, je l'aurais reçue.

10. _____ Viens avec moi chez ma copine Lucie. Je ne sais pas où elle habite.

a. Si jeunesse savait, si vieillesse pouvait.

b. Si j'avais le temps, je sortirais aujourd'hui.

c. Tu vas voir que je les ai faits. Tiens, les voilà!

d. Vouloir c'est pouvoir.

e. Voir c'est croire.

f. Elle vit avec ses parents dans la rue Dufour. Je connais l'adresse.

g. Rira bien qui rira le dernier.

h. Il faut manger pour vivre et non pas vivre pour manger.

i. C'est une voiture neuve et tu la conduis bien. Je t'ai vue plus tôt.

j. Crois-moi; je t'ai bien écrit une lettre.

Exercise 150

Chloé's French class. *Le cours de français de Chloé.* Translate the verb in parentheses into French using the correct form/tense/mood to find out what went on in Chloé's French class.

1. Hier je _____ à mon cours de français. (*I went*)

2. _____ qu'on allait avoir un examen, j'ai beaucoup étudié. (*Knowing*)

3. J'_____ écrire une longue rédaction. (*I had to*)

4. C'_____ très difficile. (*was*)

5. J'_____ les instructions. (*I followed*)

6. Je _____ que j'ai bien réussi. (*I believe*)

7. On _____ quand la prof rendra les examens. (*will see*)

8. Je _____ savoir tout de suite. (*I would like*)

9. Mais _____ attendre. (*it is necessary*)

10. Je _____ demain si j'ai une excellente note. (*I will know*)

Exercise 151

La maman de Jean-Paul téléphone à son fils. *Jean-Paul's mom calls her son.* Find the most appropriate reply to each question or statement and write the letter corresponding to that answer next to the question to reconstitute the conversation between Jean-Paul and his mother.

1. _____ Qu'est-ce qu'il y a, Jean-Paul?

2. _____ Tu avais promis de m'appeler!

3. _____ Il est 8 heures. Tu sais que je me fais du souci.

4. _____ Quel temps faisait-il hier soir quand tu es arrivé?

5. _____ D'habitude en août il fait orageux.

6. _____ À quelle heure pars-tu au travail?

7. _____ Tu ne devrais pas te préparer alors?

8. _____ Tu vas être en retard au rendez-vous!

9. _____ Comment va ton oncle Luc?

10. _____ Tu lui feras la bise de ma part.

a. Si, mais il fait à peine jour.

b. Oui, maman. Je vais faire ma toilette maintenant. Je t'embrasse.

c. Oui, c'est vrai. Mais quelle heure est-il?

d. Il est à l'étranger. Il revient dans trois jours.

e. Je suis assez grand pour me débrouiller, voyons!

f. Oh rien! J'ai encore sommeil.

g. Ma première réunion a lieu ce matin à 9 heures.

h. Mais non, ne t'en fais pas!

i. Pas en ce moment. Il fait doux et sec.

j. Il faisait beau et doux.

Exercise 152

Lucie a passé une mauvaise nuit. *Lucie had a bad night.* Translate the following conversation between Lucie and her husband about Lucie's bad dream into French.

1. Hi sweetheart! How are you today?

2. I am still a little sleepy.

_____

3. Did you have nice dreams?

_____

4. Not at all! I dreamed that I had broken a leg while skiing.

_____

5. Oh no! Did I come to rescue you?

_____

6. All I can say is that I was terribly frightened.

_____

7. It probably hurt a lot.

_____

8. It goes without saying.

_____

9. It was nothing but a dream. Your leg doesn't hurt you now.

_____

10. No, but I do have a headache.

_____

Final Review

Exercise 153

C'est le week-end. Il faut faire les courses. *It's the weekend. We must go shopping.* In the following sentences, fill in each blank space with the appropriate article (definite, possessive, or partitive). Leave the space blank if no article is required, and remember to use contractions when required.

1. Aujourd'hui, c'est _____ samedi.

2. _____ samedi, je vais toujours faire les courses. Je prends

3. _____ liste et je vais

4. _____ supermarché Carrefour qui est dans mon quartier. Là, j'achète

5. _____ lait,

6. _____ céréales,

7. _____ charcuterie, mais pas

8. _____ pain ni

9. _____ légumes. Je préfère acheter

10. _____ fruits et

11. _____ légumes au marché du coin. J'achète

12. _____ pain frais tous les jours chez

13. _____ boulanger favori. Il s'appelle Marius et il a

14. _____ meilleur pain

15. _____ monde.

Exercise 154

C'est la rentrée. Il faut acheter des fournitures scolaires. *It's back-to-school season. We have to buy school supplies.* In the following sentences, fill in each blank with the appropriate article (indefinite, possessive, demonstrative, or interrogative).

1. *Maman:* Regarde, Laurie, voilà _____ beau sac à dos!

2. *Laurie:* _____ sac à dos, maman?

3. *Maman:* _____ sac à dos bleu et noir, là-bas.

4. *Laurie:* Ah oui! Il n'est pas mal mais je préfère porter mes affaires dans _____ vieux sac en toile.

5. *Maman:* Oh Laurie! Tu as vraiment besoin d'_____ sac neuf!

6. *Laurie:* Je t'assure, maman, je veux garder le sac de toile. C'est _____ porte-bonheur (*lucky charm, m*) depuis si longtemps!

7. *Maman:* Bon! Allons voir si nous pouvons trouver _____ nouvelle imprimante pour ton ordinateur.

8. *Laurie:* Je crois qu'il y a _____ bonne sélection ici! Merci, maman.

9. *Maman:* Après, il faut acheter aussi tous _____ livres que ton prof de français recommande.

10. *Laurie:* _____ livres, maman?

Exercise 155

On sort avec des amis. Il faut se détendre. *We are going out with friends. We have to relax.* In the following dialogue, fill in each blank with the appropriate adjective.

1. *Eric:* J'ai _____ projets ce weekend. (*a lot of*)

2. *Miriam:* Ah oui? Tu veux me donner _____ idées? (*a few*)

3. *Eric:* Bien sûr! On peut commencer par appeler _____ amis et aller au centre Beaubourg! (*some*)

4. *Miriam:* Oh! Je n'ai pas envie d'aller au musée. De plus, il ya toujours _____ de monde là-bas. (*too many*)

5. *Eric:* Je ne parle pas d'aller au musée. C'est l'endroit _____ amusant pour faire du skateboard. (*most*)

6. *Miriam:* Ah! D'accord. Ce n'est peut-être pas encore _____ animé que d'habitude tôt le matin. (*as*)

7. *Eric:* Et puis, on peut boire _____ de soda à la terrasse d'un café. (*a glass of*)

8. *Miriam:* Bon. Bonne idée! Je suis _____ enthousiaste que toi mais ça va. (*less*)

Exercise 156

On va au gymnase. Il faut rester en forme. *We go to the gym. We have to stay in shape.* In the following sentences, fill in each blank with the appropriate adjective or adverb.

1. Il est _____ 14 heures. (*already*)

2. Allons _____ au gym! (*quickly*)

3. _____ je vais faire une promenade. (*Otherwise*)

4. _____ je ne vais plus avoir le courage ou la force. (*Later*)

5. _____ j'adore aller au gym. (*Frankly*)

6. Tous les membres du gym pratiquent _____ des sports. (*diligently*)

7. Beaucoup de ces gens sont _____ des amis. (*evidently/of course*)

8. _____, moi, je ne vais pas assez _____ au gym. (*Unfortunately, often*)

9. Mon copain Fabrice y va encore _____ que moi. (*more rarely*)

10. C'est parce qu'il travaille _____ que moi. (*as hard*)

Exercise 157

Le gymnase. *The gym.* Translate the following sentences using the vocabulary provided in parentheses. Take care to structure the sentence appropriately and make adjectives agree when necessary.

1. My gym is big and spacious. (le gym/grand/spacieux)

   _____

2. There are many machines. (la appareil)

   _____

3. People walk on modern treadmills. (Les gens (m)/marcher/moderne/le tapis roulant)

   _____

4. People are athletic, muscular, and in good shape. (Les gens/athlétique/musclé/en bonne forme)

   _____

5. Indoor activities are generally as important as outdoor activities. (l'activité (f)/en salle/ important/généralement/en plein air)

   _____

6. Women go to the gym as often as men. (la femme/aller/souvent/l'homme)

   _____

7. I sometimes stay at the gym longer than my friends. (quelquefois/rester/longtemps/l'ami)

_____

8. For me, the best time of day to exercise is the morning. (le moment de la journée/faire de l'exercice/le matin)

_____

Exercise 158

C'est le weekend. Nous allons au cinéma. _It's the weekend. We are going to the movies._ In the following dialogue, fill in each blank with the appropriate object pronoun.

1. _Michel:_ Il y a un nouveau film qui joue au cinéma. Tu veux _____ voir? (_it_)

2. _Thomas:_ Tu as vu la critique? Tiens, je te _____ montre. (_it_)

3. _Michel:_ Tu n'as pas besoin de me _____ montrer. Je sais qu'elle est bonne. (_it_)

4. _Thomas:_ On peut inviter Jean. Tu veux _____ envoyer un texto? (_to him_)

5. _Michel:_ D'accord. Mais il faut aussi inviter tes cousines. Alors, toi, tu _____ envoies un texto ou tu _____ téléphones. (_to them, them_)

6. _Thomas:_ Oh zut! Où est mon portable? Tu sais, je _____ oublie toujours quelque part. (_it_)

7. _Michel:_ Eh bien. Tu n'_____ as pas besoin. Regarde! Voilà tes cousines là-bas. Appelle-_____ vite! (_it, them_)

8. _Thomas:_ Arielle, Josée, vous voulez _____ accompagner au ciné? (_us_)

9. _Michel:_ Si vous voulez venir, dépêchez-_____, les filles! (_reflexive pronoun_)

10. _Thomas:_ Oui, allons-_____ ! (_there_)

Exercise 159

C'est la rentrée. Nous faisons la connaissance de nos camarades de classe et de nos professeurs. _It's back-to-school time. We get to know our classmates and our teachers._ In the following dialogue, fill in each blank with the appropriate stress or object pronoun.

1. _Michel:_ Dis donc, Thomas, qui est la fille assise devant _____ ? (_you_)

2. _Thomas:_ C'est Gisèle, une nouvelle élève. Je vais te _____ présenter. (_her_)

3. *Michel:* D'accord. Et qui est le garçon à côté d'_____? (*her*)

4. *Thomas:* Ça, c'est Luc. Il travaillait avec _____ dans le labo physique l'an dernier. (*me*)

5. *Michel:* Je ne _____ connais pas du tout. (*him*)

6. *Thomas:* Chut! Tais-_____ ! Je veux entendre le discours du directeur. (*reflexive pronoun*)

7. *Michel:* Tous ces discours au début de l'année! Ça _____ ennuie. Il y _____ a trop! (*me, of them*)

8. *Thomas:* Écoute! Pour _____, les administrateurs, c'est important de _____ donner des renseignements. (*them, us*)

9. *Michel:* Je sais, Thomas. Tiens, je crois qu'il va _____ présenter les nouveaux profs. (*us*)

10. *Thomas:* Oui, écoutons-_____! (*him*)

Exercise 160

Les nouveaux profs. *The new teachers.* In the following paragraph, fill in each blank with the appropriate preposition or prepositional phrase from the list provided. Some may be used more than once.

à	à côté de	à propos de	au
au centre de	car	de	derrière
du	en	pendant	

M. le directeur présente les nouveaux professeurs 1. _____ ses élèves.

2. _____ ses présentations, les étudiants écoutent attentivement

3. _____ ils sont curieux. M. le directeur est debout 4. _____ le

podium, 5. _____ la salle. Les professeurs sont alignés 6. _____

lui. Il les présente un à un et dit quelques mots 7. _____ chacun d'eux. Thomas dit

8. _____ Michel 9. _____ cesser de parler. Un des nouveaux pro-

fesseurs vient 10. _____ Tunisie, un autre vient 11. _____ Maroc.

Moi, je ne suis jamais allé ni 12. _____ Tunisie ni 13. _____

Maroc, seulement 14. _____ Algérie.

Exercise 161

Les conséquences de mes excès. *The consequences of my excesses.* Complete each sentence with the present participle form of the verb in parentheses.

1. En _____ trop vite, je fais des erreurs. (écrire)

2. En _____ trop vite, je me fatigue. (courir)

3. En _____ et en _____ trop vite, je me fais mal à l'estomac. (manger, boire)

4. En _____ l'escalier trop vite, je tombe. (monter)

5. En _____ trop vite, je dis des bêtises. (répondre)

6. En _____ trop, je me stresse. (réfléchir)

7. En _____ trop de choses, je fais des dettes. (acheter)

8. En _____ trop vite, j'ai des amendes. (conduire)

Exercise 162

Ne faites pas comme moi! *Don't do as I do!* Using the plural imperative form of the verb, tell your friends not to indulge in any of the excesses mentioned in the previous exercise. The first one is done for you.

1. N'écrivez pas trop vite!

2. _____!

3. _____!

4. _____!

5. _____!

6. _____!

7. _____!

8. _____!

Exercise 163

Je veux savoir! *I want to know!* Ask your best friend the following questions. Pose each question in two different ways, first with **est-ce que** and then with *inversion.*

1. Why do you write too fast?

   a. _____?

   b. _____?

2. When do you run too fast?

    a. _____?

    b. _____?

3. Do you always eat and drink too fast?

    a. _____?

    b. _____?

4. How do you go up the stairs?

    a. _____?

    b. _____?

5. (To) whom do you answer too fast?

    a. _____?

    b. _____?

6. In what circumstances (*la circonstance*) do you think too much?

    a. _____?

    b. _____?

7. What do you buy and where do you buy it?

    a. _____?

    b. _____?

8. At what time do you sometimes drive too fast?

    a. _____?

    b. _____?

Exercise 164

Que peut-on et que ne peut-on pas faire à la piscine publique? *What can one do and what can one not do at the public pool?* Using the verbs **pouvoir** and **devoir** in the present tense, and the vocabulary in parentheses, translate the following sentences.

1. We can swim and dive into the deep end. (nager/plonger/le profond)

_____

2. We can sunbathe and rest in the lounge chairs. (se faire bronzer/se reposer/la chaise longue)

_____

3. We can go to the restrooms and take a shower. (aller/les toilettes/prendre une douche)

_____

4. Children can play and have fun in the little pool. (jouer/s'amuser/la piscine)

_____

5. Everyone must obey the lifeguard. (tout le monde/obéir/le maître nageur)

_____

6. Children must stay with adults. (l'enfant/rester/l'adulte)

_____

7. Nobody must put other people in danger. (personne/mettre les gens en danger)

_____

8. We must shower before going into the pool. (prendre une douche/la piscine)

_____

Exercise 165

Que fera-t-on après la piscine? *What will we do after the pool?* Complete the following paragraph by writing the verbs in parentheses in the future tense.

Jean-Luc et moi, nous 1. _____ chez nous (rentrer). Nos parents nous

2. _____ rendre visite à la tante Pauline (emmener). Notre tante nous

3. _____ un gros dîner (faire). Nos cousins nous 4. _____ leurs

nouveaux jeux vidéos (montrer). Nous 5. _____ probablement faire une promenade

en ville (aller). Il y 6. _____ beaucoup de touristes dans les rues (avoir). Nous

7. _____ sûrement des glaces (acheter). Maman 8. _____ s'arrêter

dans des galeries d'art (vouloir) et papa 9. _____ envie de boire un café (avoir).

Nous 10. _____ une soirée très agréable (passer). Nous 11. _____

bien contents mais fatigués en fin de soirée (être). Nous 12. _____ vers minuit

(se coucher).

Exercise 166

Mon année de terminale. *My senior year.* Complete each sentence with either the **passé composé** or the **imparfait** of the verb in parentheses as deemed appropriate.

L'année dernière quand j' 1. _____ (être) au lycée, je 2. _____

(devoir) travailler régulièrement et sérieusement pour avoir de bonnes notes. Au mois de décembre

j' 3. _____ (envoyer) mes dossiers de candidature à plusieurs universités qui m'

4. _____ (intéresser). Deux universités m' 5. _____ (donner)

une réponse positive assez rapidement. La troisième 6. _____ (attendre)

jusqu'au mois d'avril pour me répondre. La lettre 7. _____ (arriver) le premier

avril! J' 8. _____ (avoir) horriblement peur de l'ouvrir. Finalement

j' 9. _____ (prendre) mon courage à deux mains et je l' 10. _____

(ouvrir). Heureusement que la réponse 11. _____ (être) positive. Après cela, le temps

12. _____ (passer) si vite!

Exercise 167

L'année dernière au lycée et cette année à l'université. *Last year in high school and this year in college.* Fill in the first blank in each sentence with the **imparfait** form and the second blank with the present tense of the verb in parentheses.

1. L'an dernier, j'_____ cours tous les jours et cette année, je

   n'_____ cours ni lundi ni jeudi. (avoir)

2. L'an dernier, je _____ des devoirs aux profs tous les jours et cette année, j'en

   _____ deux ou trois fois par trimestre. (rendre)

3. L'an dernier, je _____ partie de trois équipes de sport et cette année, je _____

   _____ partie seulement de l'équipe de tennis. (faire)

4. L'an dernier, je ne _____ pas, mais cette année je _____ au

   centre d'information. (travailler)

5. L'an dernier, mon déjeuner _____ cinquante minutes, mais cette année il

   _____ au moins deux heures. (durer)

6. L'an dernier, j'_____ seulement l'espagnol et cette année, j'_____

   aussi le français. (étudier)

7. L'an dernier, je _____ toujours mes devoirs le soir même, mais cette année je

   les _____ après quelques semaines. (finir)

8. L'an dernier, j'_____ encore lycéen et cette année, je _____

   étudiant universitaire. (être)

Exercise 168

Si j'habitais encore à la maison. Les pour et les contre. *If I still lived at home. Pros and cons.* Translate each sentence from English into French using the conditional tense.

1. Mom would make my dinners.

_____

2. Dad would tell me when I have to go to bed.

_____

3. My little sister would constantly ask for help with homework.

_____

4. I would get up at 5:30 each morning.

_____

5. My friends could not come over after 7 P.M.

_____

6. I would never play music late at night.

_____

7. My parents would wake me up in the morning.

_____

8. I would go out at night only on the weekend.

_____

9. I would have breakfast and dinner with my family.

_____

10. I would have less freedom.

_____

Exercise 169

Les regrets et les joies d'André. *André's regrets and joys.* Use the past infinitive of the verb in parentheses to complete each sentence.

1. Je regrette de _____ ce travail plus tôt. (ne pas finir)

2. Je regrette d'_____ souvent pendant la semaine. (sortir)

3. Je regrette de _____ plus souvent à ma famille. (ne pas téléphoner)

4. Je regrette d'_____ au café chaque jour. (trop dépenser)

5. Je suis content d'_____ à mes examens. (réussir)

6. Je suis content d'_____ chez moi pendant les vacances. (rentrer)

7. Je suis content d'_____ mes amis au retour à l'université. (retrouver)

8. Je suis content de _____ à la maison. (se bien reposer)

Exercise 170

Ma routine quotidienne à l'université. *My daily routine at the university.* Complete each sentence by writing the reflexive verbs in parentheses in the present tense.

1. Je _____ entre une et deux heures du matin. (se coucher).

2. Je _____ quelquefois quand il y a des fêtes bruyantes dans mon dortoir.
   (se réveiller)

3. Mais je _____ assez vite. (se rendormir)

4. Je _____ vers dix heures du matin. (se lever)

5. Je _____ , je _____ les dents et je _____ .
   (se laver, se brosser les dents, s'habiller)

6. Je _____ que j'ai cours. (se rappeler)

7. Je _____ . (s'en aller)

8. Quelquefois je _____ sur cet immense campus. (se perdre)

Exercise 171

Mon université. *My university.* Translate each sentence by using the verb in parentheses in the passive voice.

1. My university was built in 1858. (construire)

_____

2. The courtyard was added in 1910. (ajouter)

_____

3. The information center was renovated last year. (rénover)

_____

4. A new restaurant is going to be opened on the campus very soon. (ouvrir)

_____

5. The student parking will be extended next year. (agrandir)

_____

Exercise 172

Description d'Irène, ma camarade de chambre. *Description of my roommate Irène.* Complete each sentence by translating the phrase in parentheses.

1. Irène est intelligente et elle _____. (*has presence*)

2. Le matin, elle _____ de faire du jogging même quand il _____.

   (*is used to, is bad out*)

3. Elle _____ énergique chaque fois qu'on la rencontre. (*looks*)

4. Elle _____. (*is never in a bad mood*)

5. Après son jogging, elle _____. (*grooms herself*)

6. Elle _____ pour être au cours à l'heure. (*does her best*)

7. Quand elle voit ses amies, elle leur _____. (*gives a kiss on the cheek*)

8. Elle _____ toujours _____ de bavarder avec ses amies.

   (*has the time*)

Exercise 173

À qui est-ce? *Whom does it belong to?* Complete each sentence with the word(s) in parentheses.

1. La brosse à cheveux d'Irène est sur le lavabo de la salle de bains. _____ est
   à côté de mon lit. (*mine*)

2. Son lit est à côté de la fenêtre. _____ est contre l'autre mur. (*mine*)

3. Elle a accroché plusieurs jolies affiches au mur. Moi, je préfère _____ de la
   Tour Eiffel. (*the one*)

4. Elle me laisse jouer à des jeux vidéo très cool. J'adore _____ qui présentent des
   problèmes bizarres. (*the ones*)

5. Elle téléphone souvent à ses parents. Moi, j'appelle _____ une fois par semaine.
   (*mine*)

6. Elle a de belles photos sur son bureau. J'aime bien _____ où elle est entourée
   d'éléphants. (*the one*)

Exercise 174

Pour bien réussir à l'université. *In order to do well at the university.* Complete each sentence with the present subjunctive of the verb in parentheses.

1. Il faut absolument que vous _____ les devoirs à temps. (rendre)

2. Il vaut mieux que vous _____ absents des cours. (ne pas être)

3. Il serait bon que vous _____ aux discussions. (participer)

4. Il serait utile que vous _____ du travail indépendant. (faire)

5. Il est nécessaire que vous _____ bien votre temps libre. (gérer)

6. Les profs suggèrent que vous _____ bien vos sujets de travail indépendant. (choisir)

7. Les profs doutent que vous _____ le temps de faire vos recherches. (ne pas avoir)

8. Les profs seront contents que vous _____ à vos examens. (réussir)

9. Vous devez être patients jusqu'à ce que vous _____ de bons résultats. (avoir)

10. Vous devez poser des questions et tester vos connaissances avant que vos profs vous _____ passer de gros examens. (faire)

11. Vous devez faire tout le travail nécessaire sans qu'on vous le _____. (dire)

12. Il faut persévérer bien que ce _____ difficile. (être)

Exercise 175

Pauvre Sophie! *Poor Sophie!* Complete each sentence with the past subjunctive of the verb in parentheses.

1. Marc doute que Sophie _____. (se dépêcher)

2. Il est désolé qu'elle _____ en retard. (être)

3. Il regrette qu'elle _____ une mauvaise note à l'examen. (avoir)

4. Il est possible que Sophie _____. (ne pas étudier)

5. Il se peut qu'elle _____ avec des amis hier soir. (sortir)

6. Il souhaite qu'elle _____ la soirée avec lui. (passer)

7. Il est vraiment triste qu'elle _____ de mauvais choix dernièrement. (faire)

8. Il n'est même pas sûr qu'elle _____ les conséquences de ses actions. (comprendre)

Exercise 176

Sophie va mieux! *Sophie is doing better!* Choose the appropriate relative pronoun in parentheses to complete each sentence.

1. Sophie est la fille _____ ne travaillait pas et sortait tout le temps s'amuser. (qui, que)

2. Ah oui! Marc m'a parlé d'elle. C'est elle _____ on ne voyait jamais aux cours. (qui, qu')

3. C'est ça! Mais elle a eu de très mauvaise notes _____ l'ont choquée. (qui, que)

4. Eh bien! Heureusement qu'elle a vu que _____ elle faisait ne pouvait pas continuer. (ce qui, ce qu')

5. Oui, le jour _____ Sophie a échoué à un examen important, elle a soudain changé son style de vie. (que, où)

6. Tu vois, les gens peuvent changer. C'est le genre de choses _____ je te parlais. (dont, où)

7. Les amis parmi _____ elle se trouve maintenant sont beaucoup mieux. (lesquels, que)

8. Marc est son meilleur ami. C'est celui _____ l'a toujours aidée le plus. (lequel, qui)

9. C'est le genre d'ami _____ tout le monde a besoin. (qui, dont)

10. C'est la raison pour _____ je l'admire. (que, laquelle)

11. Sophie fait beaucoup de progrès _____ Marc est très content. (de qui, dont)

12. Tout est bien _____ finit bien! (qui, que)

Answer Key

Exercise 1

1. la 2. le 3. le 4. la 5. le 6. la 7. la 8. le 9. le 10. la 11. le 12. la 13. le 14. la 15. la

Exercise 2

1. Légume/le 2. Légume/le 3. Fruit/la 4. Arbre/le 5. Fruit/l' (f) 6. Légume/le 7. Fruit/la 8. Légume/le 9. Arbre/le 10. Arbre/le 11. Légume/l' (m) 12. Fruit/la 13. Arbre/l' (m) 14. Légume/le

Exercise 3

1. U 2. E 3. D 4. S 5. M 6. D 7. L 8. L 9. U 10. E 11. M 12. S 13. E 14. S 15. E

Exercise 4

1. the sail of the boat/la 2. the death of the poet/la 3. the physical appearance of the athlete/le 4. the pound of bread/la 5. the teaching position/le 6. the woman's veil/le 7. the village post office/la 8. the guided tour of the museum/le 9. the dead man in the coffin/le 10. physics and chemistry/la

Exercise 5

1. l' (m) 2. l' (f) 3. le 4. la 5. le 6. l' (m) 7. l' (f) 8. le 9. l' (m) 10. le 11. le 12. la 13. le 14. le 15. la 16. le 17. le 18. la 19. la 20. le 21. la 22. la 23. le 24. la 25. le 26. le 27. le 28. la 29. le 30. le

Exercise 6

1. madame 2. Les 3. samedi 4. en 5. aux 6. des 7. à la 8. des 9. Le docteur 10. Le petit 11. monsieur 12. La/la 13. l' 14. de 15. en 16. le 17. L' 18. Le 19. en 20. du 21. L' 22. La 23. – 24. en 25. Les

Exercise 7

1. une 2. un 3. un 4. une 5. des 6. des 7. un 8. un 9. une 10. des 11. – 12. un 13. – 14. un 15. une

Exercise 8

1. cet 2. cette 3. ces 4. cette 5. Ce 6. Ces 7. Ce 8. Cet 9. cette 10. Ces 11. Cet 12. Cette 13. Cette 14. Ces 15. Ce/ce

Exercise 9

1. mon 2. ton 3. son 4. ma 5. ta 6. sa 7. mes 8. tes 9. ses 10. notre 11. nos 12. votre 13. vos 14. leur 15. leurs

Exercise 10

1. les 2. les 3. la/les 4. les 5. les 6. le 7. les 8. les 9. les 10. le

Exercise 11

1. Quelle 2. Quelle 3. Quelles 4. Quelle 5. Quels 6. Quel 7. Quelle 8. Quels 9. Quels 10. Quel 11. Quelle 12. Quelle 13. Quel 14. Quel 15. Quels

Exercise 12

1. le 2. les 3. Les 4. des 5. Les 6. – 7. – 8. une 9. la 10. – 11. ma 12. ces 13. ce 14. ton 15. –

Exercise 13

1. I am coming from school. 2. I am going to the market with Mom. 3. Fruit is expensive in winter. 4. This fruit is still green! 5. Vegetables are always fresh here. 6. I like/love vegetable soup. 7. Buy this celery. It looks good. 8. And these carrots too. 9. Soon it is/it will be Dad's birthday. 10. He loves animals. 11. Especially dogs. 12. What do you think of this little bulldog? 13. You hate bulldogs? Too bad! 14. Where are we going to buy his birthday cake? 15. At the bakery in Rémy Street? 16. That bakery is very expensive, isn't it? 17. His birthday is on Monday, right? 18. That's good. I always stay home on Mondays. 19. We always invite all his friends. 20. What a great family!

Exercise 14

1. le dimanche 2. ce dimanche 3. leurs 4. Cet 5. leur 6. Son 7. la 8. Quelle 9. sa 10. Ses 11. l' 12. le français 13. professeur 14. des/des 15. les achats 16. une 17. Sa 18. des 19. des 20. Cet

Exercise 15

1. les crayons 2. les chaises 3. nos bureaux 4. ces dames 5. messieurs 6. mesdames 7. leurs garçons 8. ses filles 9. quels fils 10. les hôpitaux 11. les yeux 12. des morceaux 13. les généraux 14. vos bateaux 15. mes choix 16. les autobus 17. les tableaux 18. les musées 19. les portes 20. ces bijoux

Exercise 16

1. – 2. des 3. de 4. de 5. de 6. d' 7. – 8. de 9. de 10. d' 11. les 12. de 13. du 14. de la 15. du 16. d' 17. de 18. des 19. de 20. de

Exercise 17

1. Du 2. de la 3. Du 4. de 5. De l' 6. d' 7. du 8. Le 9. des 10. de 11. Some coffee, sir? 12. Yes, thank you. With some cream! 13. I'll be right there. Some bread with that? 14. Sure! But no croissants! 15. OK. Some mineral water? 16. No, no, thanks. No mineral water. 17. But bring me some orange juice! 18. Yes, sir. Our juice is very fresh today. 19. Do you have chocolate croissants (rolls) today? 20. Yes. And delicious brioches as well.

Exercise 18

1. – 2. de 3. de 4. de 5. de 6. d' 7. – 8. le 9. de 10. d' 11. les 12. de 13. le 14. de la 15. Les

Exercise 19

1. I have blue eyes. 2. I have blond hair. 3. I buy lots of sports magazines. 4. I watch soccer games on TV. 5. I like sports. 6. My son Éric looks like me. 7. He has blue eyes and blond hair like me. 8. That child knows so many games. 9. He is very extroverted. He talks to everybody. 10. He plays a lot of tricks on his friends. 11. Here are a few examples. 12. He sends fake invitations. 13. He writes amusing notes to his classmates. 14. He tells unbelievable jokes to everybody. 15. He draws very funny caricatures of his friends.

Exercise 20

1. *Éric:* Hello, ladies and gentlemen. *Waiter:* Just a minute, young man. I am serving customers. 2. *Éric:* I have a little money for a Coke. *Waiter:* Children cannot come in without their parents. 3. *Éric:* But I only want some bread and a soda. *Waiter:* Listen, little one. I am going to serve you because I don't have a lot of customers. 4. *Éric:* Thank you, sir. Is there butter on this bread? *Waiter:* No, sorry. But here is a Coke and some water. 5. *Éric:* I don't need water. *Waiter:* Finish your Coke and go home! 6. *Éric:* Can I have some ice cream? *Waiter:* What! Go home and come back with your parents!

Exercise 21

1. *Éric:* Hello, Mrs. Lebon. *Mme Lebon:* Hello, my child. 2. *Éric:* I would like some butter please. *Mme Lebon:* Butter or margarine? 3. *Éric:* Is butter yellow? *Mme Lebon:* Yes, so you do want butter. 4. *Éric:* Yes, and some

rolls also. *Mme Lebon:* How many rolls? 5. *Éric:* Two rolls and some dark chocolate. *Mme Lebon:* Here is a chocolate bar and two rolls. Is this for you? 6. *Éric:* Yes, ma'am. I love rolls with chocolate inside. *Mme Lebon:* You like good things! 7. *Éric:* I also need some apples for Mom. *Mme Lebon:* Don't you like apples? 8. *Éric:* I do, but Mom is going to make an apple tart. *Mme Lebon:* Oh! So sorry! I don't have any more apples. 9. *Éric:* Do you have apricots? *Mme Lebon:* Yes, here is half a kilo. 10. *Éric:* Thank you, ma'am. Are apricots expensive? *Mme Lebon:* Not at all. Not more expensive than apples.

Exercise 22

1. grande 2. petite 3. fatiguée 4. énervée 5. méchante 6. allemande 7. verte 8. distraite 9. grise 10. spontanée 11. japonaise 12. mauvaise 13. résignée 14. désespérée 15. française 16. jolie 17. bleue 18. courte 19. démodée 20. épuisée

Exercise 23

1. Ils sont grands. Elles sont grandes. 2. Mes frères sont petits. Mes sœurs sont petites. 3. Ils sont fatigués. Elles sont fatiguées. 4. Les petits sont énervés. Les petites sont énervées. 5. Les chiens sont méchants. Les chiennes sont méchantes. 6. Ils sont allemands. Elles sont allemandes. 7. Les gazons sont verts. Les herbes sont vertes. 8. Les profs sont distraits. Les profs sont distraites. 9. Les pulls sont gris. Les robes sont grises. 10. Ces garçons sont spontanés. Ces filles sont spontanées. 11. Ces camions sont japonais. Ces voitures sont japonaises. 12. Ces romans sont mauvais. Ces nouvelles sont mauvaises. 13. Ils sont résignés à partir. Elles sont résignées à partir. 14. Les hommes sont désespérés. Les femmes sont désespérées. 15. Ce sont des films français. Ce sont des émissions françaises. 16. Ce sont de jolis bouquets. Ce sont de jolies fleurs. 17. Voici des pantalons bleus. Voici des jupes bleues. 18. Tes shorts sont courts. Tes robes sont courtes. 19. Tes costumes sont démodés. Tes vestes sont démodées. 20. Ils sont épuisés. Elles sont épuisées.

Exercise 24

1. grande/grands/grandes 2. riche/riches/riches 3. séparée/séparés/séparées 4. blanche/blancs/blanches 5. américaine/américains/américaines 6. italienne/italiens/italiennes 7. fatiguée/fatigués/fatiguées 8. gentille/gentils/gentilles 9. basse/bas/basses 10. bonne/bons/bonnes 11. prétentieuse/prétentieux/prétentieuses 12. naïve/naïfs/naïves 13. fière/fiers/fières 14. folle/fous/folles 15. sèche/secs/sèches

Exercise 25

1. J'ai fait un voyage amusant. 2. Il me faut un stylo bleu. 3. Les films américains sont pleins d'action. 4. Ça, c'est un film passionnant. 5. C'est le seul homme avec toutes ces femmes. 6. Quelle longue journée! 7. J'ai ma propre voiture. 8. C'est la dernière fois que je t'écris. 9. J'aime mes amis français. 10. Mireille est une jolie fille. 11. C'est une petite faute. 12. C'est une actrice célèbre. 13. C'est une vieille femme. 14. Les Alpes sont des montagnes hautes. 15. Ce sont de nouvelles habitations.

Exercise 26

1. Marc est plus paresseux que Lise. 2. Jeanne est moins paresseuse que Marc. 3. Jeanne est aussi paresseuse que Joseph. 4. Joseph et Jeanne sont plus paresseux que Lise. 5. Marc est le plus paresseux des quatre. 6. Marc est le pire (le plus mauvais) en français. 7. Lise est la meilleure en français. 8. Joseph est aussi bon en français que Jeanne.

Exercise 27

1. F 2. F 3. V 4. F 5. F 6. V 7. V 8. V 9. F 10. F 11. F 12. F 13. F 14. V 15. V

Exercise 28

1. J'ai de nouveaux voisins. 2. Ce sont des gens aimables. 3. Mais ils ont un chien méchant. 4. Le vieil arbre des voisins est sec. 5. Pauvres voisins! 6. Leur fille Denise est amoureuse de Pierre! 7. Denise est attentive en classe mais Pierre est distrait. 8. Notre maître est irrité. 9. Il n'est pas patient. 10. Mais il est très indulgent. 11. Quelle belle voiture! 12. Je préfère son ancienne voiture. 13. Ces nouvelles voitures sont chères. 14. La voiture de papa est vieille. 15. Elle est bonne seulement pour les voyages courts.

Exercise 29

1. dehors 2. Autrefois 3. longtemps 4. D'abord 5. encore 6. presque 7. bien 8. beaucoup 9. si 10. vraiment 11. partout 12. déjà

Exercise 30

1. précieusement 2. tranquillement 3. réellement 4. vraiment 5. doucement 6. difficilement 7. impoliment 8. lentement 9. heureusement 10. fièrement 11. élégamment 12. prudemment 13. impatiemment 14. aisément 15. résolument 16. extrêmement 17. totalement 18. rarement 19. faussement 20. généralement

Exercise 31

1. Denise parle moins doucement que Marc. 2. Denise parle aussi doucement que Jeannine. 3. Denise parle plus doucement que moi. 4. Marc parle le plus doucement. 5. Je parle bien le français. 6. Tu parles le français aussi bien que moi. 7. Luc ne parle pas aussi bien le français que nous. 8. Toi et moi, nous parlons le français le mieux. 9. Le professeur parle le français le plus vite. 10. Luc parle le français le plus mal (le pire).

Exercise 32

1. J'aime **bien** les bandes dessinées. (*I like comic strips.*) 2. Tu as **déjà** fermé ton livre? (*Have you already closed your book?*) 3. **Quelquefois** je lis jusqu'à onze heures du soir. *Or* Je lis **quelquefois** jusqu'à onze heures du soir. (*Sometimes I read till 11 P.M.*) 4. Je fais **toujours** mes devoirs après le dîner. (*I always do my homework after dinner.*) 5. J'écoute **aussi** de la musique pop. (*I also listen to pop music.*) 6. Je pars de la maison **très** tôt le matin. (*I leave my house very early in the morning.*) 7. Mes copains et moi attendons l'autobus **patiemment**. *Or* Nous attendons **patiemment** l'autobus. (*My friends and I wait patiently for the bus.*) 8. Ginette a **vraiment** grandi cet été. (*Ginette really grew up this summer.*) 9. Elle chante **gaiement**. (*She sings gaily.*) 10. Le bus s'est **enfin** arrêté. *Or* **Enfin** le bus s'est arrêté. (*The bus finally stopped.*) 11. Je parle au chauffeur **poliment**. *Or* Je parle **poliment** au chauffeur. (*I speak politely to the driver.*) 12. **Aujourd'hui** je suis fatigué. *Or* Je suis fatigué **aujourd'hui**. (*I am tired today.*) 13. Je voudrais étudier **calmement** chez moi. (*I would like to study quietly at home.*) 14. Je vais rester à la maison **demain**. *Or* **Demain** je vais rester à la maison. (*Tomorrow I will stay at home.*) 15. Il va **régulièrement** au restaurant. *Or* Il va au restaurant **régulièrement**. (*He goes to the restaurant regularly.*)

Exercise 33

1. bruyamment 2. sûrement 3. en retard 4. partout 5. Déjà 6. Ailleurs 7. En ce moment 8. hier 9. très 10. Le lendemain 11. rapidement 12. la veille 13. si 14. beaucoup 15. tellement

Exercise 34

1. without a doubt 2. really 3. Unfortunately/too much 4. almost 5. Now/quietly/patiently 6. early 7. nothing good/right now 8. as much as 9. something 10. Usually

Exercise 35

1. vraiment/réellement 2. Heureusement 3. souvent 4. presque 5. certainement/sûrement 6. probablement 7. d'habitude/à l'heure 8. calmement 9. d'abord 10. rien

Exercise 36

1. Je 2. Nous 3. Ils 4. Elle 5. tu 6. Elles 7. Vous 8. Je 9. J' 10. On 11. on 12. J' 13. Ils 14. Nous 15. tu

Exercise 37

1. Moi 2. toi 3. toi 4. nous 5. eux 6. eux 7. toi 8. Moi 9. toi 10. eux 11. moi 12. moi 13. elle 14. nous 15. toi

Exercise 38

1. l' 2. leur 3. lui 4. l' 5. les 6. lui 7. leur 8. le 9. la 10. les 11. l' 12. les 13. leur 14. lui 15. l' 16. l' 17. le 18. le 19. les 20. le

Exercise 39

1. nous 2. te 3. me 4. vous 5. m' 6. se 7. la 8. nous 9. les 10. l' 11. te 12. vous 13. me 14. les 15. s'

Exercise 40

1. m' 2. te 3. me 4. me 5. me 6. te 7. m' 8. nous 9. s' 10. te 11. se 12. te

Exercise 41

1. leur obéis 2. le lis 3. lui téléphone 4. la finis 5. l'aiment 6. l'adores 7. les écoutes 8. leur parle 9. lui dis 10. lui dis 11. la fais 12. sais le parler 13. la vendent 14. lui demande 15. leur dire

Exercise 42

1. Touche-moi! 2. Lave-toi! 3. Demande-moi! 4. Regarde-toi! 5. Parle-moi! 6. Lavons-nous! 7. Dépêchons-nous! 8. Pressez-vous! 9. Cherchez-moi! 10. Cache-toi! 11. Réveille-toi! 12. Demandes-en ! 13. Couchons-nous! 14. Dites-moi ça! 15. Couchez-la!

Exercise 43

1. en 2. y 3. y 4. en 5. y 6. en 7. en 8. y 9. en 10. y

Exercise 44

1. y 2. y 3. en 4. en 5. y 6. y 7. en 8. y 9. en 10. y

Exercise 45

1. elle 2. nous 3. soi 4. toi 5. lui 6. vous 7. eux 8. elles 9. lui 10. elle

Exercise 46

1. Lui 2. Moi 3. Toi 4. Elle 5. Vous 6. Eux 7. Nous 8. Elles 9. eux 10. elle 11. lui 12. elle 13. eux 14. moi 15. toi

Exercise 47

1. Marie 2. sa sœur Élise 3. le sac de Marie 4. Élise 5. son sac 6. ses devoirs 7. les questions 8. les réponses correctes 9. les notes 10. la meilleure note 11. Francine 12. l'amour de sa vie 13. ses employés 14. le métro 15. le français et l'anglais

Exercise 48

1. l' 2. la 3. l' 4. la 5. le 6. les 7. les 8. les 9. les 10. l' 11. l' 12. le 13. les 14. le 15. les

Exercise 49

1. il l'écoute 2. il les entend mal 3. il les donne 4. il l'a 5. il la répète 6. il l'explique bien 7. il les comprend 8. il le fait 9. il le passe 10. il l'adore

Exercise 50

1. à ses parents, leur 2. à sa copine, lui 3. à son papa, lui 4. à Denise, lui 5. aux grands-parents, leur

Exercise 51

1. Moi/l' 2. la 3. les 4. les 5. l' 6. l' 7. y 8. leur 9. t' 10. Moi/t' 11. moi/m' 12. t' 13. Tu 14. leur/Moi 15. toi 16. moi

Exercise 52

1. y 2. y 3. t' 4. y 5. en 6. en 7. en 8. y 9. en 10. y

Exercise 53

1. *Have* you thought about my question? —Yes, I have thought about it. 2. Do you want to go to Québec this summer? —Yes, I do. 3. Good. Do you want to accompany me home now? —Sure. I'll accompany you. 4. Is your car parked in front of the café? —That's right! That's where it is. 5. Are you just back from English class? —Yes, I just got out. 6. Are you hungry? Would you like some couscous? —Certainly, I'd like a little. 7. I would like to buy some fresh bread for Mom. —OK. Let's buy some! 8. Here is a bakery! —Let's go in! 9. Good. Let's

also talk about this weekend! —OK. Let's talk about it! 10. Are we still going to Marie's party? —Of course we are going.

Exercise 54

1. vous 2. vous 3. moi 4. m' 5. moi

Exercise 55

1. le mien 2. la sienne 3. le leur 4. les nôtres 5. la nôtre 6. les vôtres 7. la nôtre 8. les siens 9. les miens 10. les leurs 11. le tien 12. la sienne 13. les vôtres 14. le vôtre 15. les siens

Exercise 56

1. celui *This tree belongs to my neighbor. Mine is over there.* 2. celle *This car belongs to Julie. Mine is in the garage.* 3. celles *These green plants belong to my mother. Mine are in my room.* 4. celui *This iPod belongs to my brother. Mine is in my car.* 5. celles *These pictures belong to my sister. Mine are not developed.* 6. ceux *My favorite poems are the ones the titles of which I underlined.* 7. celle *My friend Jeanne is the one you met last night.* 8. celles *My prettiest party shoes are the ones I just put away.* 9. celle-ci/celle-là *I can give you one of my rackets. Do you want this one or that one?* 10. Celui-ci/celui-là *Which movie are we going to watch? This one or that one?* 11. celui *The math teacher is the one you see sitting behind his desk.* 12. celle-ci/celle-là *Which one of these two dresses is the most beautiful, this one or that one?* 13. celle-ci or celle-là *You need a tie? I can lend you this one (or that one).* 14. celle *My favorite radio show is the one on Radio France at 10 P.M.* 15. celui *The best poem is the one by Lamartine.*

Exercise 57

1. Lequel *I have a blue pen and a black pen. Which one would you like?* 2. Lequel *Here are a gray sweater and a white sweater. Which one fits me best?* 3. Lesquels *I love white grapes and red grapes. How about you? Which ones do you prefer?* 4. Lequel *I can serve white or red wine. Which one is the best?* 5. Lesquelles *I have good Italian pasta and good German pasta. Which one should I make?* 6. Auquel *You want to speak to an employee? —To which one?* 7. Duquel *You need a book! —Which one?* 8. Auxquels *You want to go to two concerts this month. But (to) which ones?* 9. Auquel *You are going to give a gift to one of your friends? To which one?* 10. Lequel *Here are two nice chickens. Which one are you going to buy?*

Exercise 58

1. du *What name are you making fun of? —Not yours, don't worry!* 2. aux *To which of your friends do you give gifts? —To the best (friends), of course!* 3. des *Are you talking about your last year's vacation? —No, I'm talking about yours.* 4. aux *What homework are you thinking about? —About ours, obviously!* 5. du *Which high school are they talking about? —About theirs.*

Exercise 59

1. celle 2. Celle/mienne 3. celle 4. lequel 5. celui 6. Duquel/celui 7. celui 8. Laquelle/tienne

Exercise 60

1. qui 2. que 3. qui 4. que 5. que 6. qui 7. que 8. qui 9. qui 10. que 11. qu' 12. qu' 13. qui 14. que 15. qui 16. que 17. qui 18. qui 19. qui 20. que

Exercise 61

1. qui *The friend with whom you play tennis is very athletic.* 2. qui *The gentleman for whom you work is generous.* 3. laquelle *Your mother is the (one) person without whom you cannot live.* 4. qui *The big boy behind whom I'm walking is my brother.* 5. lequel *This is an instrument without which I cannot do my work.* 6. lesquelles *The flowers in front of which I find myself are really beautiful.* 7. qui *The person about whom I think all the time is my fiancé.* 8. laquelle *The day I think about all the time is my wedding day (that of my wedding).* 9. auquel *The moment I think about all the time is the moment when I'll say «I do».* 10. qui *He*

is the person with whom I want to spend the rest of my life. 11. auxquelles *The things to which you are the most attached are only things.* 12. qui *The friend on whom you can count the most, that's me.* 13. lesquels *I appreciate those people without whom I would not be where I am.* 14. qui *The gentleman next to whom you are going to be seated is a well-known artist.* 15. laquelle *There is the façade on which his name is engraved.* 16. qui (or quoi) *I never know whom you are thinking about (or what you're thinking about).* 17. lequel *Is this the piece of jewelry for which you paid so much?* 18. qui *Do you know by whom this poem was written?* 19. qui *Tell me to whom you are going to give this.* 20. qui *To whose right will he be seated?*

Exercise 62

1. Le jour où 2. l'hôtel où 3. jour où 4. le mois où 5. où

Exercise 63

1. Those ten days in Tahiti are the vacation that I will remember all of my life. 2. This horrible adventure is something I would rather not remember. 3. My French book is the book I need every day. 4. This Ferrari is the car I have been dreaming of forever. 5. Rats are the animals that scare me the most. 6. This teacher is the one from whom I learned the most. 7. What I would like is a new bracelet. 8. The most talked-about people are movie stars. 9. Beware of (Do not trust) hypocrites. 10. There is the gentleman whose car disappeared last night. 11. There is the young lady whose purse was stolen. 12. Do you remember the boy I told you about? 13. Look! It is the house with the red tiled roof. 14. That is the teacher about whom everybody complains. 15. The dates you must remember are on this calendar.

Exercise 64

1. ce qui *I don't know what is happening.* 2. ce que *I don't know yet what I am going to study.* 3. ce dont *I am going to tell you what I need to make dinner tonight.* 4. ce dont *Tell me what you want.* 5. Ce qui *What fascinates me is your imagination.* 6. ce dont *I am going to tell you what I am the most afraid of.* 7. ce que *Guess what I want as a gift.* 8. ce qui *I can tell you what is wrong.* 9. ce qu' *I wonder what she wants.* 10. ce qui *Show me what is in the box.*

Exercise 65

1. quoi *You do not always know what I am thinking (about).* Or qui *You do not always know about whom I am thinking.* 2. où *The place where I feel the most at ease is my house.* 3. où *Soon I am going to see again the city where I was born.* 4. dont *The city of which I showed you pictures is my birthplace (the city of my birth).* 5. dont *The person of whom I am the proudest is my father.* 6. où *The day when I see my hometown again, I will be happy.* 7. dont *The childhood friend I always tell you about is going to come today.* 8. quoi *We are going to eat, after which we are going to take a walk.* 9. où *The restaurant where we are going to eat is excellent.* 10. dont *The dessert I crave is the crêpe my grandmother used to make.*

Exercise 66

1. qui 2. que 3. dont 4. où 5. que 6. que 7. dont 8. dont 9. que 10. qui 11. où 12. qui 13. que 14. dont 15. que

Exercise 67

1. que 2. le moment où 3. où 4. qui 5. que 6. lequel 7. dont 8. que 9. dont 10. laquelle 11. qui 12. ce que 13. qui 14. ce qui 15. ce qu'

Exercise 68

1. en 2. à 3. sur 4. Pendant 5. en/en 6. près de 7. pour 8. vers *or* à 9. avant 10. sans 11. sur 12. au centre *or* près 13. de 14. entre 15. pour

Exercise 69

1. à/de 2. de *or* à/pour 3. chez/chez 4. en/en 5. à/à 6. en/en *or* de/de 7. de/de 8. aux/aux 9. à/à 10. en/en 11. en/en 12. chez/chez 13. à/au 14. au/à 15. à/au

Exercise 70

1. Je cherche... 2. J'écoute... 3. Je demande... 4. Je regarde... 5. J'attends... 6. Je paie... 7. Je commence à... 8. J'oublie d'... 9. Je t'aide à... 10. J'apprends à... 11. Je décide de... 12. Je demande... 13. Je te demande de... 14. Je te dis de... 15. Je cesse de...

Exercise 71

1. la 2. l' (f) 3. le 4. le 5. X 6. la 7. l' (f) 8. la 9. l' (f) 10. X 11. les (m) 12. X 13. le 14. X 15. l' (f) 16. les (f) 17. la 18. la 19. la 20. l' (f)

Exercise 72

1. à 2. en 3. à 4. en 5. à 6. en 7. à 8. en 9. à 10. en 11. à 12. au 13. à 14. aux 15. à 16. en 17. à 18. au 19. à 20. au

Exercise 73

1. de 2. d' 3. d' 4. d' 5. de 6. du 7. des 8. de 9. du 10. du 11. de 12. d' 13. d' 14. du 15. du 16. du 17. du 18. d' 19. du 20. de

Exercise 74

1. de l' 2. du 3. de la 4. des 5. d' 6. de l' 7. de la 8. du 9. de l' 10. du 11. du 12. de la 13. de la 14. de l' 15. de la 16. de l' 17. du 18. de la 19. du 20. de la

Exercise 75

1. Au contraire 2. au lieu de 3. à cause de toi 4. à l'improviste 5. à gauche 6. au fond 7. à temps 8. à voix haute 9. À la rigueur 10. à la maison 11. À bientôt/Au revoir/À tout à l'heure 12. à l'étranger 13. À l'avenir 14. à la fois 15. à peine

Exercise 76

1. du violon 2. de fatigue 3. d'abord 4. de rigueur 5. de la trompette 6. de long 7. de jour 8. De rien 9. de bon cœur 10. De grâce

Exercise 77

1. de plus en plus 2. à droite 3. à l'heure 4. De rien 5. De bon cœur 6. à la fin 7. Au bas 8. à l'improviste 9. de l'orgue 10. à voix basse 11. à la maison 12. au lieu de 13. de bon appétit 14. d'abord 15. à la montagne 16. à travers 17. à la fois 18. à peine 19. à propos 20. à temps

Exercise 78

1. From time to time, my husband is a daredevil. 2. Last year we went to the Alps where mountain climbing is absolutely necessary. 3. At first I participated willingly. 4. But after a while I got tired of walking. 5. I must say that the view over the plain is very beautiful during the day. 6. But when I saw Henri reach the summit of the mountain, I trembled with fear. 7. I walked back and forth because I was nervous. 8. He planted a big flag two meters long and two meters wide. 9. He was at five hundred meters altitude. 10. He was not at all tired; on the contrary he was full of energy.

Exercise 79

1. par contre 2. et 3. ou 4. Pourtant 5. surtout

Exercise 80

1. bien que *Grammar is difficult for you even though you study a lot.* 2. dès que *Go to sleep as soon as you arrive.* 3. parce que *I am going to help you learn French since/because I speak it well.* 4. Quand *When you speak it well, you will come to France with me.* 5. alors que *I do the cooking while you watch TV.* 6. Lorsque *When I am tired, I go to sleep.* 7. parce que (puisque) *I go home for (because/since) it is late.* 8. Aussitôt que *As soon as you help me, I will finish the exercise.* 9. alors que/tandis que *You always play while your brother works.* 10. quoiqu'/malgré qu' *You pass your exams although they are difficult.*

Exercise 81

1. de peur des 2. sans 3. Après que 4. jusqu'à ce que 5. pour 6. Pendant 7. avant 8. sans 9. de peur que 10. pour que 11. pour 12. pendant que 13. avant qu' 14. Après 15. jusqu'à

Exercise 82

1. de 2. Et 3. à 4. pour 5. Et *or* Mais 6. sur 7. Pourtant *or* mais 8. pendant 9. puisque 10. surtout/pour que

Exercise 83

1. pour moi 2. de Paris 3. pendant 4. sans lui 5. pour 6. Pourtant 7. Grâce à 8. Donc *or* Alors 9. près de 10. jusqu'à

Exercise 84

1. persistant *You succeed in life by persisting in your efforts.* 2. étant *You do not succeed by being lazy.* 3. pratiquant *It is by practicing that you make progress.* 4. réfléchissant *Upon thinking it over, I realized that I was wrong.* 5. pensant *While thinking about you, I was moved.* 6. roulant *He fell while riding the bike.* 7. Ayant *Having a lot of patience, I do a good job as a teacher.* 8. regardant *I never do my homework while watching TV.* 9. marchant *I saw Suzie while walking to the bakery this morning.* 10. attendant *While waiting for the bus, we chat.* 11. passant *While passing by the park, I met a friend.* 12. restant *By remaining quiet, we do not disturb people.* 13. faisant *By being careful, we avoid accidents.* 14. choisissant *By choosing one's friends carefully, one shows good sense.* 15. prétendant *By pretending to agree, he is a hypocrite.* 16. dormant *You do not earn a living by sleeping.* 17. mangeant *You get hungry while eating.* 18. forgeant *It is by doing blacksmith work (forging) that you become a blacksmith.* 19. enseignant *It is by teaching that you learn.* 20. voyageant *It is while traveling that you learn to travel (become a traveler).*

Exercise 85

1. INF/to choose 2. INF/to speak 3. CP/we speak 4. IMP/Finish! 5. INF/to finish 6. CP/one speaks 7. CP/you finish 8. IMP/Study! 9. CP/they speak 10. INF/to study 11. CP/they finish 12. IMP/Speak! 13. CP/I speak 14. CP/she sells 15. IMP/Sell!

Exercise 86

1. présente	2. oublie
présentes	oublies
présente	oublie
présentons	oublions
présentez	oubliez
présentent	oublient

Exercise 87

1. chantes *you sing/are singing* 2. parle *I speak/am speaking* 3. écoutons *we listen/are listening* 4. cherchez *you look for/are looking for* 5. porte *one wears/is wearing* 6. apportent *they bring/are bringing* 7. j'adore *I love* 8. restent *they stay/are staying* 9. danse *Paul dances/is dancing* 10. arrivent *my parents arrive/are arriving* 11. Écoute *Listen, Marie* 12. Regardez *Look, children* 13. félicitons *Dear friends, let us congratulate the wedded couple!* or félicitons (. . . *let's congratulate* . . .) 14. Embrassez-vous *Kiss each other!* 15. Dînons *Let's dine, you and I, Paul!*

Exercise 88

1. choisis	2. finis
choisis	finis
choisit	finit
choisissons	finissons
choisissez	finissez
choisissent	finissent

Exercise 89

1. réussis *you succeed/are succeeding* 2. rougis *I blush/am blushing* 3. grandissons *we grow/are growing* 4. guérissez *you heal/are healing* 5. ravit *she delights* 6. réfléchissent *they think/are thinking* 7. Choisis *Choose your occupation!* 8. saisissez *My friends, seize the opportunity!* or saisissons (. . . *let's seize* . . .) 9. ne rougis pas *Paul, don't blush!* 10. Obéissons *Let's obey our parents!*

Exercise 90

1. réponds	2. attends
réponds	attends
répond	attend
répondons	attendons
répondez	attendez
répondent	attendent

Exercise 91

1. attends *you wait/are waiting* 2. défends *I defend or forbid/am defending or forbidding* 3. perdons *we lose/are losing* 4. entendez *you hear/are hearing* 5. répond *she answers/is answering* 6. vendent *they sell/are selling* 7. Descends *Come down the ladder, Paul!* 8. perdez *My friends, do not lose patience!* or perdons (. . . *let's not* . . .) 9. réponds-moi! *Luc, answer me!* 10. Attendons *Let's wait for our friends!*

Exercise 92

1. je vais regarder 2. vous allez punir 3. on va entendre 4. nous allons danser 5. tu vas chercher 6. elles vont choisir 7. ils vont attendre 8. je vais répondre 9. elle va rougir 10. nous allons écouter 11. je vais faire 12. tu vas apprendre 13. vous allez mettre 14. ils vont être 15. on va avoir

Exercise 93

1. j'apporterai 2. vous préférerez 3. on défendra 4. nous compterons 5. tu chercheras 6. elles choisiront 7. ils attendront 8. je répondrai 9. elle rougira 10. nous peignerons 11. tu réussiras 12. ils penseront 13. elle viendra 14. je laverai 15. nous prendrons 16. vous étudierez 17. il décidera 18. elle plaira 19. ils défendront 20. je rirai

Exercise 94

1. il aura répondu 2. nous aurons accompagné 3. tu auras saisi 4. vous aurez bâti 5. j'aurai commandé 6. ils auront ajouté 7. on aura présenté 8. j'aurai guéri 9. cela aura ravi 10. j'aurai chanté 11. tu seras arrivé(e) 12. elle sera née 13. il sera mort 14. nous serons allés/allées 15. vous serez retourné(s)/retournée(s)

Exercise 95

1. je bavarderais 2. vous cacheriez 3. on entendrait 4. nous nourririons 5. tu mériterais 6. elles cesseraient 7. ils attendraient 8. je descendrais 9. elle réfléchirait 10. nous rendrions 11. elle donnerait 12. je dirais 13. ils écriraient 14. nous rencontrerions 15. tu mangerais 16. il enseignerait 17. vous attendriez 18. j'apprendrais 19. elles arriveraient 20. tu chanterais

Exercise 96

1. Je vais parler 2. Je répondrai à 3. tu vas attendre 4. Tu feras la connaissance de 5. Elle va arriver 6. Je te présenterai 7. vont rater 8. Ils auront attendu 9. Ils vont marcher 10. nous allons déjeuner 11. Nous aurons fini 12. Elle ne va plus tarder 13. Elle resterait 14. Tu ne le regretterais pas 15. elle te plairait

Exercise 97

1. rencontriez *you used to meet/were meeting* 2. souhaitais *I used to wish/was wishing* 3. perdaient *they used to lose/were losing* 4. j'épousais *I was marrying* 5. remplissais *you used to fill/were filling* 6. applaudissions *we used to applaud/were applauding* 7. regrettait *we used to regret/were regretting* 8. remerciiez *you used to thank/were thanking* 9. trompait *she used to deceive/was deceiving* 10. quittions *we used to leave/were leaving* 11. brossais *you used to brush/were brushing* 12. j'expliquais *I used to explain/was explaining* 13. désobéissait

she used to disobey/was disobeying 14. travaillaient *they used to work/were working* 15. punissait *she used to punish/was punishing* 16. écrivions *we used to write/were writing* 17. disiez *you used to say/were saying* 18. choisissait *she used to choose/was choosing* 19. tombais *you used to fall/were falling* 20. retournais *I used to return/was returning*

Exercise 98

1. tu as fermé 2. elle a cherché 3. nous avons trouvé 4. j'ai attendu 5. on a répondu 6. vous avez fini 7. ils ont choisi 8. j'ai entendu 9. tu as réussi 10. elle a étudié 11. on a aimé 12. elles ont joué 13. nous avons perdu 14. tu as désobéi 15. j'ai donné 16. vous avez bâti 17. ils ont parlé 18. on a regardé 19. nous avons téléphoné 20. j'ai vendu

Exercise 99

1. chantée 2. faits 3. achetée 4. vu 5. jetés 6. mangée 7. prêté 8. sorties 9. vus 10. lue

Exercise 100

1. J'ai **écouté** la radio. 2. Cette musique que tu as **jouée** dans la voiture est très belle. 3. Nous avons **entendu** la sonnette. 4. Les films que vous avez **regardés** hier soir sont très vieux. 5. La vieille dame que tu as **aidée** était très aimable. 6. Les exercices de Français? Moi, je les ai déjà **finis**. 7. Tu as **lu** le même livre que moi. 8. Ils ont **porté** leurs lunettes de soleil. 9. La réponse que tu m'as **donnée** est bonne. 10. Tes vêtements? Je les ai **lavés**. Ils étaient sales.

Exercise 101

1. est sortie 2. es allée 3. est arrivé 4. sommes descendus/descendues 5. suis entré(e) 6. êtes parti 7. sont venus 8. es tombée 9. suis rentré(e) 10. sont morts 11. est allée 12. sont retournés 13. est née 14. est devenue 15. sont restés

Exercise 102

1. j'ai brossé 2. tu as fini 3. vous avez répondu 4. nous avons rencontré 5. il est tombé 6. elle est arrivée 7. on a attendu 8. ils sont montés 9. tu es allé(e) 10. nous sommes sortis 11. j'ai oublié 12. on a présenté 13. tu as défendu 14. vous avez rougi 15. elle est venue

Exercise 103

1. est passée 2. avons sorti 3. sont sortis 4. avez passé 5. est descendu 6. sommes montés 7. as descendu 8. as monté 9. ont sorti 10. a passé 11. sont passés 12. ai sorti 13. avons rentré 14. est montée 15. sont rentrées

Exercise 104

1. Il étudiait quand le professeur est entré. 2. Elle a rougi quand il a parlé/Elle rougissait quand il parlait. 3. Ils parlaient français. 4. J'étudiais beaucoup. 5. Elle a invité son ami(e). 6. Elle a embrassé sa mère. 7. Je regardais la télévision tous les jours. 8. Quand tu es arrivé(e), je dînais. 9. Nous sommes monté(e)s et nous avons joué aux cartes. 10. Nous jouions quand Lisa a appelé (téléphoné).

Exercise 105

1. Si vous rencontriez le président, vous n'oublieriez pas ce jour-là. 2. Si vous parliez plus de langues, vous voyageriez plus. 3. Si vous finissiez maintenant, vous regarderiez la télé. 4. Si je posais une question, est-ce que vous répondriez? 5. Si nous marchions beaucoup, nous maigririons. 6. Si elle l'aimait, elle l'attendrait. 7. Si vous jouiez contre moi, je gagnerais. 8. Si elle écoutait, elle entendrait. 9. Si j'étais là, j'expliquerais. 10. Si vous perdiez la balle, nous la chercherions.

Exercise 106

1. être rentrés 2. avoir chanté 3. avoir gagné 4. avoir entendu 5. avoir bâti 6. avoir perdu 7. avoir fait 8. avoir marché 9. avoir raté 10. être parties 11. être arrivé 12. être descendu 13. avoir fait 14. avoir oublié 15. être sortis 16. être rentrée 17. avoir lavé 18. être sortis 19. être montée 20. avoir réussi

Exercise 107

1. I love to play ball with my friends. 2. But I also like to discuss things. 3. When I speak, it is to express my thoughts. 4. I am trying to finish an exercise. 5. In the evening I study. 6. My girlfriend stays here to help me. 7. She does me a favor. 8. Mom is having the car fixed. 9. The mechanic makes her wait. 10. We have dinner at 8 o'clock.

Exercise 108

1. J'accompagne 2. Nous aimons 3. lave et coiffe 4. Elle raconte/travaillant 5. nous bavardons 6. nous rentrons 7. admire 8. déjeune 9. je mange 10. vous passez

Exercise 109

1. Ils bâtissent 2. nous attendons 3. remplissent 4. grandit 5. bâtir/choisir 6. J'entends 7. défendent 8. désobéis/ punir 9. perdre 10. attendant/obéis

Exercise 110

1. La famille finissait le dîner quand je suis arrivée. 2. Mais Chloé parlait au téléphone quand je suis entrée. 3. Elle parlait français. C'était sûrement sa cousine française. 4. Elle lui a dit au revoir quand elle m'a vue. 5. Elle m'a invitée à prendre le dessert. 6. Je suis restée un peu. 7. J'ai même parlé un peu français avec Chloé. 8. J'ai passé un bon moment avec elle. 9. Quand je suis partie, la famille était encore à table. 10. J'ai pris le bus à 20 h.

Exercise 111

1. a étudié 2. a terminé 3. souhaitait 4. finissait 5. lisait 6. a réussi 7. féliciterais 8. a annoncé 9. finirais 10. aimerais

Exercise 112

1. avoir travaillé 2. avoir parlé 3. avoir bavardé 4. avoir persuadé 5. avoir conseillé 6. être allés 7. avoir discuté 8. avoir passé

Exercise 113

1. choisisse 2. aimions 3. rencontriez 4. rende 5. sois 6. ait 7. saisissent 8. réponde 9. remplissent 10. vendes 11. explique 12. racontiez 13. nourrissent 14. souhaite 15. chantions 16. réfléchisse 17. descendions 18. montes 19. peigne 20. attende

Exercise 114

1. ait vendu 2. ait attendu 3. aies donné 4. ait perdu 5. ayez guéri 6. ait répondu 7. ait trouvé 8. ait dîné 9. soit partie 10. ait rencontré 11. aies échoué 12. ait obtenu 13. aies été 14. ayons perdu 15. ait refusé 16. ayez réussi 17. soit passée 18. soient allés 19. soit arrivée 20. ayons rencontré

Exercise 115

1. je m'amuse 2. tu t'amuses 3. il/elle/on s'amuse 4. nous nous amusons 5. vous vous amusez 6. ils/elles s'amusent

Exercise 116

1. je me fâcherai 2. tu te fâcheras 3. il/elle/on se fâchera 4. nous nous fâcherons 5. vous vous fâcherez 6. ils/elles se fâcheront

Exercise 117

1. je me reposais 2. tu te reposais 3. il/elle/on se reposait 4. nous nous reposions 5. vous vous reposiez 6. ils/elles se reposaient

Exercise 118

1. je me suis promené(e) 2. tu t'es promené(e) 3. il/elle/on s'est promené(e) 4. nous nous sommes promené(e)s 5. vous vous êtes promené(e)(s) 6. ils/elles se sont promené(e)s

Exercise 119

1. We meet girlfriends. 2. We meet at the square. 3. They always lose their belongings. 4. They get lost in this big city. 5. I tweezed my sister's eyebrows. 6. I tweezed my eyebrows. 7. Mom put the baby to bed. 8. Mom went to bed. 9. The phone woke him up. 10. He woke up at 8. 11. A judge married them. 12. They got married before a judge. 13. This clown will amuse the children. 14. The children will have fun with this clown. 15. Shave your beard, Dad! 16. Dad is going to shave. 17. Renée walked the dog this morning. 18. Renée went for a walk this morning. 19. Jacqueline bathed little Luc. 20. Jacqueline bathed/took a bath.

Exercise 120

1. The door opens easily. 2. This is how this dish is prepared. 3. You drink an apéritif before the meal. 4. "Bon voyage" is used in many languages. 5. This book is sold in every bookstore. 6. We break eggs to make an omelet. 7. The exercise will soon be finished. 8. This president was liked by everyone. 9. True happiness is rarely found. 10. French is spoken here.

Exercise 121

1. Il ne joue pas. 2. Nous n'applaudissons pas. 3. Ils n'ont pas vendu la maison. 4. Nous n'avons pas obéi. 5. Je n'attendrai pas. 6. Elle n'écoutait pas. 7. Il n'a pas répondu. 8. Tu n'étais pas là/Vous n'étiez pas là. 9. Je ne souhaitais pas cela. 10. Ces plantes n'ont pas jauni.

Exercise 122

1. Elle ne réfléchit jamais. 2. Je n'en veux plus. 3. Nous ne disons jamais rien. 4. Il ne porte que le noir. 5. Ils n'aiment jamais rien. 6. Je ne désobéirai jamais plus. 7. Tu n'as entendu (Vous n'avez entendu) personne? 8. Elle ne danse plus nulle part. 9. Je ne descends pas encore. 10. Nous ne montons jamais plus.

Exercise 123

1. Est-il monté? 2. Écoutes-tu? 3. Porte-t-elle une robe? 4. Parlent-ils/elles français? 5. Est-ce que j'ai réussi? 6. Avons-nous aidé? 7. Attend-elle? 8. Descendez-vous? 9. Est-ce que je danse bien? 10. Aime-t-il les films français? 11. Entendez-vous? 12. Sommes-nous arrivé(e)s? 13. Sont-ils/elles sorti(e)s? 14. Est-il ici? 15. Les enfants étudient-ils? 16. (Est-ce que) J'ai bonne mine? 17. Rachelle a-t-elle aimé la musique? 18. Montons-nous? 19. Tes parents sont-ils restés? 20. Finis-tu?

Exercise 124

1. i 2. j 3. e 4. a 5. h 6. c 7. f 8. b 9. g 10. d

Exercise 125

1. préférais, préfère, ai préféré 2. t'appelais, t'appelles, t'es appelé(e) 3. jetait, jette, a jeté 4. espéraient, espèrent, ont espéré 5. achetais, achète, ai acheté 6. payaient, paient (payent), ont payé 7. neigeait, neige, a neigé 8. gelait, gèle, a gelé 9. annonçait, annonce, a annoncé 10. levais, lève, ai levé

Exercise 126

1. préférerais, préférerai 2. t'appellerais, t'appelleras 3. jetterait, jettera 4. espérerions, espérerons 5. achèteriez, achèterez 6. paieraient (payeraient), paieront (payeront) 7. neigerait, neigera 8. gèlerait, gèlera 9. annoncerait, annoncera 10. lèverais, lèverai

Exercise 127

1. je fais 2. elle va 3. nous sommes 4. tu as 5. ils/elles ont 6. je faisais 7. elle allait 8. nous étions 9. vous aviez 10. ils/elles avaient 11. je ferai 12. elle ira 13. nous serons 14. tu auras 15. ils/elles auront 16. j'aurai fait 17. elle sera allée 18. nous aurons été 19. vous aurez eu 20. ils/elles auront eu 21. Il faut que je fasse 22. Il faut qu'elle aille 23. Il faut que nous soyons 24. Il faut que tu aies 25. Il faut qu'ils/elles aient

Exercise 128

1. je lis 2. vous lisez 3. elle a lu 4. ils/elles ont lu 5. nous lisions 6. je lisais 7. tu liras 8. ils/elles liront 9. elle aura lu 10. Il faut que je lise 11. Ils faut qu'ils/elles lisent 12. Il faut que je dise 13. elle a dit 14. il disait 15. nous

dirons 16. tu écris 17. ils/elles écrivaient 18. il a écrit 19. il aura écrit 20. Il faut qu'elle écrive 21. elle conduit 22. j'ai conduit 23. Il faut que nous conduisions 24. ils/elles conduiront 25. ils/elles conduisaient

Exercise 129

1. je suis 2. ils/elles suivent 3. elle a suivi 4. nous avons suivi 5. vous suiviez 6. Suis! 7. Suivons! 8. Il faut qu'elle suive 9. Dommage qu'il ait suivi 10. ils/elles vivent 11. Vivons! 12. Vis! 13. Vivez! 14. nous vivions 15. j'ai vécu 16. il a vécu 17. Il faut que je vive 18. il faut qu'ils/elles vivent 19. Il est bon qu'elle ait vécu 20. Il est bon qu'ils/elles aient vécu

Exercise 130

1. je comprends 2. ils/elles apprennent 3. nous surprenons 4. tu prends 5. j'ai compris 6. ils/elles ont appris 7. ils/elles prenaient 8. Prends! 9. Prenez! 10. Prenons! 11. Il faut qu'elle prenne 12. Il faut que nous prenions 13. Dommage que j'aie pris 14. Dommage que tu aies surpris 15. Il est bon qu'il ait compris 16. j'apprendrais 17. ils/elles apprendraient 18. je prendrais 19. ils/elles surprendraient 20. elle comprendrait

Exercise 131

1. je mets 2. nous mettons 3. ils/elles mettent 4. je mettais 5. j'ai promis 6. ils/elles ont promis 7. ils/elles ont permis 8. Mets! 9. Mettons! 10. Il faut que nous permettions 11. Il faut qu'elle permette 12. Il faut que nous promettions 13. Il est bon qu'elle ait promis 14. Il est bon qu'il ait permis 15. je permettrais 16. ils/elles permettraient 17. vous promettriez 18. je promettais 19. elle mettait 20. je permettais

Exercise 132

1. ils/elles plaisent 2. nous plaisons 3. il se tait 4. vous vous taisez 5. ils/elles ont plu 6. il s'est tu 7. tu t'es tu(e) 8. je me tairai 9. Il faut que je plaise 10. Taisons-nous!

Exercise 133

1. je sers 2. nous servons 3. ils/elles mentent 4. tu mens 5. je sors 6. il sort 7. il dort 8. nous partons 9. vous partez 10. j'ai servi 11. nous avons dormi 12. nous avons servi 13. ils/elles ont menti 14. elle est sortie 15. nous sommes sorti(e)s 16. je suis parti(e) 17. ils/elles partaient 18. je mentais 19. il mentait 20. je dormais 21. Partez! 22. Servons! 23. Dormons! 24. Il faut que tu dormes 25. Il est bon que nous dormions

Exercise 134

1. je vois 2. vous voyez 3. ils/elles croient 4. je crois 5. je dois 6. ils/elles doivent 7. nous devons 8. tu reçois 9. elle reçoit 10. ils/elles reçoivent 11. j'ai vu 12. vous avez vu 13. ils/elles ont cru 14. j'ai cru 15. j'ai dû 16. ils/elles ont dû 17. nous avons reçu 18. ils/elles ont reçu 19. je devais 20. ils/elles devaient 21. je recevais 22. nous recevions 23. je verrai 24. ils/elles recevront 25. je devrai

Exercise 135

1. j'ouvre 2. ils/elles ouvrent 3. tu offres 4. nous offrons 5. il couvre 6. ils/elles ont couvert 7. nous avons offert 8. il a découvert 9. elle offrait 10. ils/elles couvraient 11. Ouvre! 12. Ouvrons! 13. Couvrez! 14. Il faut que j'ouvre 15. Il est bon qu'il ait découvert 16. Dommage qu'elle ait couvert 17. nous couvririons 18. ils/elles ouvriraient 19. j'offrirais 20. tu offrirais

Exercise 136

1. il veut 2. nous voulons 3. je veux 4. vous pouvez 5. ils/elles peuvent 6. je peux 7. j'ai pu 8. j'ai voulu 9. ils/elles ont voulu 10. nous pouvions 11. elle pouvait 12. je voulais 13. ils/elles voulaient 14. tu voudrais 15. nous voudrions 16. ils/elles voudraient 17. je pourrais 18. il pourrait 19. ils/elles pourraient 20. Il faut que je veuille 21. Il faut que nous voulions 22. Il faut qu'elle puisse 23. Il faut qu'ils/elles puissent 24. Il est bon que nous ayons pu 25. Il est bon que nous ayons voulu

Exercise 137

1. je tiens 2. elle tient 3. il vient 4. nous venons 5. tu deviens 6. ils/elles deviennent 7. je reviens 8. j'ai tenu 9. vous avez retenu 10. ils/elles sont devenu(e)s 11. elle est revenue 12. nous tenions 13. tu tenais 14. ils/elles

venaient 15. elle revenait 16. Reviens! 17. Tenons! 18. Venez! 19. Il faut qu'elle revienne 20. Il faut qu'ils/elles retiennent 21. Dommage que nous soyons devenu(e)s 22. Dommage que je sois revenu(e) 23. je me souviendrais 24. ils/elles se souviendraient 25. elle se souviendrait

Exercise 138

1. Je sais quelle heure il est. 2. Ils/Elles savent mon nom. 3. On sait la vérité. 4. Elle sait la réponse. 5. Nous savons compter. 6. Tu sais jouer. 7. Il sait chanter. 8. J'ai su que c'était un mensonge. 9. Elle a su que j'étais là. 10. Je savais chanter. 11. Sache que… 12. Sachez que… 13. Nous savions parler français. 14. Il faut que je sache. 15. Il faut qu'ils/elles sachent. 16. Dommage que vous ayez su. 17. Il est bon que nous ayons su. 18. Je saurai ce nom. 19. Vous le saurez. 20. Ils/Elles sauront le faire.

Exercise 139

1. Ils/Elles connaissent la ville. 2. Je connais ton/votre prof. 3. Nous connaissons beaucoup de gens. 4. Je l'ai connue pendant quelque temps. 5. Ils/Elles connaissaient mon oncle. 6. Vous le connaissiez. 7. Nous le reconnaîtrons. 8. Ils/Elles connaîtront tout le monde. 9. Il faut qu'il me reconnaisse. 10. Il est bon que tu m'aies reconnu(e).

Exercise 140

1. Il neige maintenant. 2. Il pleut en ce moment. 3. Il faut que nous écoutions. 4. Il a plu hier. 5. Il a neigé hier. 6. Il a fallu écouter. 7. Il pleuvait il y a une heure. 8. Il neigeait. 9. Il fallait partir. 10. Il pleuvra demain. 11. Il neigera bientôt. 12. Il faudra oublier. 13. Il faudrait partir. 14. Il pleuvrait. 15. Il neigerait.

Exercise 141

1. ai besoin 2. a envie 3. as la parole 4. avons envie / avons l'habitude 5. Qu'est-ce qu'il y a 6. a de l'allure 7. avez de la chance 8. avoir le temps 9. a l'air 10. as mal 11. ont peur 12. ont du courage 13. as… ans 14. a lieu 15. Il y avait une fois

Exercise 142

1. ça y est 2. nous sommes 3. est de garde 4. être de retour 5. es des nôtres 6. quelle heure est-il 7. est de bonne humeur 8. j'y suis 9. Il est 10. mauvaise humeur

Exercise 143

1. fait la bise/fait attention 2. fait sa toilette 3. se sert 4. fait de son mieux 5. s'en va/fait du sport/fait des courses 6. fait la connaissance 7. fait des courses 8. fait un tour 9. fait attention 10. fait mal 11. fait du sport 12. se casse 13. fait des voyages 14. fait des progrès/fait de son mieux 15. se rappelle

Exercise 144

1. Je suis désolée que Monique soit malade. 2. Je ne suis pas sûre que son mari ait reçu mon message. 3. Pourvu qu'il ait reçu le message, il sera bientôt là. 4. Je suis heureuse qu'elle m'ait téléphoné. 5. Je souhaite qu'elle guérisse vite. 6. Le médecin voulait qu'elle dorme. 7. Je doute qu'elle l'ait écouté. 8. Je vais rester ici bien que ce ne soit peut-être pas nécessaire. 9. Il faut qu'elle soit patiente. 10. Il est temps que je mange quelque chose.

Exercise 145

1. s'est passée 2. se souviennent 3. se promenaient 4. s'est approché 5. s'appelle 6. s'est arrêtée 7. se sont parlé 8. s'amusaient 9. se sont mariés 10. s'aimeront

Exercise 146

1. We are easily deceived by what we love. 2. To be appreciated, you must die or travel. 3. You are praised without flattery when you are absent. 4. Those who cannot get angry are fools; those who do not want to get angry are wise. 5. What you fear will happen more easily than what you hope for. 6. The law forces us to do what is said (on the books), not what is just.

Exercise 147

1. 10. 2. 7. 6. 8. 3. 9. 4. 5.

Exercise 148

1. Why are you late, Chloé? —I went to the school library. 2. What time did you leave school? —Around 4:30. Why didn't you call? —We can't use phones in the library. 4. Who is with you? —This is my friend Jean who is going to help me with homework. 5. And who is going to help me with Dad's birthday cake? —Oh Mom! I forgot! 6. What! How can you forget something that important? —I am really sorry, Mom. 7. Can your friend come and study with you on Saturday or Sunday? —Which day can you come back, Jean? 8. For me either Saturday or Sunday is fine. Which do you prefer? —Come on Saturday! 9. What time? —At 2 P.M. 10. Will you keep a piece of cake for me? —Naturally!

Exercise 149

1. c 2. e 3. g 4. d 5. a 6. i 7. b 8. h 9. j 10. f

Exercise 150

1. suis allée 2. Sachant 3. ai dû 4. était 5. ai suivi 6. crois 7. verra 8. voudrais 9. il faut 10. saurai

Exercise 151

1. f 2. c 3. e 4. j 5. i 6. g 7. a 8. h 9. d 10. b

Exercise 152

1. Bonjour chérie! Comment vas-tu (ça va) aujourd'hui? 2. J'ai encore un peu sommeil. 3. Tu as fait de beaux rêves? 4. Pas du tout! J'ai rêvé que je m'étais cassé la jambe en skiant. 5. Oh non! Est-ce que je suis venue à ton secours? 6. Tout ce que je peux dire c'est que j'avais terriblement peur. 7. Ça faisait probablement très mal. 8. Ça va sans dire. 9. Ce n'était rien qu'un rêve. Ta jambe ne te fait pas mal maintenant. 10. Non, mais j'ai mal à la tête.

Exercise 153

1. — 2. Le 3. ma 4. au 5. du 6. des 7. de la 8. de 9. de 10. des/les 11. des/les 12. du 13. mon 14. le 15. du

Exercise 154

1. un 2. Quel 3. Ce 4. un/mon 5. un 6. mon/un 7. une 8. une 9. les/ces 10. Quels

Exercise 155

1. beaucoup de 2. quelques 3. des 4. trop 5. le plus 6. aussi 7. un verre 8. moins

Exercise 156

1. déjà 2. vite 3. Autrement/Sinon 4. Plus tard 5. Franchement 6. diligemment 7. évidemment/bien sûr 8. Malheureusement, souvent 9. plus rarement 10. aussi dur

Exercise 157

1. Mon gym est grand et spacieux. 2. Il y a beaucoup d'appareils. 3. Les gens marchent sur des tapis roulants modernes. 4. Les gens sont athlétiques, musclés et en bonne forme. 5. Les activités en salle sont généralement aussi importantes que les activités en plein air. 6. Les femmes vont au gym aussi souvent que les hommes. 7. Quelquefois je reste au gym plus longtemps que mes amis./Je reste quelquefois au gym plus longtemps que mes amis. 8. Pour moi, le meilleur moment de la journée pour faire de l'exercice est le matin.

Exercise 158

1. le 2. la 3. la 4. lui 5. leur, leur 6. l' 7. en, les 8. nous 9. vous 10. y

Exercise 159

1. toi 2. la 3. elle 4. moi 5. le 6. toi 7. m', en 8. eux, nous 9. nous 10. le

Exercise 160

1. à 2. Pendant 3. car 4. derrière 5. au centre de 6. à côté de 7. à propos de 8. à 9. de 10. de 11. du 12. en 13. au 14. en

Exercise 161

1. écrivant 2. courant 3. mangeant, buvant 4. montant 5. répondant 6. réfléchissant 7. achetant 8. conduisant

Exercise 162

1. N'écrivez pas trop vite! 2. Ne courez pas trop vite! 3. Ne mangez pas et ne buvez pas trop vite! 4. Ne montez pas trop vite! 5. Ne répondez pas trop vite! 6. Ne réfléchissez pas trop! 7. N'achetez pas trop de choses! 8. Ne conduisez pas trop vite!

Exercise 163

1a. Pourquoi est-ce que tu écris si vite? 1b. Pourquoi écris-tu si vite? 2a. Quand est-ce que tu cours trop vite? 2b. Quand cours-tu trop vite? 3a. Est-ce que tu manges et tu bois toujours trop vite? 3b. Manges-tu et bois-tu toujours trop vite? 4a. Comment est-ce que tu montes les escaliers? 4b. Comment montes-tu les escaliers? 5a. À qui est-ce que tu réponds trop vite? 5b. À qui réponds-tu trop vite? 6a. Dans quelles circonstances est-ce que tu réfléchis trop? 6b. Dans quelles circonstances réfléchis-tu trop? 7a. Qu'est-ce que tu achètes et où est-ce que tu l'achètes? 7b. Qu'achètes-tu et où l'achètes-tu? 8a. À quelle heure est-ce que tu conduis quelquefois trop vite? 8b. À quelle heure conduis-tu quelquefois trop vite?

Exercise 164

1. Nous pouvons/On peut nager et plonger dans le profond. 2. Nous pouvons/On peut se faire bronzer et se reposer dans les chaises longues. 3. Nous pouvons/On peut aller aux toilettes et prendre une douche. 4. Les enfants peuvent jouer et s'amuser dans la petite piscine. 5. Tout le monde doit obéir au maître nageur. 6. Les enfants doivent rester avec les adultes. 7. Personne ne doit mettre les autres gens en danger. 8. Nous devons/On doit prendre une douche avant d'aller dans la piscine.

Exercise 165

1. rentrerons 2. emmèneront 3. fera 4. montreront 5. irons 6. aura 7. achèterons 8. voudra 9. aura 10. passerons 11. serons 12. nous coucherons

Exercise 166

1. étais 2. devais 3. ai envoyé 4. intéressaient 5. ont donné 6. a attendu 7. est arrivée 8. avais 9. ai pris 10. ai ouverte 11. était 12. a passé

Exercise 167

1. avais, ai 2. rendais, rends 3. faisais, fais 4. travaillais, travaille 5. durait, dure 6. étudiais, étudie 7. finissais, finis 8. étais, suis

Exercise 168

1. Maman me ferait mes dîners. 2. Papa me dirait quand je dois me coucher (aller au lit). 3. Ma petite sœur me demanderait constamment de l'aide avec les devoirs. 4. Je me lèverais à cinq heures trente (et demie) chaque matin. 5. Mes amis ne pourraient pas venir chez moi après sept heures du soir. 6. Je ne jouerais jamais de musique tard le soir. 7. Mes parents me réveilleraient le matin. 8. Je sortirais le soir seulement le week-end. 9. Je prendrais le petit déjeuner et le dîner avec ma famille. 10. J'aurais moins de liberté.

Exercise 169

1. ne pas avoir fini 2. être sorti 3. ne pas avoir téléphoné 4. avoir trop dépensé 5. avoir réussi 6. être rentré 7. avoir retrouvé 8. m'être bien reposé

Exercise 170

1. me couche 2. me réveille 3. me rendors 4. me lève 5. me lave, me brosse, m'habille 6. me rappelle 7. m'en vais 8. me perds

Exercise 171

1. Mon université a été construite en 1858. 2. La cour a été ajoutée en 1910. 3. Le centre d'information a été rénové l'an dernier/l'année dernière. 4. Un nouveau restaurant va être ouvert sur le campus très bientôt. 5. Le parking des étudiants sera agrandi l'an prochain/l'année prochaine.

Exercise 172

1. a de l'allure. 2. a l'habitude, fait mauvais 3. a l'air 4. n'est jamais de mauvaise humeur 5. fait sa toilette 6. fait de son mieux 7. fait la bise 8. a, le temps

Exercise 173

1. La mienne 2. Le mien 3. celle 4. ceux 5. les miens 6. celle

Exercise 174

1. rendiez 2. ne soyez pas 3. participiez 4. fassiez 5. gériez 6. choisissiez 7. n'ayez pas 8. réussissiez 9. ayez 10. fassent 11. dise 12. soit

Exercise 175

1. se soit dépêchée 2. ait été 3. ait eu 4. n'ait pas étudié 5. soit sortie 6. ait passé 7. ait fait 8. ait compris

Exercise 176

1. qui 2. qu' 3. qui 4. ce qu' 5. où 6. dont 7. lesquels 8. qui 9. dont 10. laquelle 11. dont 12. qui